Liberalism
is Not
Enough

Marian Rubins Davis
Horace Bancroft Davis

ACKNOWLEDGMENTS

I would like to thank the many people who helped me with this book. Rachel Louise Stocking, for her work in editing the many versions, the Orcas (Tomás and Arianna Stocking) for producing the actual book, and the entire Bear clan who helped in one way or another, or even just gave me moral support. I am indebted to Tom Caulfield for producing the intermediate computer printouts, and to Al Hénon for his friendly advise.

HBD

Table of Contents

PART 1

DIRECTION

by

Marian Rubins Davis

I

England

The turning point came for me on a Saturday night in January--or was it February--of 1927. Mrs. Featherstone had asked me to go marketing with her, to buy the food for the coming week. Her husband has just turned over his pay, or as much of it as she ever saw. He kept something back, she knew, but probably not much, from his full time wages as a carpenter; what she got was 3 pounds 10s., far more than most Middlesbrough housewives had that winter to see them through the week. And of course we were paying guests; this gave her extra mouths to feed but also extra cash. She stepped confidently into the big market.

It was bitter cold. Yorkshire winters are always cold and this year, marked by the unsuccessful coal strike and the long effort of the general strike in brave but unavailing support of the miners, the weather seemed on the side of the bosses, bent on giving a sharper edge to misery. The wind was coming in, that Saturday night, from the river, and even in the thick crowds around the lighted stalls it was searching, keen. Walking from one section of the market to another took all one's breath and courage.

We had heard of longshoremen in Middlesbrough who went to the docks in the morning hoping for work and whose wives pawned the bedding to be sure there would be dinner when they got back; if their men were chosen from the line and came back with a day's pay they got the bedding out of hock and slept warm that night. We had seen pinched faces and barren homes, as we visited steelworkers' families. We had read the figures: the number of unemployed in Yorkshire, in England; had learned something about the inadequacy of the "dole." But until that night I had not looked on hunger.

It was toward the end of our evening. Mrs. Featherstone, nearly finished, was doing her last bit of bargaining at one of the fish stalls. I wandered away from her, drifted to the end of the stall, turned my back on the crowds and blazing electric bulbs, and looked into a sky lit with stars and with the glare of blast furnaces along the Teeside. Glancing down I saw the barrels at the end of the stall, barrels into which the fishmongers had flung the guts, the offal, from the bloody chopping blocks on which they had cleaned the fish they sold. This refuse froze quickly in the winter air. The barrels were many. They were higher than ordinary barrels and only part full. Bending over several of them were children, perhaps eight, perhaps six years old, some of them so small they balanced on their stomachs, feet in the air, so they could reach the frozen fish guts in the barrel. They were after food. And when they had it they ate it, there, frost and all, taking great frantic bites, their eyes roving for a market guard or fishmonger who might chase them away or turn them in. This was want.

I could have seen its counterpart on the lower East Side before we took ship for England. I had read possibly more than most sheltered young American intellectuals about human need. But up to that time I had not looked on it, and all the eloquent words that compassionate writers can pile in purposeful prose possess less force than a sudden glimpse of reality. From that moment, wavering, wondering was over. I knew that this sort of thing must not be.

What a person could do about it was an intricate problem, one with many facets, one that would grow incredibly with the doing. But this was clear: something must be done.

You may wonder why it had not been clear to me before. To the two men closest to me, my father and my husband, it had long been clear.

Father had never known stark want but he had left high school to help support his widowed mother and her family of three sons and whether it was the working class background of her grandfather, a boatbuilder on the clydeside, or Father's own scrounging for small wages as a boy, or simply his broad human sympathy and alert eyes I never knew, but he was aware of need and cared and in his own ways did what he could. We saw from a distance some of the ways: Family Welfare Board, Urban League, and, more vital and more costly, firm determination to deal with the unions to which his employees belonged when he had an interior decorating business and the Open Shop drive of the early twenties was on. The struggle was real. The banker who lunched with him at Minneapolis Club refused, an hour later, to renew his note unless he "broke with the union." Father did not break with the union. Nor was his social philosophy a recent acquisition or a shallow thing.

At times I thought it was shallow, for example when I read and rejected copies of the *New Republic* that he brought home and left on the living-room table. I was studying the orthodox economists then and the *New Republic* did not parse. Years later I recalled his sharp and detailed criticism of American imperialism in the Spanish-American war, of marines in Nicaragua, of intervention in Mexico. Mother went along, as she did in all things, but Father was the spokesman. He read Henry George; was a single taxer. He was close to, though not of, the Farmer-Labor Party. He had never been a farmer but he understood the movement that swept Minnesota and the Dakotas, knew with precision through his earlier connection with the grain business just how the elevator companies mulcted the farmers. He inveighed against the railroads and Wall Street, his sallies were always richly documented with facts. He supported Wilson but opposed the entrance of the United States into the First World War and broke, finally, with the friends who were leaders of the Protestant churches at home because they swung so quickly into line, preached war, condoned, indeed urged the killing of one's fellow men. I learned much from him. I could have learned far more.

My husband's recognition of the need for social change stemmed from a very different boyhood and had carried him, by the time we met in 1924, considerably farther. Briefly, his mother's Quaker convictions and his father's independence of thought had made an affluent New England family distinctly better to grow up in than its secure social standing and firmly rooted Harvard tradition might lead one to expect. He was too young for the draft. The Friends Service Committee gave him fellowship in France with young American and English men and women-- convinced Friends and birthright members of one meeting or another and sympathizers--at a time when Europe was shaken by change as well as by war. Economics at Harvard and later at Columbia sent him to see life for himself as third helper on the open hearth in the mills at Braddock, Pennsylvania. A year with the International Labor Office gave him insights into the European labor movement. By the time I knew him he was a confirmed trade unionist, friendly to the British Fabians but not convinced that they had the answer. He was himself determined to find the answer and was at home with working people wherever he found them. I married a man who was convincing in a basic, inexplicable way but also--and this won me as much as anything I can put into words-- unswervingly honest, however harsh and costly the honest appraisal and honest answer might prove.

Through him I met some of the young intellectuals who, at that time, were flocking to jobs for the labor movement in America. The ILGWU and the Amalgamated in New York had cultural as well as organizational verve and we visited Brookwood where I had brief but intriguing acquaintance with people who were working for the ILG, the Amalgamated, and other left-wing unions, or training themselves to do so. Their talk, vigorous as any college

4

bull session and far closer to reality, gave me glimpses of a world more active and more furiously divided than I had guessed. It was 1924. Communist leadership, especially in textiles, was certainly discernible and reactions to it were as sharp as they were varied.

I had read Marx in a course at Smith on classical economic theory. A teacher, whose incisive thinking had given me the most powerful stimulus of a rich undergraduate life, had not convinced me that Marx's theoretical reasoning was fallacious; she had introduced me to it and to the indictment of the English factory system in the first volume of *Capital*, though we had time to do no more than dip into it. My curiosity was whetted and when I returned to full time study after two years on research and teaching fellowships I sat for days on end in the library at Columbia, digging deeper. Only classes interrupted me, and I was acclaimed by the fellow student who spurred me on, a young Jewish upward-mobile son of an immigrant family. Later he drifted to a quiet berth in a Washington agency, thinking Lord knows what about his early enthusiasm for Marx. I am just touched with sadness when I remember now his earnest face, his slightly blurred speech that made such excellent sense, and what I owe to him. So I read. After I met Horace (and even before, among Columbia graduate students) I heard a lot of talk "about it and about" but reserved judgment.

Here was something obviously important, a vast literature. Of course *Capital*, a natural beginning for a person interested in economic theory, gave only part of the documentation for a program of change, and, in a precise sense, not the most moving part. The *Theses on Feuerbach* I did not find then and the *Manifesto* I dismissed, I think, until Engels' *Peasant War in Germany* taught me, years later, that here was an approach to the massive confusion of history. From that confusion I had fled, literally, to economic theory, and it was the best, most rigorous work I had done in studying economic theory that led me to Marx and made it possible for me to read him intelligently.

The first year of our marriage, 1925-26, was spent in Ithaca. I learned exactness, working with Willcox; had fun sparring with "Cope" and even exchanging words with Davenport in theoretical discussions at economic department gatherings where I, as wife and research assistant, was allowed to kibitz (Davenport had been a name in gold letters on the back of a rather hefty and meaty volume that I had worried voraciously as a dog does a bone; now he was a man and I could talk to him straight). I ate a banana split in company with William Green when he came to lecture at a trade

5

union gathering (we attended AF of L city central meetings as Teachers' Union members). Pregnant, I carried a suitcase part way up the enormous hill to campus for Anna Louise Strong when she came (at my husband's invitation) to talk to Cornell students about her children's colony on the Volga. After the end of the academic year, in August, we welcomed baby Chan and prepared to carry him with us on a fellowship jaunt to Europe to study living standards of steel workers. We set off in early October.

The trip took us, eventually, to Middlesbrough and the Featherstones who put us up because Ellen Wilkinson had asked them to. Ellen Wilkinson, later Minister of Education in the Labour Cabinet, was then sitting for Middlesbrough. Mrs. Featherstone had helped put her into Parliament, organizing back-yard meetings for her in block after block of Middlesbrough's working class neighborhoods. Ellen, herself born to a working class family in the Midlands, had been in the Communist Party and had left it but remained friendly. Before we went to Middlesbrough she had asked us to dinner in London and we had met there a number of Party people, including Tommy Jackson, witty and incorrigible in person as he is in print, and Maurice Dobb, a rosy-cheeked lad at that time, engaging and a bit diffident for all his enthusiasm. At that merry dinner as on other occasions in London I got the distinct impression that while talk about theoretical and tactical differences ran free, there was in England an accepting and understanding co-existence of Party and non-Party (including ex-Party) people that was not known in America. Ellen, asked on one occasion whether a certain man was impartial, replied "Yes, as between the Left and the Extreme Left, he's in the Middle of the Road."

We had a serious talk with Page Arnot one day in London. I had felt pushed toward some kind of decision, concerned to develop a firmer orientation even while we were in Ithaca. Watching through the labor press, during that Cornell year, the developments in the Passaic strike, I remember thinking, probably saying, that it would be comfortable to be a Communist because you would know then where to stand, you'd be told. The Party, on whose face I had not really looked, beckoned, I felt, as Catholicism must beckon to one buffeted by the winds of doctrine. Needless to say Horace disparaged this motive and I, without catching his unwillingness for the fold, could not move without conviction. Now, in London, I had a nearer, clearer view of the Party and of Party thinking. Page Arnot was impressive. I do not recall his words, know only that our talk ranged far and we asked many questions. He had a grasp and a quiet, convincing analysis of whatever he discussed. This gave one the feeling of firmness, of systematic linking of many situations, of syntheses continually being forged by a man whose purpose had, of course, long been to change the world. I listened. Reserved judgment.

In Middlesbrough we found politically sophisticated workers for the most part more concerned about the Labour Party and the Independent Labour Party than about the program of the Communist Party, and we found everyone, sophisticated and unsophisticated, the unskilled, the semi-skilled and the labor aristocracy, concerned about unemployment and the obvious inability of the antiquated British steel mills to compete with the newer, technically superior German mills. For steel was basic to Middlesbrough's economy and even very simple people could understand that British mills were old and inefficient and British steel not selling as it must if people were to hold their jobs.

Sometimes with my baby in my arms or pushed before me in his "American pram," sometimes without, I took a turn occasionally at the family visiting that yielded the monthly estimates and records of expenditures on which part of my husband's study was based. One incident sticks in my memory. On a sunny morning we visited the drab home of a man who had been severely injured on the job shortly after his marriage (he had ten children at the time of our visit so presumably the marriage had taken place some time before). The accident had incapacitated him for the rather highly skilled job he had then held, but the company had kept him on in a minor capacity (as an American steel company would not have done), and apparently he earned enough to feed the family in some fashion. Pretty scantily, though, to judge from their budget. I saw only the kitchen of their tiny home on one of Middlesbrough's grimmest streets and it was bare indeed. The mother of the family was worn but spirited. She gave me a figure of expenditure per pound on tea that drew an exclamation from me before I quite realized that I was voicing my astonishment. She bought better tea than I had thought I could afford when I was keeping house a month or so earlier in London. Her answer to my surprise was conclusive, if not devastating: "When you live a life like ours you need good tea. I'll buy the best to the end of the chapter. Folks with enough of other things may be able to manage on poor tea. I'll not."

Another experience came not in the line of duty but because I had gone with Mrs. Featherstone to a city-wide meeting of the Women's Auxiliary. It was a good meeting with a fine lot of alert and vigorous speeches and some competent parliamentary handling of points of controversy, the whole far more intellectual and informed than meetings I attended in the United States later of the League of Women Voters and the AAUW, and of course fascinatingly different in class background and general purpose. As it was closing, members were asked to visit at a home not far from the meeting hall; an unemployed worker's family was having a particularly hard time. Mrs. Featherstone and I decided to go. There were two rooms in this home, one that served as kitchen and scullery, one a bedroom that opened on the street. In the one big bed lay a gaunt woman who looked fifty but was probably in her late thirties. A little girl of eight or nine was sitting by the bed and did not take her enormous eyes off us the whole time we were there. The woman was in a daze but spoke occasionally in answer to our questions. In tiny improvised coffins on the table near the door were the corpses of two premature babies born that afternoon to the woman. She had thought she had a tumor, that she couldn't be "that way" again. There was literally nothing to eat in the house but a half cup of sugar in a bowl on an otherwise empty shelf. The infants had been starved in the womb, the child was abject, the mother beyond tears. We left a little money and as we were going out the door the little girl, who had scooped the coins up from the table, passed us, off to buy some fish and chips.

A third vivid memory of Middlesbrough is gay but has intrinsically the same import. I was sure that Chan should have his daily swig of orange juice so we bought oranges for him. This did not go unnoticed by the two younger Featherstones, Marjorie, thirteen, and Roy, eleven. One day Roy came in from school and said he had to get off to the Cubs (he pronounced it Coobs). But he wondered, being hungry, whether he might have something to eat before he went.

"It's too early for tea. Your dad's not home yet," said his mother.

"Sure, it's early for tea, but, Mother, would you have an orange?"

"An orange!" exclaimed Mrs. Featherstone in surprise not unmixed with wrath. "Do you think I'm Rothschild?"

The oldest Featherstone child was not a child but a wage-earner. At fifteen Charles could work in the steel mill on the night shift only because he had lied successfully about his age. But he had, and he did. We saw little of him, a short, spare, tight-faced lad. He brought home some fantastic pay like 30s a week and turned it all over to his mother except for bus fare and one shilling for cigarettes.

8

One morning Mrs. Featherstone told me that Charlie had not gone to work the night before, had complained of pain in his stomach and had just then thrown up a very strange-colored mess. We went upstairs, to the little back bedroom with its three beds for the three young Featherstones (in a working class home, typically a two-bedroom dwelling, it was simpler to have all your children of one sex when they reached their teens, but this could not always be arranged). Charlie looked very ill and we suggested a doctor. Mrs. Featherstone gave us a worried glance. One didn't get a doctor into the house on slight provocation and Charlie was far too sick to go to the clinic where he could have had free medical care. We insisted that she let us pay and in the end she did. When the doctor came he said "ruptured appendix" and within a few hours Charlie was on the operating table. He pulled through. A little later and he wouldn't have. His mother loved him. She hadn't guessed, of course, that his life was at stake. Neither had we. But to us a person in serious pain required a doctor whether or not his life was threatened. We could act on that code; she couldn't.

In spite of Marjorie's gay strumming on the piano and her parody of *Men of Harlech* ("Romans came across the Channel, All dressed up in tin and flannel, Half a pint of woad per man'll Clothe us more than these . . ."), and in spite of Mrs. Featherstone's good bread and the family's unfailing friendliness, things got a bit thick with eight people living in a house that had been small for five. We went on a ten day trip to Guisbrough (shades of Robin Hood's Guy of Guisborne in that village on the moors) and shortly thereafter to London again. After a month which Chan and I spent in Shepherd's Bush and Hockey mostly in the British Museum, we were off to South Wales.

This time William Green's letter to the WEA got us an introduction; we lived with a miner and his wife in Ebbw Vale. Mr. and Mrs. Jones were childless but took Chan to their hearts. I remember the day when Mrs. Jones wrapped Chan in her shawl and carried him over the moors for tea with her cousins in the next village. Remember too the Sunday when we all climbed up along the Tredegar Road to the hills that rose to the west and found there families gathered from miles around, all come on foot, literally thousands of people, miners and steelworkers and their wives and children for a "Hands Off India" rally. There were a number of speakers at various points on the vast expanse of open moor. Around each of them some hundreds of people gathered--as many as could get near enough, close-packed, to hear the shouted and militant words. Others wandered from one group to another. It was at once a holiday and a fervent demonstration against British imperialism chaired by Anevrin Bevan, then sitting for that district. I thought of it years later when I read Jürgen Kuckinski's discussion and statistical analysis of the growing misery of the working class. These Welsh families knew poverty themselves and they saw beyond their moors and rivers, beyond Europe and strange seas, to other workers impoverished by the same capitalists, felt kinship with them, and asked in June, 1927 that the British government take hands off India.

During our month with the Joneses, Fisher, Horace's younger sister, came out to spend a week-end with us. She had been in London and wired from there that she was coming. The telegram arrived when we were out of the house and created consternation. Only for deaths did working people of Wales send telegrams. The Joneses were frankly astonished when they learned that the message was simple and pleasant. Their surprise at the wire was matched by their surprise that anyone would travel all that expensive way from London just for a week-end holiday. But they accepted Fisher on sight and asked her to go with them to an evening party where an ardent young ISP lad undertook to educate her on the evils of American capitalism. Fisher, half socialist already, loved a good argument, and undertook to tell off the British imperialists; we gathered things were hot and heavy. She was asked to return for more.

We got to know some of the Ebbw Vale people fairly well, heard innumerable tales of Benjy, a real miner whose experiences were wonderfully expanded so that you heard straight-faced accounts of incredible events. In Benjy's garden, for example, he grew cabbages so big that when he sent one to Cardiff to the fair, the flat car that bore it couldn't get past the place where the track goes close to the cliffs down Cwm way until the cabbage had been pushed off. Benjy came down Tredegar Road on his bike one day so fast that the wheels were still turning the next morning when he looked out and saw the bike hanging there on the peg where it belonged just by the door.

In the small stone houses of Ebbw Vale we saw poverty quite as stark as in Middlesbrough's brick rows. I tried to scrub the floor one day for a pregnant little wisp of a woman whose husband had been injured in an accident at the Works. The floor was stone, with mortar that crumbled under my brush. I did a very bad job, but when the baby came she named it for me.

We had many talks with Mr. Jones. Mrs. Jones kibitzed. She was the quiet devoted type but the one remark of hers that I recall struck deep. He had to leave the house at 5:30 to catch the train to Cwm and his job. "Do you get up at that hour to give him his breakfast?" I asked. "Always. I go back to sleep when he leaves, of course. He could get it himself. But I always think if I shouldn't get up to give him his tea that would be the day he'd not come back." About a year before there had been a mine disaster at Cwm costing over 300 lives.

Mr. Jones loved to talk. About everything. But most about the lives and conversation of the men with whom he worked. One of his friends had been made a foreman. "He's a friend of mine no more." I protested and had my first lesson in class consciousness. If you let yourself get promoted to foreman you stepped out of your class. No matter if a foreman's wages seemed pitifully low to an American. You became a boss. Friendship from those you bossed was more than you could look for. "I still speak to him on the street," said Mr. Jones, "but I can't respect him. He let himself be bought for one pound ten a week extra, he did, and a soft job." Mr. Jones was a hearty young man, but he worked in a three-foot seam. Mrs. Jones wrote to us later that he died, five years after our visit, of miner's asthma.

II

France

Off to France. Barbara was on her way so I had *mal de mère* during the Channel crossing. But I thoroughly enjoyed the stewed rabbit dinner we were given by the Jacobe family who had found us a lodging in Maisons-Alfort and welcomed us into their crowded little home for our first meal on the continent. Georgette, the unmarried daughter, was in her late teens, a millinery worker. She was most friendly to us throughout our stay, took me in to hear Mistinguette one evening, and was our faithful guide in many areas of living out of gratitude to Fisher, with whom she had had a school-girl correspondence during the war. One of her brothers was in the Party and had a radio set--rare among Parisian workers at that time. On it he listened avidly to newscasts and political speeches. The Jacobes in their family ran the gamut from left to center and had so much goodwill and such equable acceptance of differences that one detected no evidence of friction.

While Horace worked in the library in Paris, Chan and I became acquainted with Maisons-Alfort, a working class suburb up the Seine. We lived in a *maison meublée* where the fact that we rented two rooms marked us as rich. Every other family, including those with two children, lived in one. Each room was bare but clean; contained a double bed, an armoire, a table, two chairs, a wash basin with running cold water, a two-burner gas plate. With two rooms and a borrowed crib we had the luxury of a bedroom distinct from a kitchen-living-dining-room and could keep clothes in one armoire, linen and food in the other. People attributed this lavish behavior to our being American and accepted us in spite of it. Those who might have looked askance were won by Chan, a friendly little boy whose first three words, spoken in late August, were French.

My French was very scant, Horace's excellent; after long conversations with our neighbors he would cue me in. There was the family of three in the corner room next to ours. Italians. CGTU and vehemently so. I could never get the translations fast enough to follow the argument but the father of that family put the case against the CGT on every possible occasion, and gave us union papers and notices of demonstrations. He also sang one aria after another when we went as two families to take our babies for an outing in the fields on the other side of the boulevard from our

12

maison meublée. He had loved opera in Milan before he migrated to France to look for work. Down the hall from us was another Italian family. The man was an ornamental plasterer by trade, had come to Paris with his young wife, his daughter Rosetta, aged five, and his son Lino, aged three, only to find there was no work there in the depression for a plasterer. He and his wife hired themselves out as laborers in a market garden and left every morning before the children woke up. Rosetta rose in due course, dressed herself and Lino, got breakfast and later lunch for them both and took care of the little boy until the parents returned at 4:30. One day, in lighting the gas to warm their cocoa, she had dropped the match and the *logeuse* who rented rooms and cleaned the stairs and halls arrived barely in time. This had happened before our arrival, and thereafter the *logeuse* had warmed the cocoa, a function I gladly took over for the joy of Rosetta's and Lino's companionship. Rosetta in return for my lighting the stove, operated our insect spray. "Pour les puces, Madame!" she would shout with glee as she spotted the fleas that infested our bed and doused them with the spray. Day after sunny day that summer Chan and I spent hours in the fields with Rosetta and Lino. Their parents, working six days a week were too fagged to talk much; the mother washed on Sundays the outfits that had to do for all week long. Sweeter people and a happier closer family group I have yet to find anywhere.

In Ivry-sur-Seine, a nearby suburb, the Communists had won the last election and installed a city government geared to make changes on behalf of working people. We had letters from a friend of Cousin Charlotte's to Dr. Hazemann, head of the Department of Health and to the young mayor, a most open, friendly and talkative person. They both came to dinner with their wives one night, quite a thing for me to manage but I borrowed two chairs and made it somehow. The mayor had been a sailor in the French fleet in the Black Sea off Odessa just after the October Revolution. His account at points was too fast and enthusiastic even for Horace to follow.

When we visited Ivry we were struck by the progress made by the new municipal government in the period of less than a year since it had come to power. There was, for example, a new city hospital housed in what had been a mansion for a wealthy family, four stories high, the lavish drawing rooms converted into bare white-washed clinics and operation rooms, the walled garden a rest and living space for some thirty tubercular patients who would have otherwise been in tiny working class rooms or flats. Dr. Hazemann's talk was full of the needs that were unmet as yet, and

13

of the recent accomplishments. In his eagerness to show us the place he ran upstairs three steps at a time and we did our best to follow at his pace. Sanitary, well-planned, respected, the hospital and clinics were in brilliant contrast to the "well baby clinic" I had visited in another *arrondissement* of Paris, where children urinated freely against the columns of the ancient rooms and the floors appeared never to have been washed in the centuries of their existence. From Dr. Hazemann's hospital, from the mayor's talks of his plans for the community, from the gay abandon of Bastille Day at the Bois de Garche where we watched children throwing balls at caricatured figures of Mussolini and Foche, and from long serious talks with the Communist hardware store man who was our neighbor, I had a vivid impression of reality, mass support and constructive vigor in the French movement.

We were in Maisons-Alfort in August 1927. Harry Dana had been our dinner guest and had told us much about the last weeks of the struggle to save Sacco and Vanzetti. Esther Lowenthal, Smith teacher and friend, came for lunch one day and spoke of William Allen Neilson's indignation at A. Lawrence Lowell's appalling role. Two Sundays before the execution we went in to Paris to the Bois de Vincennes. The scheduled demonstration had been cancelled, according to all the Sunday papers, because official permission had been withdrawn. The word nevertheless got around-- even to us out in Maisons-Alfort. We were late. I had insisted that Chan's two o'clock feeding be on schedule and the parade had been underway an hour when we arrived. Men, women and children eight abreast, marching as close as they well could and still keep their ranks, shouting in unison: "Vanzetti! Vive Sacco!" they were still coming when we left at five, no end in sight. Arrived at the great open meadow they flowed about as had the Welsh crowd on the moor above Ebbw Vale, congregating near one or another of many speakers. Here was the same intent concern, the same outflowing of people. The Parisian demonstration was much larger of course, more organized, sharper in its message, but in a sense the two were one.

A generation later a German friend of ours, a man who had lectured on Kathe Kollwitz in Berlin in 1932, happened to be in Paris on June 19, 1953, and saw "on every lamp-post" a painted sign: "Eisenhower, assassin." The Rosenbergs, like Sacco and Vanzetti, were mourned by all decent people. The conscience of the world, roused and roused again, must someday be heard even in Washington. The struggle against colonial oppression, against the corporate power that metes out misery to millions, is part and

14

parcel of the struggle for the lives of brave, uncompromising individuals who set themselves against oppression or who are singled out, as Sacco and Vanzetti and the Rosenbergs were, in a vain effort to prove what is not provable, that there is evil in the fight for freedom. Sharp political differences are characteristic of the French left. They were submerged when it was urgent that the people go into the streets and lift their voices for Sacco and Vanzetti.

III

Germany

In Germany we went first to the Ruhr. We lived in Dortmund in the home of an official of the Deutscher Metallarbeiter Verband. Herr Kramer, a portly man in his fifties, lived with his vivacious young wife and two young daughters in a comfortable modern four-room apartment at Werderstrasse 19. We gathered that his post gave him far more the psychology of the *Beamten* than of the steelworkers he represented.

In figure and ideology Herr Kramer was strikingly like an English Blastfurnacemen's Union official whose home we had visited at Saltburn-on Sea just out of Middlesbrough. Mr. McKenna had a larger home, to be sure, and a much larger family. Theirs was a four-story house. The dining-room and kitchen were on the ground floor a few steps down from the sidewalk. The kitchen was enormous with a fire-place into which the six-year-old son could walk without bending his head. A sewing-machine was all but lost in one corner of that kitchen. In the center was a bench on which the mother of the family was usually sitting, smoking her pipe or drinking cup after cup of scalding, strong tea. She didn't at all enjoy the status of a union official's family, and looked back with nostalgia at the time when her man had a job in the works. She suffered, one gathered, from the cleavage between her notion of life and that of her well-dressed daughter who had a clerical job and exulted in all the furniture in their enormous drawing rooms.

Herr Kramer, like Mr. McKenna in person, was also like him in having a wife who was remote from union affairs. Frau Kramer was not aging and nostalgic, but young and sophisticated. But the tradition of *Kinder* and *Küche* (if not of *Kirche*) kept her as far as Mrs. McKenna was from her husband's chief concerns. (Herr Kramer, quite unperturbed by the division, had a word for it: "Sie hat ihre Sache, ich habe meine Sache.") The Kramers practise of sleeping all in one bedroom, keeping the other for guests (ourselves during our stay) and reserving the parlor for sheer display, actually limited them to a two-room apartment for all practical purposes. Frau Kramer kept it immaculate. The big sunny kitchen was the true heart of the home and compared favorably in size and modernity with that of a middle-class American dwelling.

What marked it as German was the coal range and Herr Kramer's unchallenged domination, Frau Kramer's willing subservience.

One afternoon she took me and Chan and her two little daughters for a visit to her mother's home on the other side of the city. As four o'clock approached she hustled us all rather desperately back to Werderstrasse 19. Herr Kramer would be getting home from the office and would want his coffee. Only that. The coffee was made and the pot standing along side of the shining range. In the range was a fire neatly banked; it needed only to have the drafts opened. The coffee needed only to be moved to the hot part of the range, the cream and sugar fetched, but Frau Kramer took it for granted that she should break up a merry party and rush home to perform these chores. A man who helped at home was a Pantoffelheld.

In the course of our month in Dortmund, the service I asked (and got) from my husband did not go unnoticed by Frau Kramer (nor indeed by her husband who became a bit glum at times, looking on). Nor did Horace fail to observe the advantages of the German system. Later, in Frankfurt-am-Main, he would come home from a serene day in the University Library, sit in a comfortable chair, stretch his legs before him, glancing at the shoes I should obviously kneel to remove, and say gently but firmly, "My slippers." Pantoffelheld!

Even sadder to me than the subservience of the German wife was her willingness to let men talk of union and civic matters without participating in the conversation. Horace talked with Herr Kramer over coffee, over dinner, about everything under the sun; at times I pitched in, hoping to prepare the way for Frau Kramer to do the same, at times remained aloof, either to keep her company or because my German was woefully inadequate. Frau Kramer, alert, untouched by it all, stuck happily to "ihre Sache."

From Dortmund we went to Frankfurt-am-Main. The first few days there we spend in the guest room at the Institut für Sozialforschung on Viktoria-Allee. Here the talk at table was fast indeed. Even to follow it was rather more than I could manage, but Horace dubbed in later for me most of what I had missed. The Institut was Marxist, most of its staff if not Party members then at least so oriented, I gathered. They were obviously on good terms with men in their own fields at the University of Frankfurt. We were to learn twenty years and an anti-Nazi war later, in 1947, at the University of Kansas City, from Dr. Eugen Altschul, former Professor of Economics at the University of Frankfurt, how truly cordial the relations were between a critic of Marx, like himself, and the men working vigorously in research along strictly Marxist lines at the Institut. The cordiality ran deep. It stemmed from a thoroughgoing belief in freedom of thought that permeated the German Universities, according to Altschul, something of which most American academicians have not the vaguest notion, unused as they are to controversy. It was significant that when Horace was under attack at the University of Kansas City in 1953 as the result of his being an uncooperative witness before the Jenner Committee, it was Altschul, old, completely dependent on his somewhat shabby job at the University and outspoken in his opposition to much of what Horace thought and taught, Altschul who came forward to defend him.

In the Institut we met Karl August Wittfogel and his wife Rosa. Karl August has been a Wunderkind, graduating very young from the University; in his early twenties he was holder of a doctorate and leading theoretician as well as an honored figure in the German Party. We had many good talks with him, heard something of his theory of Chinese economic development. This theory was presented in his *Wirtschaft und Gesellschaft Chinas* published in Leipzig in 1931. It was appallingly distorted by his own hand in a recent work published in America. Karl August is a tragic figure of our time. In those Frankfurt days we did not foresee it. He seemed to have everything: youth, strength, wit, erudition, confidence. He had mastered with apparent ease the rigorous training offered in the academic Germany that had so impressed Seligman and other American scholars. He had too all the concern and elan and insight of the new ideology that seemed truly to have in it the seeds of tomorrow. We were warmed and flattered that he cared to talk with us, that he befriended us. Rosa, less brilliant, was no less friendly. We felt rich indeed.

Ellen Wilkinson, in England, had given us of that country's best. Karl August, in Germany, ushered us into the circles we were most eager to know. And Germany then was close to the Soviet Union. There were the new Soviet novels in quick translation, all the fire and fun of the *Blaue Bluse*, with Party guards in uniform keeping order in the vast audience so the municipal police could be, and were entirely dispensed with. British mills were old, furnaces and techniques antiquated, output limited. German mills had been built for the most part in recent years because Germany had industrialized late; they had used superior techniques and equipment. Was it fanciful to think that by a curious parallel, German workers were following, with an alertness and vigor quite impossible to their discouraged and blighted English contemporaries, the current of new ideas flowing so strongly westward out of the Soviet Union?

Actually we were at one remove in Frankfurt. We saw the crowds of working people as well as intellectuals at the *Blaue Bluse*, caught their enthusiasm. We read Party literature as well as the *Frankfurter Zeitung* (whose editor entertained us once at dinner, a memorable occasion). But the kind of intimate acquaintance with working class families that we had enjoyed in Middlesbrough and Ebbw Vale was limited here to the George Geisels. Luckily the Geisels, like the Jacobes, were a large family and ran the gamut politically.

Frau Geisel came to us once or twice a week as *Putzfrau*. A spare, tall woman with a ready smile, she won us completely as well as keeping our two rooms immaculate and teaching Chan to "putzen." Toward the end of our stay he had us to dinner in her home. It was a tiny, dark apartment on the third floor of a huge rambling building that one reach by crossing a courtyard. The courtyard comes back to me when I look at the Fille drawing of the little girl holding a weeping baby brother in her arms in a courtyard in deep shade between high stark walls while a distracted mother calls from a window high in one of those walls, "Hold him in the sun until he dries!"

The Geisels had seven children. Frau Geisel loved them all, obviously, but it was hard to feed them in those days. There was a depth of earnestness in her voice when she looked at Barbara, born that January of 1928, *dritte Klasse* in the city hospital, and gave me advice that I wisely did not take: "Und jetzt ist Schluss!"

One of Frau Geisel's sons was a Party member. Because of the acute shortage of dwellings at that time he and his young wife had to live in one room of his parents' already crowded apartment. This was an apparently amicable arrangement although there were frequent political arguments, another son being a Social Democrat and the father and mother centrist.

It was in January that we visited them, only five years before the Reichstag fire. I have often wondered whether we were fantastically blind that we were all but unaware of the Nazi movement. The scatter-brained young son of our landlady sat at their piano and sang the Horst Wessel Song as well as *Deutschland Über Alles* while his mother, a doctor's widow impoverished by the inflation, scuttled about in the kitchen trying to concoct a meal from far too little food, but he was not a serious person, had let a number of jobs slip through his fingers. A working class family like the Geisels seemed not to consider ominous, at that time, the sporadic street fighting of groups of young Nazis. The Geisels' political spectrum was broad; it did not, of course, include those insane folk. The Geisels thought of them as demoralized middle class ne'er-do-wells and did not consider them a serious menace. Bob Brady, whom we had known in Ithaca, went to Germany a year or so later than we did and found the situation greatly changed.

To us the problem before the German people seemed to be one of consolidating the social welfare gains of the Republic under a stronger government, one that would include the Communist Party, which obviously enjoyed the confidence of a large sector of the working class and of the most brilliant and concerned intellectuals. We enjoyed the sharp irony of anti-Hindenburg brochures and caricatures and were so stirred by the political vigor of the movement that it seemed inevitable that the strong would survive, the differences between Social Democrats and Communists not so much ironed out as sharpened and constructively resolved, and the German working class emerge from its obvious difficulties and stand in a position to advise, in detail, Englishmen and Americans who wanted to build for themselves a better life.

My own feeling of being at home in Germany had been strong from the moment our train crossed the border en route from Liege to Dortmund. It was based, I presume, on the romantic stories my German grandmother had told me of her early childhood in Baden, whence the family had fled in 1848 because her father, an officer in the Landswehr, would not fire on his countrymen involved in the revolution. My grandmother's sense of being German, her loyalty to the country she had left at the age of four, had been so strong that she found herself arguing almost alone against the canards about German atrocities that gained eager credence in the United States during World War I. This sense of being German was part of my heritage from her, quite as definite though not as consciously learned as her skill in baking cherry pie. Reinforced surely by the obvious cultural likenesses in German life to the American life I knew, it gave me instant confidence in the German people and an awareness of kinship. This feeling of belonging and understanding was deepened by my experiences when Barbara was born.

Being a foreigner I was unable to arrange that my maternity fees be covered by the system of social insurance introduced by the new republic. But by going third class I got the delivery and ten days in the hospital for twelve marks, a modest sum indeed compared with what I had paid for similar care in Ithaca. I shared a room with two other mothers and in the long hours between feedings we talked intimately, as one does in a maternity ward. One of them was having her third baby; the two older ones, in their teens, inspired her slightly sardonic "Kleine Kinder, kleine Sorgen, grosse Kinder, grosse Sorgen." The other mother was herself not quite out of her teens, married to a young garage mechanic who looked like a rather bewildered high school boy when he came to visit. Her bills were all met by his insurance which covered also the entire cost of a layette and whatever extra food the baby might require for the first six months together with several check-up visits and possible post-natal care after leaving the hospital. Had the mother been employed herself at the time she had become pregnant she would have got six months on maternity leave with pay, part before, part after delivery.

In several respects the maternity care differed from what I had seen in Ithaca and was to see later in other American hospitals. The delivery room was equipped to admit three patients at a time and was staffed by highly trained midwives rather than by private doctors engaged by the patients. But when a problem arose in my case I noticed that in a very short time not one but two doctors came on call and saw me through. There was no anaesthesia. This pleased me; it was accepted as routine by the other patients and I was deeply interested in the stoic calm in which they all went through labor--no shrieking as of souls in torment as one heard in an American maternity ward. Another contrast was in the after care. Barbara was born just before supper so I got back to my room, after my glimpse of a baby who looked exactly like Mother, just in time for that meal and was called on for no further effort that day. But the next morning at 6:30 a little nurse came briskly in, threw up the window to a chill January day and announced gaily, "Jetzt treiben wir Gymnastik!" This was for me as well as for the others. The first few days I was given very light, slow exercises, but exercises I did, both morning and evening, and fairly soon I was up and about--enjoying the regime American hospitals were to adopt approximately a generation later. Moreover, the staff, busy as they were, showed warmth, a direct and unaffected kindliness that was most cheering. In the face of it I could not feel a stranger. Nor could I but wish then and later that young working class mothers in our country could receive such excellent care as part of their husband's earning under a state that was committed to a broad program of social insurance.

Germans suffered that winter. The lack of housing was the most obvious problem, but one also caught indications of widespread unemployment. Things were far from simple and people had by no means forgotten the deprivations suffered during the war nor regained physical strength lost then. I remember serving rutabagas with noon dinner one day to two young students we knew (they were living together as man and wife but couldn't afford to get married, they said). The girl--the more outspoken of the two--turned down that vegetable. "If you knew," she said, "how I ate them for breakfast, dinner, supper, as a child during the war . . . nothing but rutabagas for days at a time . . . ." What I found in Germany was certainly not plenty, nor socialism, nor even sure economic progress. I found bitter need and chaos born of war and inflation. But there was also a government which, for all its errors and weaknesses did seem pledged to meeting the basic economic problems of the people as a state duty. This seemed eminently right.

Also correct, I though, was the determination of Party people, workers and intellectuals, to push the government to more vigorous efforts--including forthright socialization of basic industries like steel.

It was during our stay in Germany that Litvinov, speaking to the world, announced that peace was indivisible and called, in behalf of his government, for general disarmament, a call strikingly like that of Krushchev more than thirty years later (perhaps it makes no sense to count over the friends who would probably be walking the earth today if that call had been heeded, or to consider what suffering the people of all continents would have been spared). The speech was published in full in the *Frankfurter Zeitung* and obviously woke earnest echoes among the German people, including the upper strata of intellectuals. We were to discover on our return to the USA no evidence that the call had made on Americans an impression of anything like the same magnitude. Many otherwise intelligent persons seemed not even to have been aware of it, or, aware, had discredited it completely.

We left Germany reluctantly, in early April. On our way to Hamburg we stopped off for a few days' visit at Walkemühle, a left-oriented but non-Communist cooperative agricultural colony near Kassel. The members of the community were most cordial. It was something for the mother of two young children to be met on arrival by a competent colonist who took over both kids at once and cared for them joyously and most successfully during our entire stay. "So that you may be free to participate fully in activities at Walkemühle," she said to me. Life in the colony was communal, healthy, simple. The purpose of the venture was to train young people to go into the labor movement as leaders and at the same time to give the experience of group living. Farm activities were engaged in for support--the food consumed in the colony was most of it raised on the place and the colonists were vitamin-conscious and sternly addicted to Rohkost (I am sure that Chan acquired at Walkemühle his taste for raw oatmeal). Their political philosophy, for all the earnest expounding I heard during our stay, seemed to me a bit nebulous. Where those people went in the later years, into the underground and the concentration camps or into the NSPD I suppose I shall not ever learn. But they were lively, critical, dedicated, at the time we were there as guests.

The S.S. Albert Ballin took us out of Hamburg for a long trip home across an Atlantic all too lashed by spring storms. Chan and the Bear were excellent sailors. I alas was not. My morale was sustained however by our stewardess. She would catch me every morning as I came dashing back to our cabin to upchuck my breakfast. A few minutes later she would appear with a second breakfast on a tray and, glancing at Barbara asleep in the Kozykar, would remark to me sternly, "Junge Frau, Sie dürfen nicht seekrank werden."

It was exciting when we finally docked and found a family delegation waiting to greet us. But for all the joy of the homecoming I was appalled by Manhattan's tempo and cold indifference, longed for the Gemütlichkeit and, yes, the sense of progressive life in the Germany we had come to love, really wished that I could take ship again at once on the Albert Ballin and return on her return voyage... in spite of the spring storms, still raging.

We spent a few days in New York City, a month in Tenafly in New Jersey and the summer at Christmas Lake, the Rubins' summer home near Minneapolis. Chan's speech shifted from German to English. I remember the moment when he was helping set the table at Christmas Lake, put down a knife, remarked deliberately, "Messer . . . knif-f-fe," and never said "Messer" again. It was a lovely summer. Having the kids in a home that had changed hardly at all since I grew up was an experience for me. Father would carry Chan downhill to bed, wrapped up in a black and white blanket (we still have one or two at Sandwich) and Chan, pointing through oak branches to the top of the summer sky would shout gaily, "See Vega!" Remembering as I did how in earlier days there had always been someone to serve as defense attorney for any tree even remotely considered as suitable to be chopped down, I was deeply impressed by the swathe that was cut in our forest to ensure Barbara plenty of sun-bathing. The kids thoroughly enjoyed their privileged position and I stayed with them into September though

Horace pushed away earlier, bent on finding us a place in which to live and work during the following year.

He had an impressive batch of material: schedules, documents, notes. His fellowship had been continued and he planned to finish the study and look for an academic post only in the following year. The country was before us; we could choose where we would live. He was naturally drawn to the Monongahela Valley, still the major site of the industry he was studying, a place rich in history as it was deep in ore dust and one he knew, at least in part, from his year at Braddock. Gary was another possibility. I was still in a daze and though we discussed the pros and cons of Pittsburgh, Gary, even Birmingham, I left the decision to him.

When he was gone I was suddenly intensely lonely. We have acted in most cases as I still think best, even in "hindsight," but I regret every day we've spent apart and there have been too many of them. One thing I did accomplish in that interval. Chan's birth had interrupted my work for Willcox. I wrote, agreeing to put the gist of my results into a memorandum; so, at the generous wage of $5 the clocked hour, I sat down on the porch in Christmas Lake woods, dug into the old notes and finished a paper that eventually got published by the National Bureau, a workmanlike job--one could not be less than workmanlike for Willcox--but arid, it seemed, in comparison with the ideas now teeming in my head.

IV

Pittsburg

Horace decided on Pittsburgh and found a house for us, a typical row house in the lee of the Jones and Laughlin mill--so we got plenty of cinders--but high on a ridge overlooking Schenley Park. Not only that. He rustled me a job, part-time, at the University of Pittsburgh, under my old friend of Columbia days, John Cover, who had undertaken a survey of meat consumption in the area. Its purpose was to determine what demand there was in what income and nationality groups for packaged meats. John, I am sure, was a bit discomfited by the commercial motivation of the survey and knew that I'd be even more so. He set up his staff so that I could concentrate on the sampling procedures and the direction of the house to house interviewing. It was fun. I got a widowed mother of slightly older children to spell me off at home and gave three afternoons a week to the job, walking over and back across a corner of Schenley Park and plunging so happily and thoroughly into the work that I'd literally forget that I had children until 5:30 came and I set off for home.

My stand-in would have supper on the table when I got there and she would slip away to her own family. We'd all eat supper together, then I'd bathe the kids and tuck them away after a romp and stories. By doing all the housework but noon dinner dishes and supper preparation myself before I walked out, I left my helper free for Kinderpflege. As any working mother could guess, it was fine as long as everyone was well. The kids always seemed serene when I got back. The rough time held off until February. Then the Bear was off on a three week jaunt to Birmingham with Art Shields and Esther Lowell, my dozen interviewers were deep in their survey and needed more help so I stepped up my schedule until it was almost full time and Barbara came down with what I thought was a heavy cold until it became so frightening one night of agonized struggling for breath that bronchial pneumonia seemed a wiser diagnosis. The survey was ditched temporarily as far as I was concerned and I pulled my baby through. What the illness cost her I shall never know. Just after her first birthday she could not tell me in words. But the whole experience gave me pause, a keen sense of my own fallibility and compassion for all women who carry the double burden, all children whose mother's thoughts are partly elsewhere. Of course if Horace had been at home it would not have happened. However deep he might be in work he has always had a sharp awareness of health problems, has always acted on it promptly.

The chief joy of our Pittsburgh home, in a way, was the Duffy family next door. Jimmie and Mary Katherine, five and three, seemed to us very grown up indeed, assumed a fond and occasionally parental attitude toward our kidlets and enjoyed with them our pocket-handkerchief sized back yard and its sandpile. They were sweet kids, talked freely (I hoped that their gorgeous young policeman father and lovely blonde young mother were not aware that Jimmie told me one day, before I could think how to stop him, just what an exciting thing it had been the night before when he woke up to see his parents doing something very strange in their bed in the next room).

We liked living near Schenley Park and developed the habit of taking long Sunday walks there, Barbara in the Kozykar, Chan on the Bear's shoulders. By early spring we had another companion on those walks, Joe Dallet. Horace was doing occasional stories for Federated Press and Joe, just out of Dartmouth and an FP correspondent too, had been told to look him up. Joe enjoyed dropping in for meals, for talks, came willingly to babysit when we had a yen to take in a movie, and joined us in those walks in the park. Joe was moving much faster then we were in the direction of the Party, perhaps because he was younger, had built up fewer intellectual reservations, perhaps he was by temperament more impetuous, perhaps because being single he had more chance to hang around with Party people and be persuaded.

Early that fall we had gone to a meeting for Foster--taking the kids along. It was a dramatic period. As the National Textile Workers' Union was active in textiles, so was the National Miners' Union in coal. Only against the background of the moribund United Textile Workers and the machine-ridden United Mine workers was dual unionism a reasonable procedure, but it surely seemed so then. In perspective the CIO itself (still more than six years in the future in 1928) might well be considered fruit of the same kind of determination to organize the unorganized as infused these left wing unions, a determination to go forward in defiance, if need be, of an existent but inactive union already in the field. I remember a crowded hall that night in late September at the Foster meeting --a rather barren hall, full of shabby people with eager faces, warm greetings, the shifting interplay of talk that tells of acquaintance and common interests and a sense of urgency. The Bear knew many of them. Scattered, practically lost among the

26

workers, were a handful of young intellectuals from the University. It was shortly after a violent raid by UMW goons on a scheduled meeting of the National Miners' Union in the same hall. This had occurred just before I reached Pittsburgh. Horace had been present when the attack occurred, had reported it for the FP.

Well, here was the Party, and here, as the main speaker of the evening, was the man who best represented the American Party then and for years to come. We went with Charles Moody to hear him in 1946 and saw then, in Charles' rapt attention and heard in his deliberate praise--praise from him was rare--the same deep respect we felt for William Z. Foster that night. He looked even at that time a bit worn with struggle. After all it had been eight years before in 1919 that he had led the strike in steel and he had not rested in the meantime. He was a thin man, strong, relaxed, genial, with talk as quick and greetings as warm as any in the room, but when he stepped to the platform you felt his concentration, and the speech that came in considered, even measures from his lips and penetrated without stress and without mike to every listener, was as magnificently organized as a lecture by Laski and even fuller of concrete, supporting evidence of the points he made. Pat was there, as I've said, his Irish eyes not only smiling but lit with a devil of daring as well as zeal, and Fanny was there, his tiny, dark-haired wife, eager, friendly, flitting from group to group. Horace pointed out others in the minutes before the meeting was called to order. When Foster spoke there was profound silence, respected luckily by Chan and Barbara who drowsed in exemplary fashion through most of the session.

We couldn't do that often however, and with a fellowship to stretch out over family living for a year and my wages going largely to pay my stand-ins, we would have been reluctant to hire babysitters even had we known competent ones. Joe, later, was invaluable, but he developed a flair too for Party meetings, so as babysitter at the time of such gatherings he wasn't much help.

Horace went around a lot getting stories for FP and generally keeping in touch. He brought home what he garnered and I had plenty of vicarious experience. I was flattered to have the movement walk in at our own door a couple of times when Fanny and I got some projects moving and she would come over in the evening to plan. In fact we observed in Pittsburgh as it would have been impossible to observe in a larger center how Party people keep in touch with progressive action already in motion, how they suggest action, how the "vanguard" really operates when it is active and conscientious and imaginative.

This, 1928-29, was the year of the Lovestone doctrine of American exceptionalism--a doctrine battled effectively by theoreticians like Foster long before it was shattered for all time by October 1929. It was the year of the Gastonia textile strike. We heard Ella Reeve Bloor, fresh from the textile area of North Carolina, tell with all her verve and militancy and wisdom, just how the struggle was shaping up. It was the year in which the Pennsylvania Coal and Iron Police aroused a broad movement of liberals as well as miners and steelworkers to call for a repeal of the statute under which they were maintained. Colston Warne was in the fight, and Bill Chalmers, later at the University of Illinois, and Bill Nunn, and, strangely enough, Fred Woltman, then a militant young assistant and graduate student, later a journalist, "expert on communism," paid informer and rat of the lowest stripe. If his scholarly career had not been cut short by his expulsion for taking up the cudgels against the Coal and Iron Police he might conceivably have gained enough maturity to have stood firm when temptation eventually came, as it undoubtedly would have done, in any case, a few years later. Leaving out Fred, best forgotten, the little group of intellectuals weathered well. Colston and the two Bills, all teaching at the University, all fathers with wives who followed but not very fast, all non-Party and consistently so, worked valiantly and selflessly in the campaign in close cooperation and frequently friendly altercation with the Party forces. As teachers the three were of course under heavy attack at the University.

It was also the year of a nationwide campaign to free Tom Mooney who was in Alcatraz, ill, on a life term for a crime he had obviously not committed (an ignorant freshman at Smith, I had first heard of Tom Mooney from my math teacher, Pauline Sperry, on a walk in the spring of 1917. She was an excellent math teacher, left shortly thereafter for the University of California where she had a long and honorable career and was cut out of her last year of teaching before retirement by her refusal to sign the loyalty oath. I wrote her a fan letter at that time and learned how steadfast she was and how sad to lose those last precious months of teaching. She was not a Party person at all, but she valued freedom of thought, and defended it). A meeting for Tom Mooney was scheduled on the University campus and held just off campus when permission was withdrawn for the original site. It reminded me of a meeting for the same purpose held under similar conditions in 1923 just across Amsterdam Avenue from Columbia University.

Sponsorship of the Mooney meeting even more than participation in the campaign against the Coal and Iron Police "made the cheese binding" when John Cover recommended Horace that summer for a job under University auspices and was told that if Horace Davis were the Angel Gabriel he'd not get a job at the University of Pittsburgh (such remarks were common parlance in the Monongahela Valley. The mayor of Duquesne had said some five years earlier during a steel organizing drive that Jesus Christ himself couldn't hold a meeting in Duquesne. One should give these speakers credit for recognizing who stood on the side of the angels).

Such a lovely job it would have been, that job for which John had been asked to name his candidate. John was not involved either in the Mooney meeting or in the campaign against the Coal and Iron Police, though he was fully aware of them both and sympathetic in his quiet way. In the course of my work on his project and through occasional visits to our home for dinner and talk, he learned a fair bit about Horace's European study, his contacts with the labor movement and his power to set up and carry through a research job of some magnitude. When John was asked to name a director for a planned five year study of unemployment in the Pittsburgh area beginning in the summer of 1929 he said unequivocally that Horace Davis was the only man he knew capable of handling the job and that he was eminently qualified. The funds, ample funds, were on hand. No one knew at the time how important such a study would have proved but we knew enough to lick our lips at the thought of it, and John had, in effect, been given the naming of the director. Horace would have designed and directed the study with anywhere up to a dozen trained people working under him. What disqualified him? In large measure he was disqualified by the very acquaintance with the labor movement, knowledge of the area and ease in approaching working people that in John Cover's mind constituted important qualifications. That a person of perception and integrity cannot be close to the labor movement without developing an attitude toward it, that a social scientist can no more than any other honest citizen look on injustice without protesting, these are truths that many refuse to recognize. Horace was turned down and a lesser man given the job--the man John had picked as one who might make a competent assistant under Horace's direction. This man worked on the project a few months, found its magnitude and problems confusing and frustrating, failed even to get it set up properly and had a nervous breakdown. As far was we ever knew the whole thing was abandoned. "It was too big for him," John reported. "I knew it would be."

I have said that we learned a lot that year. This is no place to record systematically all that we learned, but let me put down a few items. On the Birmingham trip Horace had uncovered, by chance, the murder of a Negro mechanic in the mill, a highly skilled man who had taught a succession of white workers the job while he worked at lower pay as the "helper." The story was published in the *Nation* of January 1, 1930, after an illuminating interview with a member of the staff of that weekly. They had checked the story of the murder with the United States Steel Corporation, controlling the Tennessee Coal and Iron Company, by whom the victim, Matt Lucas, had been employed and whose hired guards had called him from his bed at home in the company town and shot him in the yard for insolence on the job. The *Nation* man questioned the advisability of publishing the story but did not deny its accuracy (in 1942 when Horace was interrogated by security officers in connection with an OSS job, he discovered that his interest in the Matt Lucas case was in his FBI dossier). As grim, almost, as the murder itself was the fact that the story had not appeared even in the Negro press and seemed not to be known in the Negro community in Birmingham, the city where Matt Lucas had been employed and in whose suburb he had lived.

We knew some of the people involved in the attempt to organize steelworkers in Alequippa, met Milan Resetar at a picnic shortly before his incarceration. He was an Alequippa steelworker who had been sentenced with several others to five years for talking union in one room of a worker's home while a children's birthday party had been going on in another and who died in the federal penitentiary at Blawnox. Jessie O'Connor, who had a few shares of U.S. Steel rose in the stockholders' meeting to protest the conditions he confronted, ill with tuberculosis, in the prison, and to ask the U.S. Steel Corporation to get him pardoned. It made the press but did not change the policy of the company.

I swept cinders from our porch every morning and wanted to go with Horace to visit the Jones and Laughlin Mill from which it came. But the safety director of the mill explained most courteously why this could not be. He said that many of the furnaces, in fact most of them, were out of date installations without modern safety devices. They could not, of course, be replaced until they had been operated long enough to have rendered a reasonable return on the original investment, but meanwhile they were very dangerous and the company simply could not run the risk of allowing a woman to visit, as even in a tour of the mill there was chance of a serious accident. Horace went without me and found conditions quite as bad as the safety director had indicated. We both wondered how the safety director felt spending his unearned salary.

Pat Toohey and some of our other friends were working among the coal miners in the unorganized bituminous mines of West Virginia and southern Pennsylvania. One week-end Horace went with them on an expedition to Morgantown, West Virginia, where a little later Pat and a couple of others were actually besieged in a farmhouse, a dramatic incident in a running battle between NMU organizers and UMW men. I wanted him to go and cannot believe it made any difference in the event, but things got a bit thick for me at home before his return and the little brother or sister who might have been was lost, only two months along. A miscarriage is only a miscarriage, and I know that the gynecologists say soothingly and no doubt correctly that if things are not right with a pregnancy it will be terminated and better early than late. Every time, however, it is a sad loss. So it was then. We wanted another bearkin.

The job on the unemployment survey in Pittsburgh was definitely lost, and it was late to get a good academic post. Only some time after this did we learn that Don English, titular head of the department the year Horace was at Cornell, had in letters of recommendation, damned him not only with faint praise but with the definite accolade of being "pro labor." Whether for this reason or for another he got no very alluring offer and we settled on Southwestern, a small denominational college in Memphis. Matt Lucas gave us warning; I remember this strange feeling when our train, at night, in early September, crossed into Kentucky and we were in the South.

V

Memphis

Memphis seemed at first quite an ordinary American city, and our acquaintances on the campus seemed reassuringly like modest academic folk in any number of modest colleges over the country. Coming, as we did, from a milieu where news from Gastonia was lapped up eagerly, and stricken, as we had been, by the shooting there, by the murder shortly after of Ella Mae Wiggins, during the opening days of the trial of the union leaders, we found it strange to hear Ponni Davis (young faculty wife and our good friend before the year was out) commenting on the same events in her lovely, cultured Virginia voice from a point of view poles away from ours. This one must say for Ponni: from the first, and notably so in this most controversial matter of Gastonia, she presented with admirable clarity her own view of a subject and then listened, with objectivity and a delightful, young willingness-to-be-convinced to a view diametrically opposed to her own. Her husband, a former Rhodes Scholar, was less articulate and less open to conviction.

We found a pleasant boarding place in which to stay during our house-hunting. I phoned some Smith friends and true to the Northampton tradition one of them called on us even before we moved to our new home. This was a four-room frame dwelling on a quiet street. No cellar. No foundation even. Just brick pillars for the house to rest on and board siding from floor to ground. In the following winter, one of the most severe in years, our plumbing was to suffer from the exposure, but of that we had no foretaste in September. We were assured that Tennessee homes needed no cellars and it was lovely to have no furnace to care for, only a big stove in the children's room and fireplaces in our room and the dining-living room. The house was simple but charming, held us and our things, had an ample yard, and, as we soon discovered, a mockingbird given to midnight serenading.

Lillie Mae Harris, the fourteen-year-old daughter of one of the kitchen staff at Southwestern, was part of our household from the beginning. She had left school for day work and while she did not by any means come to us every day she was with us at least two days a week to help with kidlets and household chores, a trim, self-respecting, competent young person whose friendliness was real. Through her we kept in touch too with her mother, whom we had liked on sight.

32

The Harrises, mother and daughter, invited us to go with them to visit their relatives in the country, a rare experience for white folks, and proof, we felt, or almost proof, that they accepted us. The welcome in the farm home was warm, talk was free. The only flaw was that they served us at their table but would not sit and eat with us in spite of our urging. So far their courage did not reach. It was a memorable day. Included, among other things, a long talk for Horace with another tenant farmer, a white man and apparently a friendly neighbor of Lillie Mae's uncle. The two tenant farmers, white and black, discussed their problems freely with Horace, the terms of their tenancy contracts and the state of agriculture on the red and badly eroded land. But they did it separately. Lillie Mae's uncle introduced Horace to his white neighbor, then himself strolled away as if it would have been improper somehow for him to join the conversation between two white men. Our children rode one of the farm horses, saw cotton in full glory at the point of being picked, watched a sorghum press in operation.

Through Lillie Mae we learned much. One day she did not come to work when I expected her. She had been with us the day before, was to have returned. Her mother called at noon to apologize, said her daughter was ill and could come back in a few days. I got the real story only by insisting. Lillie Mae had left work with us and taken supper with a friend. Waiting for a bus to go home after dark, she was accosted on a lonely corner by two young white men in a car. They forced her into their car, drove to a still more lonely spot, raped her and left her somewhere near the bus line to find her way home as best she could. Her mother hoped we would not speak of the affair. It could only hurt her daughter. There would be no way of getting the attackers punished though Lillie Mae remembered the license number.

Later, much later, after we had spent a night in jail and were on the point of leaving town, Lillie Mae wanted to see us to say good-bye. We persuaded her leave it at a phoned good-bye as our house was being watched and we feared repercussions for her. But there she was, loyal, firm. We are only sorry that our paths did not cross again. Not much more than ten years older than our Chan, she was, but a woman already and a brave one.

In Memphis we learned and learned that year. Even the daily paper was a source of enlightenment. It reported, e.g., the case of a Negro passenger on a streetcar who had the gall to question the change he was given when he paid his fare. The conductor-motorman shot him dead on the front platform of the car in the presence of witnesses and was apparently not even indicted for murder. He was sentenced to a month in jail for carrying a gun without a permit. One day the paper reported an attack upon a young white woman by a Negro. The date of the hearing was announced and I persuaded Dean Hartley's wife, a Yankee and a member of the AAUW, to go to it with me to hear what might be said. The procedure was extremely brief, tucked in between a minor traffic violation and a petty theft. Some of the details of the incident had been given in the press release; others we picked up from testimony in court. The woman in the case worked with her husband in a small grocery store that the two of them owned. It was in a Negro neighborhood. About noon one day her husband happened to be out of the store and the defendant came in to make a purchase. There was an argument and she told him to get out; as he left, by the front door, she started screaming. He ran around by the alley at the side of the store and when a policeman, alerted by the screams, gave chase, the Negro hid in a lumber yard about a block away. Soon after he was apprehended, put in jail and charged with attempted rape. It looked on the face of it like a frame-up since neither in the press release nor in the court testimony was there any detail to suggest an attack. The defendant claimed that the argument was over a debt of his to the store.

Mrs. Hartley and I were interested. We went to the store, walked around and saw the alley and the lumberyard. The neighborhood was one of small frame houses set close together. That noon-time when we were there, it was full of people going to and fro. Presumably it was not more lonely on the day of the alleged attack. We went to the defendant's address, a boarding-house a few blocks away, and talked with his landlady. She said he was a young man, very steady, quiet and hard-working and as far as she knew had never been in trouble before. He had recently come to Memphis from a farm home in Arkansas and was on his lunch hour when he went to the store that day. Even through the normal screen of reticence any Negro observes when talking to any white person, a screen immeasurably thicker than usual in circumstances like these, one gathered that the landlady thought the storekeeper's wife had been malicious.

My husband went to the jail and asked to talk with the defendant, explaining that it seemed to him that the man needed and deserved legal counsel. He was not released at once but the case was eventually dropped.

The neighborhood of the store and the boarding-house was close to one that bordered on a struck plant where there had been violence charged against pickets and where we had done some visiting one Sunday morning, trying to pick up from conversations with neighbors the issues in the strike and the actual course of events. This method of casual inquiry was a technique the Bear had developed and used effectively in the Matt Lucas case in Birmingham (in 1959 Art Shields was to use it with brilliant success in Poplarville, Mississippi; how much of it Horace caught from Art in 1929, how much Art from Horace, how much both of them from Esther Lowell, probably no one can say. Some of it, however, I know was indigenous with the Bear). Accustomed to the readiness with which Welsh miners, French laborers, steelworkers of Yorkshire, the Ruhr and the Monongahela Valley opened their hearts and minds to the quiet questioning of my husband, I was prepared to have Negro workers in Memphis respond with equal candor. On the whole they did, though the veil was always there. It was over a generation later, during a second sojourn in the Deep South, that I heard our people spoken of as "the opposite race" and came to understand how truly remarkable it was that people in Memphis, Negro people, trusted Horace as they did.

We enjoyed a good deal of casual and not-so-casual interviewing first and last, both in the city and on Sunday jaunts in a rented car to the plantations of the Mississippi Delta. The kids went along and here, as in Europe, we found that a child was a disarming companion, giving one entree where adults alone might have been unwelcome.

Dwelling by dwelling, talk by talk, we built up a picture, fragmentary no doubt but moving, of what it meant to be a Negro in that region. Much that we had learned from Negro sharecroppers in the Delta was confirmed, interestingly enough, by the husband of one of my (white) Smith classmates when we were invited to their rather lavish home for dinner. "You Northerners just don't understand our problem." This came, as we had learned to expect it, quite early in the conversation and out of the blue. We had purposely said nothing about racial issues, finding it far pleasanter to stay on other subjects when talking with white Southerners, and after all, these people had been friendly to us. "You Yankees just don't understand the nigras as we do. We were raised with them. . . ." He launched, with no encouragement from us, into a tale about one cropper's family with whom he had trouble on one of his plantations in the Delta. As landlord he tried to visit each estate at least once a year, although of course all details were handled by the local manager whom he hired to run it. In this case he passed, in his car, a cropper's house that stood near the road; he knew there was a new family there that year and as he went by he glanced, out of curiosity, at the woman sitting on the porch. To his amazement and wrath he saw that she seemed to be white. Another glance, down the field beside the house, showed him a man, obviously black, cultivating rows of cotton. When the landowner reached the manager's office he asked him, he said, "in no uncertain terms what he meant letting land to a nigra cropper with a white wife."

"She swears she's a nigger," the manager had replied.

"They have to go," our host had told him. "Tomorrow at the latest."

At this even the manager demurred. "But they've put in a crop."

This, of course, could make no difference, our host explained. He had insisted that they go at once. Even if she had been able to prove that she had some Negro blood it wouldn't have looked right, having her there.

Home from dinner the Bear said he wouldn't put his knees under that man's table again. I saw my classmate, Ann, when she called to see me, but managed to evade further invitations.

Ponni Davis was another story. Unlike Mrs. Hartley, she had no damyankee background, but she followed fast. We saw the Davises a lot that winter--when they took us to Bach concerts, when they came for dinner and bridge, when they baby-sat for us; around the edges we talked. Often about the subject that concerned us most--the status of the Negro in the South. Ponni borrowed books, including a richly illustrated little volume by Scott Nearing, called *The American Negro*, if I remember correctly. This she had on her living-room table one day when some other Southwestern faculty people called. The man spied the book, skimmed through it, and accused Ponni of turning into a "nigger lover." Ponnie replied with spirit and asked us for more books like it.

Our next door neighbors to the east were named O'Connor, a childless couple in their forties and most friendly. Our kids could always get a cookie in Mrs. O'Connor's kitchen. Once a week there came to these neighbors, to do their washing and cleaning, an old woman who had been born on Mrs. O'Connor's grandfather's plantation in Mississippi. Her name was Tillie; what more, I never knew. She was bent and very dark, with a wrinkled, kindly face. Often when she left she carried a small bundle of food or clothing. Whether this was a generous addition to adequate wages or the usual grudging supplement to wages so low they made even a white employer feel guilty, one could only surmise. However that may be, the following story is true, I am sure. Mrs. O'Connor told it to me immediately after the event.

On one of "Tillie's days," late in February, it was bitter cold with driving rain. Mrs. O'Connor went shopping and on her return she found Tillie unconscious on the kitchen floor--a stroke. Mrs. O'Connor finally brought her to, but Tillie was terribly weak. Mrs. O'Connor called her husband to come home early from work. They set up a bed in the barn and carried her out there to stay until she recovered enough to make her own way home.

"In the barn?" I asked, incredulous. "On such a cold day!"

"Yes," said Mrs. O'Connor, "what else could I do? I've known Tillie ever since I can remember. She used to be my mammy when I was a baby. You know I'd never be able to walk into my kitchen again if Tillie were to die in there. I just wouldn't be able to bear it."

The O'Connors had a guest room--never used during the time we knew them.

Tillie recovered and was back at work the following week. She and I used to hang out clothes at the same time, some days. She washed in the old tub in the O'Connors' back yard, I in my new washing machine, but we called across to each other as we were hanging out the clothes. We borrowed back and forth, chatting occasionally. In the course of the spring Tillie, at Horace's request, got some friends together in the small bare yard behind her house one evening to hear him tell about an organization in New York that was trying to set up branches in the South, an organization for Negro rights. The gathering was not large, in the little bare yard between clustering frame houses. It opened and closed with prayer, though this we had not planned. As Horace talked, the listeners, dark, and darker as the evening deepened, were intent. No organization developed, but the ideas found a reception that was impressive. Ready verbal response would have indicated less concern than the silence, the pondering, the occasional thoughtful words, the sudden, almost startled agreement. They believed in us although we were white.

All that spring unemployment was growing. It was more dire than the flooding Mississippi River, though that was appalling enough.

"Times is tight," said one young Negro woman as she ironed her husband's shirt while we sat in the only chairs in her one-room home and watched and listened. She ironed with exquisite precision and somehow emphasized her terse phrases with the firm repetition of her strokes, pausing only to put a cooling flat-iron back on the top of the Franklin stove and to pick up the other, the heated one. "Times is tight." She had had a job as "off-bearer" in a saw mill, ten cents an hour, ten hours a day, carrying boards from the saws to the lumber piles. She still worked occasionally, but seldom for a whole day. Her husband expected to be laid off too in a week or so. Didn't think he'd be able to find anything else. "We been married three years. I always used to be sad we didn't have no babies. Now . . ."

Even on our modest street beggars stopped to ask for a bite or a dime. Some of them had come in from the country, all of them said they were moving on, but seemed to have no hope of finding work. Just kept moving on .

We read in the *Daily* (that came daily) about the March 6th demonstration of the unemployed in New York City. And through the pleasant southern spring, through days of kidlets playing in the sun with our puppy, Peter, through Munga's visit and Chan's learning to read and Barbara's contented little calls on Mrs. O'Connor in her welcoming, lonely home, I felt a sort of inexorable gathering of evidence. America was no exception. We had seen starker poverty in Delta croppers' shacks, their unpainted board walls papered with old newspapers, than in Middlesbrough slums in the depths of that earlier winter. It was late in coming to the United States because of the Federal Reserve system perhaps and other factors, but here, inevitable, was the Depression, and even during these early months of the first year one could see that it was far more formidable than those other depressions I had followed through Mitchell's statistically documented pages. Hoover and the Dean of the Business School at the University of Minnesota had been sure it couldn't happen here. Even Mitchell with all his objectivity and his flair for pursuing economic causal relations had not traced a convincing pattern. (Willard Thorp, working full time under Mitchell's guidance with the National Bureau of Economic Research straight through the years 1929-32, was in New York City at our home one evening in 1932. We asked him what had caused the depression. "You know," he said, with a frustrated look on his little-boy face, "we never really found out.")

There was more for the economist-questioner, far more, in the Marxian analysis. Living as we did in touch with working people, seeing the problem of growing unemployment written in human lives, we felt ourselves in the center of converging forces. All our love of our fellow men, all our sense of the strength and charm and unique and inestimable worth of individual people, joined now with what had become, to me at least, inescapable conviction about the laws of social development, the way things were moving and must move, given the organization of the American economy. I'm sure I'd have been convinced in Pittsburgh too, but perhaps in Memphis the class picture was especially clear, superimposed as it was on the violence of holdovers from the days of chattel slavery. I was beginning at last to understand the world; I wanted to change it. I clipped a printed form from the *Daily* and wrote to East 12th Street asking for information about the Communist Party.

In the course of the trade union drive of the National Textile Workers Union south from Gastonia and Marion, a half dozen organizers had been arrested in Atlanta for holding an unsegregated meeting. To have white and Negro workers sitting in a hall together, side by side, violated a state law. The organizers were held incommunicado, awaiting trial. Almost simultaneously Horace received a letter from Bob Dunn in New York and I received one from Tom Johnson, the Party District Organizer in Birmingham, asking that we get up a meeting in Memphis to protest the arrest of the organizers, their prosecution, and, indeed, the whole divide-and-rule policy of segregation that was proving a serious bar against effective union organization as well as a rank injustice in itself.

Ann Burlak was one of the arrested organizers. We knew her name. In her early twenties she was already a heroine of the American movement. We had never seen her, could, of course, have no slightest notion what good friends we'd later become or that her daughter and our daughter born in 1943 would be even closer friends. We considered the request as a simple organizational proposition and proceeded to take steps to carry it out.

Memphis had practically no union movement. The few stalwart AF of T members we knew were not to be pulled into this kind of effort. We looked around. Found one liberal clergyman, a rather meek Unitarian minister who defected later when the going got tough, and a small group of Jewish sympathizers organized in the Workmen's Circle, who stuck bravely to the end, and that was that. At one point I definitely lost heart, suggested that perhaps we'd better drop the whole idea. I can see the Bear now, leaning back against the kitchen wall, his chair tilted, his eyes thoughtful, his speech deliberate. It was only a week or so before we were to leave Southwestern at the end of the second semester--leave permanently with nothing but FP in New York to go to; we couldn't stick it any longer in the South.

"I somehow don't want to go away from this place," he said, "without taking some kind of a stand against the kind of things we've seen here."

We went on with the meeting.

We found that an indoor meeting unsegregated could not be held, so we got a permit for an outdoor meeting in a park overlooking the Mississippi. It was set for a Friday evening in early June. Thursday afternoon Horace gave a written announcement to the press and picked up the leaflets we had ordered from the printer. He got batches to the Jewish friends, a few to Tillie, and after supper we took the rest door to door in the working class neighborhoods we knew, most Negro. We took the kids with us. Chan gave out a good many leaflets on the street. He liked, too, going back to some houses he remembered visiting earlier on our news gathering trips. The last one we went to was more spectacular by night than by day. Great swathes of wallpaper were peeling off the wall in a tiny room. The one kerosene lamp, set on a table, threw fantastic shadows. We left leaflets there and drove the kids home to bed.

On our porch was a reporter waiting for a story. As I remember it, we gave him a "mouthful," ranging from increasing severity of business cycles, through freedom to organize, "work or wages" and equality for the Negro, to building a new society in the Soviet Union, free of unemployment.

It came out full, accurate, even glowing, the paper the next day, but long before we saw the paper we were wakened by the hostile, anonymous phone calls. Tom Johnson, who was to speak at the meeting, arrived from Birmingham. I left him at a late breakfast talking things over with Horace while I went off to put out the very last leaflets, house to house in a white working class neighborhood with one of the Jewish women comrades. She was a right wing Socialist and I--since Tom Johnson had greeted me that morning and, smiling, pushed a card into my hand--was a Communist. But we were comrades. We finished giving out the leaflets about noon; she drove me to the market where I picked up food for lunch, then left me at my door.

The phone calls had continued sporadically during my absence but Tom and Horace had taken them in stride as they did the personal call from the discomfited Unitarian minister who withdrew from sponsorship and declined the place he had previously accepted on the program. The kids had been playing outdoors. Lunch was under way, almost eaten, when the phone rang once more. Cliff Davis, Chief of Police, had a message for

40

Horace: the permit was withdrawn. Two hundred legionnaires were said to be gathered to break up the meeting if it should be held. "I'll be right down," said the Bear, "I want to talk to you about that." He took off with Tom Johnson, and I put the kids to bed for naps.

Barbara went serenely enough, but Chan was disturbed, fighting back tears. "Billy's mother sent me home this morning," he said. Billy was almost six, Chan's idol. He lived two houses down the street and had always been happy to have Chan go there to play. "She said I couldn't play with Billy ever any more. She said you should get me a little nigger to play with."

"We don't use that word."

"No, but Billy's mother did."

"Well, Billy's mother doesn't understand. We think Negroes should have just as good houses as white folks and every family should have a house as big as it needs, like this house for us. Billy's mother hasn't thought about things that way; she doesn't understand. You go off now and have a good rest. Don't worry about it."

My son, not yet four, looked up at me, his brown eyes earnest and bright. "Yes, but I _do_ worry. And I think we should take Billy's mother and show her that house with the paper coming off the wall and _then_ she would understand."

After Chan went to rest things moved rather fast. I called Mrs. Hartley and arranged to have her come and pick up the kids after rest. It seemed wise for them to play with little Hartleys this afternoon. When she came she remarked understandingly that they had some new toothbrushes at their house and plenty of kidlet pyjamas; if things got still thicker than they were already, she could keep the children over night. And she drove off with hers and mine, a happy crowd.

I got in touch with the movers who were to come for our furniture the following week. It seemed only smart to have them take the few choice pieces now, just in case . . . . So they did--our sideboard, the chest that Cousin Charlotte had carved, the Cynthia chair. The men who moved the furniture to the truck had dark brown skin, and sombre eyes. They said nothing but I felt stronger for their prompt response to my appeal and for their presence during the minutes it took them to do the work. When they were gone I washed the dishes. I was on my way back to empty the ice-box pan when the ring came at the front door. Two cops.

"Your husband and Tom Johnson are under arrest. You goin' ahead with that meetin'?"

They were pushing without ceremony into our tiny front hall. I said something about a search warrant as one of them picked a book out of the book-case. They laughed raucously and strode on in.

"So. Better tell us. You goin' ahead with it?" They stood there looking rather threatening. I certainly did not intend to say no at once, but things were obviously not going to be simple. I called Mrs. Hartley's number intending to confirm the plan that she keep the kids over night. No answer. She had said something about an expedition to the zoo. Then I called the woman I'd been with that morning and got the name and phone number of a good lawyer. The men stood towering over me as I sat there phoning, so my conversation with the lawyer was brief. He was crisp and helpful, said he would try at once to see Horace in jail, thought I might be wise to give up the meeting. I thought so too, by that time. The cops were asking me to hurry and decide and they were pulling books from our shelves at random. I had barely put down the phone and turned to give them an answer when they said, without waiting for it, "You're under arrest," and marched me out to their car. They didn't even let me take time to empty the ice-box pan. I had a minute to pick up my purse. We left the house unlocked, door open.

Booking in at the jail was simple, crude, quite unmitigated by southern courtesy. "We've got the breaches on her," remarked one of them at the desk. He meant, I later discovered, that the charge was breach of the peace. Finger printing and "mugging" (taking front and side photographs) took some time so when I reached my cell it was 4:30, too late for the regular evening meal. They served two meals a day in that jail. They graciously allowed me to pay them a dollar and a quarter from my already confiscated purse and brought me for that sum the most completely unappetizing plate of food I had ever beheld. Then I had just a tiny room, a single bed, a barred window, and my thoughts.

In the course of the evening a man called me out for questioning. He suggested that I might wish to send a message to my children, asked where they were. I replied that I had no message and was sure they were all right--did not tell him where. He kept at me for some time, trying, not very skilfully, to elicit the information, but I was firm. Later I learned the wisdom of this firmness. The men at the house had, of course, taken Mrs. Hartley's number but had no name to go with it. They called the number that evening, said they had instructions from me to fetch the children and bring them to me, and asked her for her address.

She was quick-witted, noticed that they did not speak to her by name, and replied that if I really wanted them to get the children she was sure I would give them her name and address myself.

On my way back to my cell I passed two other women prisoners, Negroes, in the adjoining (segregated) section of our wing of the jail. I asked the matron (relatively decent) who was conducting me what they were in for.

"No charge," she said. "Just for questioning."   "How long have they been here?"

"Three months."

My bed was hard. I slept rather little that night.

We were wakened early for a meager and tasteless breakfast, or perhaps I should say, untasted: muddy coffee and a bowl of dirty grits with a maggot or two parading therein. It was some two hours later, perhaps at eight, that the matron admitted to my cell and the adjoining one, which was then made accessible by leaving the door between unlocked, a rather haggard young woman and her son, who looked about eight years old.

He began to cry. "We're in jail. How long do we have to stay this time?"

His mother reassured him. "What makes you think we're locked up? We can get out whenever we want to."

"No we can't. Look at the bars at the window."

She turned to me. "Honey, you wouldn't have some snuff?" It was rather a desperate appeal, but I had none. Little by little, nervously, she began asking me questions. Once the matron came in and looked at her inquiringly. She shook her head and at the matron's departure asked more questions, more nervously. My answers were evasive. At last she came out directly.

"Who was it got you to hold that meeting? What was it all about?" She was shaking, whether from lack of snuff or from fear I'd fail her again, I couldn't guess.

I turned to her frankly then and told her I wasn't going to answer any of the questions and that we'd be much happier, both of us, if she would simply give up trying. She burst into tears and said, "I told them I wasn't smart enough to get you to talk."

So I comforted her, made her lie down on my bed, covered her over with a blanket and took her little boy into the next cell. There we amused ourselves reciting *Peter Rabbit*. He knew a lot of it and between us we managed to get all the way through. We were about to start on *Benjamin Bunny* when the matron came in. She was quite cross at the situation that confronted her and took them both out. The little boy waved good-bye; his mother cast me a sorrowful glance.

Later the matron tried, quite awkwardly, to pump me herself, but gave it up. Still later I was taken out of the cell and through many corridors, up and down narrow winding metal stairs, to the line-up. On a tiny stage, facing blinding lights, I stood with Tom Johnson and Horace and had just time to tell Horace that the kids were all right and to assure myself by looking into his face that at least he hadn't been hit over the head. Our lawyer called, a vigorous young man (some four years later, when he was representing a group of CIO organizers, he was forced off the road, apparently, on a straight stretch of highway near Memphis; he was alone in his car at the time; when they found him he was dead, no witnesses). He thought we had the basis for a suit for false arrest but pointed out the difficulty in winning such a suit. He got us released at about 2:30. My purse was returned minus most of the money that had been in it, but we were not disposed to argue. Sunshine and June air, sniffed through taxi windows, seemed incredibly luxurious.

The house was a mess. The floor was thick with cigar ashes and butts and dirty foot-prints. The book-cases were gutted, and research material from the four-drawer wooden filing case I'd bought my first year in graduate school had been flung indiscriminately around the bedroom. We crammed it back in somehow and spent days and nights on and off for four months the following fall and winter trying to set it to rights. The ice-box pan had brimmed over. We didn't want to bring the kids back into that turmoil and frankly I had no desire to sleep there myself, so we got a room in the hotel where Grandpa and Munga had stayed when they came to visit us, a place that still held for the kids the aura of their visit and consequently consoled them for not going home.

Two little AF of T school teachers took us off on a picnic on Sunday, an expedition memorable for their serenity and the serenity of the early summer woods; for the vigorous argument over IT IS ME, and the stern remark of one of them, "Well, Mr. Davis, I respect you for your convictions but if you were in my English class you would be marked down for saying IT IS ME"; and memorable for the story of the child who had reported at Sunday School that morning that God ate with his left hand, and, when the teacher asked whatever made him think that, replied, "Well, you see, Jesus was sitting on His right hand."

We did a frantic job of cleaning up and packing so that we could leave Memphis on Monday night. The O'Connors were

44

friendly. Mr. O'Connor had gone to the jail and tried to see us on Friday night, we learned, but had been unable to do so. Mrs. O'Connor entertained the kids while we worked and popped in at the kitchen door from time to time, loquacious as ever. "Honey, down in Mississippi where I was raised, if you'd said aloud what you told that newspaper man they'd have strung you up by your toes!" She had us all in to lunch the last day.

Tillie was there at the house, washing. Mrs. O'Connor whispered as we left, "Please don't say anything to Tillie about all this. Nothing at all. She's old. She just wouldn't understand and anyway I don't want her to be disturbed." We said good-bye and thank you and left. Tillie, glancing back to be sure she was unobserved, followed us to our hedge. "Those same folks all met again Friday night," she said, "in my backyard. We prayed for y'all. Real lovely prayers. We knew God was with you." Her eyes were shining.

By Monday night somehow everything was done. We walked down the station platform hand in hand, the four of us, with minutes to spare before our train left. A group of men, dicks if ever there were any and you could tell by the shoes, stood chatting and combing with their glances everyone who passed. As we strode by, the kids in excited conversation about trains, one of the men lifted his head sharply as if to click us into his private IBM machine.

He turned up later in our Pullman car. When we went to the diner for breakfast he sat two tables down. The porter came to brush us off as the train was pulling into Chicago. I was sitting so as to face the car and noticed that the dick spoke briefly to the porter, who then came directly to me. As the porter brushed my jacket he asked, "You are Mrs. Davis, aren't you?" "Yes," I replied, "what did that man want to know about me?" The porter was silent, his face gone impenetrable. But he went from us directly to brush off our dick and did so standing in the aisle. As he brushed the left lapel of the man's suit coat he turned it back for a fraction of a second, revealing the badge on the pocket of the vest. Only that. But for a porter living on the Mississippi run out of Chicago it was heroism, solidarity, courage beyond the call of duty, and it was so perfectly executed as to be quite undetected by one party and quite understood by the other. One could contemplate returning to the South some day since there were people like that living there.

In Chicago we decided to try to shake our dick before taking the train to Minneapolis. We didn't want him following us to

Christmas Lake. The first move was to check all our bags and the portable typewriter at the station. Sure enough, of the two men he accosted there, one remained outside the checkroom with him. Alas, however, the other followed us. We tried walking with the kids in the park beside Lake Michigan. It soon became apparent that there was a car following us too. So Horace left to phone an ACLU lawyer and, eventually, Carl Haessler, and I strung along with the kids in the sunshine, instructed to stay in the park until he got back. They enjoyed the out of doors but were soon troubled by the obvious aimlessness of our wandering. With wonderment I could have coped. But when the demand came clear and sharp, in a piercing whisper, "Nanie, I have to go . . . ," we had no choice but to walk to the Art Museum and accomplish that task. It took a very long time. Out on the steps again I was comfortably certain I must have lost all dicks. Eventually we found the Bear who had arranged for us to spend the day with Haesslers in Highland Park, and we made our way to the suburbs apparently alone.

Carl was given the job of subtracting our bags from the check room. Bored with his current job and surburban respectability, he enjoyed thoroughly the familiar feel of danger. Arrived at the check room he quickly identified the two dicks waiting there (he checked out the bags but left the portable typewriter there to confuse them). At the el, he neatly evaded the one man who followed him. He did it with the skill of an old hand, and we had to thank him for a serene visit with the family that summer.

Serene at least for us. Father was troubled by my decision about the Party and said as much. Academic jobs were closed to the Bear for the time being and so we settled for New York City and full time with Federated Press at $30 a week, better pay then than it would be now, but even in 1930 not munificent.

VI

Sunnyside

Sunnyside, in an apartment near Sal's, was good. Chan had public kindergarten, Barbara a morning play group, and I enjoyed a swirl of new friends, my first taste of Party life, and the most leisurely pregnancy yet. Mina waited until the two older kids had finished with chicken pox and then waited further, most considerately, on a Monday in April, 1931, for me to get the blankets washed and hung to dry on the roof of our walk-up apartment building and for us all to finish lunch, before definitely starting to come. All went very smoothly, and an easy birth led into a babyhood that was exemplary indeed.

Those years, 1930-33, were crowded with impressions of New York, the working class areas of Long Island City, Sunnyside, of the Party, the bubbling life of a cooperative-minded community, hosts of new and old friends, our growing family, a world plunged ever deeper in the depression, of the Harlan strike, the Scottsboro case and our own dichotomy. I was in the Party, convinced, finding it at once larger and more impressive and more difficult than I had guessed. Horace, so much better versed in the history of the movement than I, was reluctant, had grave reservations, argued with vigor, cooperated to the hilt and did not once try to pierce my reticence on purely Party matters. It was good when he decided to come in; characteristic of him that he did not hurry.

So much happened in that Sunnyside period; we were active in so live and disparate a world that it is almost impossible to do more than sketch a series of random shots, hoping that in their sum they will somehow combine the essential ingredients of our lives in reasonable proportion.

I remember friendly face-to-face talks with Bob Dunn and with Anna and Grace, the LRA friends of Horace's whom I had never really known before. I remember Party people we met through them and the warm feeling of being accepted, of belonging. I remember the zest of building in conversation, in our reading of the press, in watching organizational moves in progress, a concept of national and world developments. It was not simple, nor limited, but there was extraordinary confidence and comfort stemming from our shared understanding of the nature of the forces at work and of the direction in which we wanted our world to change.

People were not moving our way as we were to see them do later in the 30's. It was pure romantic imagination that made every worker on East 12th Street look like a comrade. But many people did feel the conviction that had held me since that winter night in Middlesbrough when I looked at hungry children, and people who had yet to feel the political conviction were beginning themselves to feel the hunger.

I remember going to Party meetings, Tuesdays, in a frigid, barren second floor room over a store in Long Island City. The organizer was a young woman who had recently been working in Denver. She was crisp and businesslike, quite undaunted by the small number in our group and the vast territory we tried to cover with sales of the *Daily* and house to house work toward building an Unemployed Council in the area. Under her guidance we picked a point of concentration. I never did manage to get around early enough to sell the paper, but I did a fair bit of house to house visiting with one comrade or another and by May, 1932, we had found enough interest, we thought, in a block of apartments to justify our holding a street meeting outside. At this I spoke. It was unexpectedly harder to hold the attention of passersby on the street than to chat with friendly unemployed tenants in the apartments where doors were opened in curiosity or hospitality. When a milk bottle filled with water hurled from a roof toward our soap box shattered on the sidewalk near me it was startling but deserved, no doubt. Through thick and thin our young organizer worked with us. Only once her stern reserve broke enough, in private conversation, for her to confide in me her greater satisfaction with the grass-roots organization in a far smaller movement in Colorado. She thought the Party was so large in New York City, so unaware of the life and thoughts of the non-Party masses, that it was in danger of being blinded by its very success in a sectarian fraction of the population. Valid criticism. Would that it had been driven home, over the years, over the Districts. By the time we really put our ears to the ground it was late indeed.

I remember sitting at coffee after breakfast with the Lewis Coveys across the court from us in Sunnyside. I was fascinated by his talk long before I identified him with Louis Fraina--and long after. Esther was simpler, sharper in moral judgment, more organizational. She helped us from the beginning in our definitely successful building of an ILD branch in Sunnyside. The true moving spirit was the Bear, but many others gathered around, some, new to the game like Betty Scheiner, a young mother and chess widow, took hold and drew their husbands in after them; some were old hands, glad to feel the stir of organization again and bringing to each meeting assurance and warmth. Negro members we sought in Jackson heights and Flushing, and we found so many through house to housing for the Scottsboro case and in a campaign to open Harlem hospitals to Negro doctors that with no intention of forming segregated chapters--but forced by the sheer geographical spread of our contacts--we organized a second chapter. The two met jointly on occasion and shared leadership.

If the effort to build a block committee in LIC through a street meeting led to rather bleak frustration--as it did--a more competently planned street meeting, about a year later, on the Scottsboro case gave me a fine sense of what could be done to catch and hold the attention of the passer-by. I was asked to give the warmer-up talk one evening on a busy corner in Asbury Park with a well-known speaker to follow. Leaflets were good and had been fairly widely distributed; the corner was well chosen. Perhaps fifteen faithful souls were standing about when the meeting opened. And I was not scared; I was full of what I had to say and determined to let my emphasis reach the crowd which I was equally determined should gather at the sound of my voice. How much living in the Deep South had to do with my determination is hard to say. But from the first minute of talking, I was confident. And people did pause, listen, draw closer. Some of them continued on their way, of course, but many stayed. The crowd around me grew and with it my sense of delivering a vital message. When--after perhaps twenty minutes--I saw the real speaker appear, I finished the point I was making and turned over to him a fairly large and definitely interested crowd.

Two other Scottsboro memories from the many that crowd in: One was of my first sight of William Patterson--the "Pat" whose leadership has been important to the movement over the years, and unwavering. He spoke in a small Negro church on a Sunday afternoon, spoke so incisively, so warmly and so well that he won the audience completely. Listening, I was aware of his almost instinctive understanding of the simplest members of his audience, his grasp of the fine legal points of the case, and, even more important, the way in which it exposed the whole possible scope of organization of support for it.

The second Scottsboro memory is our acquaintance with Janie Patterson. This was a very special privilege accorded us simply because we had room to put her up and lived in a suburban house where she could enjoy more privacy than in a New York apartment, and because she had been on an extended speaking tour, had been

rather unpleasantly pursued by newspaper reporters and needed a
week or so of complete rest. It was early spring of 1933. Her son,
Haywood Patterson, was one of the Scottsboro boys, the one, in
fact, who, many years after, wrote, with help, the moving account
of his experiences in the penitentiary, a paperback best-seller that
presaged mournfully his own tragic later life. Mrs. Janie Patterson
was a wonderful person. She made herself at home in our family
and seemed a friend from the beginning. She and her husband were
obviously respected members of the Chattanooga Negro
community. The depression had hit them hard. Mr. Patterson, if I
remember correctly, was a building trades worker. Haywood, just
17, had left home to look for a job. He was a strong, self-
respecting lad, inexpressibly dear to them, one on whom they had
built high hopes. Without any dramatic contriving, in the simplest
and most restrained speech, Janie Patterson conveyed their
confidence in their son, the shock of his arrest and of the fantastic
charge against him and the others, the bitter, unsurprised
acceptance of the legal peril in which they stood, their gratitude
to Lowell Wakefield that they had not all been lynched, her
determination to lend all her strength to the world movement for
his freedom. To many of us, of course, this was another Sacco-
Vanzetti case, especially somber with the depression need that
sent young boys across the face of the country looking for jobs that
did not exist, and with the violence of racial antagonism from
which of course the case had sprung. Janie Patterson lived with us,
enjoyed our kids, accepted, though not completely, the notion that
she should be free of household chores--our guest. When I did the
washing, though, there was no holding her back. I had suggested,
since she would not sit idle, that she might chat with me while I
got the clothes ready to hang out. She watched me wringing them
for a while and could stand it no longer. "You don't know how to
wring clothes; let me show you." I shall always remember those
beautiful strong brown hands. She explained that at home she
washed six days a week--her own family wash first, then other
peoples' clothes. I never succeeded in wringing as superbly as she
did, but I patterned my motions on hers and have benefited
immensely thereby, during the years that have followed. I did not
see her after she left our home. She went on to do a distinguished
job speaking all over the US and in Europe for her son and the
others; I continued mothering my little family--and learning about
life.

During the summers of 1932 and 1933 we were in Croton-on-
Hudson, living in the half-cottage that had been Fred Ellis's

50

before we had it. Just off Mt. Airy Road, it was a slightly improbable but actually a very happy home. Its one room had a tiny oil stove in one corner, Chan's bed in another, a shelf hung about with a curtain for a closet in a third, and a wash tub under a shower pipe in the fourth. There was a tiny sleeping porch just big enough for Mina's crib, and a large one that held our double bed and Barbara's cot, with room enough to pass between them. Add a tiny ice-box, shelves for dishes, a table, and a chair for each of us and you have the picture. Outside were open fields, waving tall grass, and a grape arbor from whose fruit we made grape jam in the fall of 1932 when we stayed in Croton through a frosty October, and it was good to have a long project like jam to justify our burning oil enough to warm the house a bit. We loved it. To be sure, after bedtime stories Horace and I had to go walking so the kids could get to sleep and with Chan in bed in the one room, our evening reading time was cut to a minimum.

The Chapmans lived in a cottage so near that they could listen for our kids as we did for theirs. They were an entertaining, typically depression couple. He was an architect, unemployed of course. She had a job as a buyer in a women's wear shop and went to the city every day, while he took care of their two kids and did all the housework. One day when he did the wash he dyed his undershirts lavender. "To make me more attractive," he remarked, "when she comes home tired from a hard day in the office."

VII

Brazil

We were in Croton in the summer of 1933, looking forward to a rather pinched winter with Horace's only salary due from a couple of nights a week at the New School, when the job offer came from Brazil. In ten days we had decided, taken our shots, packed our clothes and boarded ship. It was a two weeks' trip south through a tranquil ocean. Near Bermuda we saw schools of flying fish. Mina made a poem and intoned it softly as she stood at the rail watching them; Horace heard it.

O my blue, blue ocean.
A fish was after my ocean.
But the fish didn't bite the ocean;
The ocean swallowed the fish.

The kids cavorted gaily on deck. Horace studied Portuguese. We both read old copies of the *Daily* in the privacy of our cabin and then chucked them out the porthole by night. Chan caught us at it and, reader of the *New Pioneer* fresh from a kidlet project in Croton that had cleared 34 cents to contribute to the Committee to Aid the Victims of German Fascism, he upbraided us for throwing away good literature that might have been passed on. We explained that in Brazil we'd have to be careful.

At Santos we were met by Cyro de Berlink, a lively young man who drove us up the Caminho do Mar and lodged us in São Paulo's best hotel. He explained that the Escola Libre de Sociologia e Politica, at which Horace was to teach, had just been founded to afford education at the college level for the "elite" of São Paolo to prepare them for taking over the national government. Horace's firm but guarded suggestion that education should be for anyone interested and qualified met with frank surprise at such naiveté. Cyro remained friendly but from that moment was cautious, his gaze inquisitive.

On our trip down we had spent a day in Rio with the Michahelles family, Germans long resident there. Through them we found our first home. It was a spacious, pleasant summer home in Freguezia do O. Here let me insert my *South American Interlude*, the truth but not the whole truth. And when you have read it I can add bits that will give more substance to it, the third dimension, one may say.

South American Interlude

Orchids in our *boticaba* trees--little daring fragile things, clinging with extraordinary tenacity to the forked and lichened branches. If I had lounged in galleries, alert, absorbed and happy, for even a few hours of a few days out of these recent years I could tell now, perhaps, what name to cite so that those who know the galleries would guess at just the ineffable French tint those orchids have. But modern painters are to me unknown--you must after all omit something when you go in for babies and scrubbing floors. I cannot say who may have been crowding his canvasses with this peculiarly lovely and arresting shade of bluish pink. I can only say that when I had my first glimpse of the blossoms in the deep gloom of foliage above the assembled twisted cords of the *jaboticaba* trunks I caught my breath. Pink, blue-pink, they are, delicately touched with blue itself. The leaves are curved and slender, like little grey-green scimitars.

Andre saw that I liked them. Instantly, with the speed and simplicity of his particularly likeable type of barefoot ten-year-old, he was up the tree to shake some down for me. They fell, reluctantly, to the grass and I picked them up unhurt, a treasure such as one can seldom have.

The *jaboticaba* trees are not really ours. We rent them and other glories of a fenced and gated stretch of woods and orchard and a rather aging house from a rather aging and rheumatic little German lawyer. When it rains, water pours through our tiled roof. The bus service to town is erratic, erring always on the same side, the side of infrequency. My husband works hard for the rent and the rest, and for this delightful but somewhat impracticable dwelling pays not only in money but in time, which he wastes tediously after lectures in long waits on the street-corner for the bus that may take half an hour or an hour to come. Sometimes it does not come at all, so that he must walk home.

The countryside is open before us and we have drunk deep of what it offers. The whisper of sunny leaves, the shrilling of cicadas at night, the songs of workers among the grapevines will echo long. But we must go.

The reasons are sharp, impelling--written clear in the lives of our neighbors:

Andre's perceptions are keen. His native endowment of pluck and wit, resourcefulness and reliability would seem to entitle him to all that modern education can offer. Here, if ever, is *mens sana in corpore sano*. Grey level eyes promise unlimited return to the

54

developing opportunities our educational specialists work so hard to devise. But the opportunities will not be his. Andre lives in a two-room house, dirt floor in a kitchen somehow immaculate, no chimney, the stove an old kerosene tin of glowing charcoal set near the kitchen door. Next year Andre will leave school and go to work and because he is clever and strong above the average he may earn five dollars a month.

Doña Maria came from Portugal six year ago, robust and hopeful with half a dozen vigorous children and a husband who had a skilled trade and a most winning, gentle manner. Skilled trade lost its meaning when his shop closed down and younger men were preferred in the shops that were still hiring. Gentle manner brought forth its like in children serene, intelligent, but it did not save the oldest girl when she was sick with typhoid, nor the second girl who died a few weeks after her; it did not save his wife's teeth, nor her health, so that now, in wasted and stricken beauty, she potters about her rotting little hole of a house, gets dinner when she has strength enough and lets the children pick at left-overs when her limbs will not lift her from her bed, pays something each week from her husband's wage of thirty cents a day for a friend to wash their few clothes, and is faintly beginning to lose her faith in the efficacy of prayer.

Up the hill, in a one-room home, is a young mother with meager cheeks flushed fever-red, who cannot carry in her arms her first baby, not yet two, because when the second was born the midwife, frightened by the mother's fainting, tore it brutally from her and all but tore with it the uterus from its moorings so that now when she lifts anything heavy, or weeps, the organ falls forward and out and she faints again. Her husband's wage will not buy her eggs and fruit; without them she cannot build up her strength for the operation that she needs, and that she could have *gratis* if she could summon the health to survive and the daring to take her into the teeming chaos of the municipal hospital, where half the patients sleep on mattresses on the floor under the beds of the other half.

A stronger mother lives in the back room of a house at the foot of the orchard. She bore three of her living five alone, rising on each occasion, after she had given birth, to tie and cut the cord herself and wrap her child up, clean and warm. Her home is orderly, a triumph, but her strong young face is lined. Her husband, with the deep, kind voice, works on the night shift at the mill, mends shoes by day, and earns too little to feed the hungry mouths. The baby born of this heroic stock was only seven months old when his father was jailed for distributing revolutionary leaflets. They wonder always how long they can keep the roof over their heads, where they will get the next needed bit of clothing.

Manoel's father has a voice that is not kind, but rasping. Manoel is often beaten. He and his brother and his little sisters all have the furtive and hardy look of children whose struggle continues at home, ends only with sleep. Manoel's father cuts *capim* (grass) on the sport field of an athletic club. But the *capim* he cuts he may not haul away. His sons cut *capim* too, wherever they can find any and carry it to their barren quintal for the cows, three cows, that are the family's only wealth. A slender yield of milk from cows who eat little else but grass, but what there is must be sold--rent, bread, rice and beans for six are hard to arrange. Manoel and Osotio, who love the cows, and whose slender, knotted little arms and shoulders ache from heavy loads of *capim*, trudge forth morning and night delivering milk and take their own coffee black.

So we must go. Not that anyone will drive us out. The neighbors want us to stay. Their friendliness recognizes class differences and builds a pleasant relationship through and above them. Our house opens serenely on terraces that face the woods and garden; our fence is strong. No one enters against our will. We have *milreis* to pay the charcoal man who gives the children a ride each time he comes, taking them down carefully with his grimy hands. We have *milreis* for the *bananeiro* whose cart is heaped not only with bananas but with grapes and tomatoes and alligator pears and the delicious hearts of the palm. We have *milreis* for the rent.

But this abundance and this beauty are built on misery itself. One must be blind who cannot see that a house so gracious and ample is more than our due, intolerable, fronted by cabins of earth and unpainted board and by the tidier but minute dwellings of brick. Orange trees, lemon trees, *jaboticabeiras*, grape-vines, young pear trees, and the soft, rubbing, elephants' ears of the banana leaves, all these are lovely, rooted in good earth, and yet, somehow, rooted in wrong. A man can buy a lot, or start to buy it, and build a house, working Sundays and holidays, plant a tree, sweat and go just a little hungry every day and pay each month and lose it all when a factory closes and the pay stops. Whence then for us this plenty?

A very little inquiry shows one with startling clearness whence it comes. Loot. Wrung from our neighbors and their like throughout this vast and prolific land. Brazil is indescribably striking for the exuberance of its vegetation, for the all but untouched magnificence of waterfall and virgin timer and mineral wealth, and for the sombre misery that looks out of the eyes of millions of barefoot, ragged, men, women, and children. Robbed from birth, they see all the incidents of their lives played against a background of stark want. And among the most astute and successful of the robbers are our own countrymen. Brazilian plantation and factory owners pay tribute in many intricate ways to North Americans, without relaxing in the least their hold on the common people of their own land. Like the lesser and more obvious barons of twelfth-century Europe, they maintain their power by force, unblushing. We simple intellectuals share in the incredible supremacy they have established, on the tacit understanding, it develops, that we close our eyes to what they are doing.

This life, so bought, has not yet lost its savor; but the price is exorbitant. Well-cooked food is "opaque" (was that not Veblen's word?), a good that cannot be questioned, and from it flows "strong blood" as they say here. But what if you think, as you sit at your table in a spacious room, of the small faces you know growing whiter and thinner each day? The *jaboticabas*, in season, fell thick to the ground--too many to pick--but give away a basketful and you felt at once the malice of the landlord and the venomous disapproval of the *gentes ricos* (the rich folk) in the valley; to give away fruit is to violate their code, is to cut out from under, by however little, all the mean and careful structure on which they have reared their security. Like the other innumerable luxuries of our class, deeply, even austerely enjoyed and proven good by our most observant and discriminating use, this ease of landed gentry appears to be intolerable. If we look upon our neighbors as human beings, brothers, it is not only irrelevant to our central purposes but impossible to maintain.

As I write, lest you find me mystic, extravagant, comes a letter on embossed stationary, couched in elegant Portuguese. My husband's contract will not be renewed. Only that. The reason is plain. My husband has discussed with candor the continuing depredations of our countrymen, the American imperialism that gives the lie to Secretary Hull's ingenuously friendly manner. The school where he teaches was founded to offer higher education to the elite of the province. He is frank about social injustice, including Brazilian injustice. It has become apparent that we do not quite play the game.

We must indeed go.

(end of **South American Interlude**)

57

Our acquaintance with Andre's family was really special. When Chan started going to school in the village school he was jeered at, even stoned, because his clothes were different (very simple, little-boy clothes from New York were elaborate, foreign, hateful to these kids). Andre was in Chan's shift. The school was crowded, so one section went from 7 to 10, one from 10 to 1, a third from 1 to 4. Chan's was the one from 10 to 1 and he passed Andre's tiny home on his walk uphill to school. Chan developed the habit of stopping off at Andre's. One day he suggested we go to call on Andre's parents. When I demurred he told me why. Andre's mother had asked us to, for one thing. And one morning when Chan was there he had pointed to the big monastery on the hill across the valley and asked her what it was. She said it was where the priests went "apprendendo bobagens" (learning nonsense). "So you see," Chan remarked triumphantly, "even if they aren't Communists (but I think they are), one thing is sure: they don't believe in God." Horace was busy and evenings together were precious. I walked around with the little girls one afternoon. Andre's mother was as cordial as her house was small. We talked about the misery of our neighbors, especially Doña Maria, and I told how Doña Maria had commented mildly, "Deus Manda" (God ordains). Doña Isabel shook her head. "Tem que lutar" (You have to struggle). So I told the Bear Chan might be right and one evening after we had put the kids to bed we walked down our drive and up the hill under the southern stars to Andre's house.

What a talk! Chan was right, we gathered. First Andre's father, big Andre, a blond, crisp, vigorous Hungarian factory worker, outlined with skill the parties of the Brazilian left--some thirteen in all. He waited with skill at crucial points for us to indicate, without actually stating, where, in the gamut of position, our choice lay. Then he told us with charming frankness that when the first of Horace's public lectures was given at the Escola Libre, against Hitler, people had been enthused (the Party and most of the sympathetic mass organizations had been illegal for some time but a representative of the only extant organization of the left had reached the Bear at the Escola and persuaded him to give a short series of public lectures under its auspices; this turned out a bold thing to have done, and a useful one. This factory worker, e.g., though he had not attended had learned the content of each lecture almost as soon as it was given). The second lecture, against Roosevelt's NRA, had plunged people in confusion. Horace had been denounced as a "Manobra do imperialism Britanico" (a maneuver of British imperialism). The third lecture was reassuring and big Andre had been told to contact this North American neighbor of his.

"How did you dare to do it? How did you know I wouldn't report you to the authorities?" asked Horace.

"Well, children as young as Chan can usually be trusted," Andre remarked.

And I remembered the day when it had rained and Chan and little Andre and Paulo had been building a Casa de Sopo (Toad Hall) in Chan's dark little bedroom (we were deep in *Wind in the Willows* then and of course it all got translated). I had shooed them onto the porch where they could be out of the rain, but in a lighter, airier play spot. They hadn't wanted to go, but at last Chan, cooperative, had supplied a motive: "Let's take the blocks, let's build the Soviet Union, a fort in eastern Siberia . . . (the talk went on in snatches while three little boys gathered up blocks and carried them to the porch and constructed the walls) . . . now, OK (all in Portuguese, of course, and me eavesdropping from the study where I pretended to read) . . . There it is and the Japanese soldiers are coming. (It was early in 1934) . . . and the Soviet soldiers call out to them from the walls "Put down your guns, comrades, come right on in. There's work enough for everybody."

Andre had reported the conversation in detail; his father consequently trusted Chan's father. That was the first of many visits. Isabel sat silent much of the time but it was not an unduly deferential silence. She put in her oar when she felt like it as few Brazilian women would have done.

A few days after this first visit Andre came to the house looking unusually earnest. He wanted to see me. "Well, here I am," I quipped, intending to go in soon and leave them all playing together.

"No, alone please," said Andre and we went into the study and closed the door.

Once sure we were unobserved he reached inside his shirt and pulled out a small newspaper, the first Party paper we'd seen, smuggled with who knows what skill and peril from Rio where it was published. I grabbed it and fell at once to reading avidly. For months we had been wanting to make real contact, to get something like this into our hands. But Andre would not leave it so. He put out his hand. "Dois tostoes," he said. He wasn't giving literature away. He was selling it.

We liked Freguezia do O but the buses got to be less and less frequent and in May we were already contemplating a move to town. One day Andre's mother Doña Isabel, appeared for a call and told me that there had been a grave turn in the fortunes of Adão's family. Adão was a thirteen-year-old living at the moment with them. He and his younger brother had been since January with other friends at the far end of Freguezia do O, ever since their 20-year-old sister had been arrested for participating in an antifascist demonstration in São Paolo. The other member of the family, a girl of 17, was in domestic service, living in, and the tiny home (they were orphans) had been closed since the arrest. The sister in prison had refused to talk, been kept for days in the *geladeira* (a tiny cell with no door or window, in which a prisoner could stand but barely sit, and into which, from time to time, cold water was poured until it reached the neck of the prisoner, standing). Still she hadn't talked. They knew all this because the prison staff of guards included many sympathizers and messages went in and out with amazing speed and frequency. But the imprisoned sister had just been deported to Europe, leaving word that wherever she went she would continue to fight the bourgeoisie. After the deportation the police apparently had made renewed efforts to find the brothers. One plainclothesman had been overheard inquiring on the bus to Freguezia do O, and consequently it had become necessary to make new arrangements for them. The younger brother was to stay a while where he was as he knew little of organizational relationships. It was thought they were after Adão, the plans for his retreat to a farm home were not complete, staying at Andre's was obviously perilous, and would we keep him at least overnight, perhaps for a day or so--until he could be fetched? Of course I said yes, and it was arranged that Horace should fetch him that night, late, going by way of the woods to Andre's house. The younger brother would continue to carry spring water for us daily (a little money-earning job we had offered him) but must not know that Adão was with us.

After our kids were in bed that night and all but Chan asleep, Horace slipped out through the woods and soon came back with a bright-eyed Adão who excitedly whispered, "My father was a soldier in the Red Army," then obediently undressed and crawled into bed with Chan, who had been cued in and was very happy about the whole deal.

Doña Casimira had also retired. I said nothing to her at the time but wondered about breakfast. Doña Casimira would be a problem. Since we had no means of knowing how long Adão would stay, we'd have to meet questions as they arose, perhaps be a bit toplofty and assume we need not explain to a servant. It wasn't easy, for I'd just left the whole family in her hands while I was away for ten days for an operation and she had earned my confidence in one way. In another she could never have it, being utterly snobbish toward her own class. Trying to persuade me to forbid working class neighbors' kids the house and the privilege of playing with our three, she had hissed out one day: "the poor man stinks always of his poverty."

Well, we got through breakfast by my simply saying to Doña Casimira that Chan had asked his friend to eat with us. He had brought no luggage, no extra clothes. She must have wondered how he happened to be there so early but asked no questions. At lunch, well, he was staying a while. Then his brother was seen approaching with the jar of spring water. Adão slipped into Chan's room and closed the door and I busied myself in the next room and maneuvered the water carrier out of doors and away. Barbara and Mina couldn't understand as much of the situation as Chan could, were told simply that we wanted Adão's visit to be a secret.

Three days slid by. Adão was now told to stay indoors because we couldn't keep neighbor kids away, nor trust them not to talk. He got bored but enjoyed typing. Did the Internationale in Portuguese over and over, so I had to keep up a continual confiscation of the copies while my eye was cocked on the front drive for untoward arrivals and he was under instructions to beat it to the woods in case they came. At the end of the third day Doña Casimira was raging. Against my unwonted employer defense of hauteur and refusal to explain, she developed an attack of indignation at the extra work imposed upon her by an extra mouth to feed. Obviously not the reason for her wrath, but that talk revealed the depth of her wrath and that night Horace took Adão back to Andre's house. We didn't see him again. We heard of his safe arrival on a tenant farm in the interior. Heard too, shortly after we moved into the city, that the police had come to our house soon after our departure and had hung around for days. Doña Casimira had told our gardener and he had told them or relayed the message to them. It was good that they were so disorganized, came so late. It had become clear that Doña Casimira had to go. We didn't even tell her to what address we were moving though she begged to be allowed to keep in touch with us. My heart was torn. She was so devoted to us personally, so impossibly far from us in her understanding. When she left I gave her the curtains we'd bought for her bedroom window because I knew she rented a bedroom in the city where she kept some belongings and to which she retired every other Sunday when she was off work. She accepted

the curtains to remember us by--especially Mina whom she adored-
-folded and patted them and smiled: "My room in the city doesn't
have any window, though."

VIII

Conclusion

It really seemed that we had come full circle when we sat in the First Baptist Church on Fayetteville street in Raleigh, North Carolina that April Sunday in 1960, the Bear had made his report as chairman on the committee to work for integration of the new County Hospital. "Your committee reports . . ." he had said, standing up before the assembly, his blue eyes intensely blue, his brows beetling, his face very white against all the dusky faces on the platform. The visiting soloist, light brown skin with a rather wildly beautiful voice, had sung her solo and sunk, a bit breathless, back into her chair. The funeral oration for Uncle Tom was yet to come, and the sober remarks about his friend Jim Crow's grave illness; it was time for greetings. A small worn young man rose, revealed himself at his first words as a "shouting" preacher, and brought greetings from Memphis where he was backing the sitdowns, and where the sitdowns, in the public library as well as at lunch counters, were going strong. "And these young people are a goin' to continue--O Lord--until victory is won." The voices of moved and responsive members of the NAACP audience shouted "Amen." He looked out at us with an earnest, troubled but unflinching face; and he was going back to Memphis almost thirty years after we had left that "city by the waters of the Mississippi river," as he intoned with pride, a pride not less for being mixed with suffering. How do I know it was suffering? He was a Negro and he lived in Memphis.

PART 2

LIBERALISM
IS NOT
ENOUGH

by

Horace Bancroft Davis

I

Family History
Father's Side, Mother's Side

Two roads diverged in a wood, and I --
I took the one less traveled by,
And that has made all the difference.
-- Robert frost, *"The Road Less Traveled."*

Louis Untermeyer comments: "The poet's 'difference' is in him from the beginning, long before he sets out on his career. The road that Robert Frost took was not only the 'different' road, but the only road he could have taken." *--The Pocket Book of Robert Frost's Poems*, ed. Louis Untermeyer, 1971, p. 222.

I think I was destined from an early age to be a dissenter, a critic, an iconoclast. Not that the way to conventional success was closed; on the contrary, it offered fairly bright prospects. But I had a moral urge for improvement, not of myself alone but of society. The question then was one of method and goal. I started off by being a liberal but became a radical. So, my story may be of some interest to others.

The daily grind, the effort to survive, is enough to occupy most peoples' lives. They seek not to make enemies, and so their critical faculties are blunted. If on the other hand they start off on a more elevated plane, with the feeling that they will survive setbacks and emerge regardless, they have the backing to take a stand and fight for a principle. My ancestry was such that I never felt the pressure of economic want, and so I was able to choose the "road less travelled" if that suited me, and it did.

Paternal Ancestors

My paternal ancestors were immigrants, on my father's side, mostly to Massachusetts. The first to arrive was Dolor Davis, in 1630; he participated in founding Barnstable and also Groton, Mass. Many others followed; by 1650 there were 35 of my ancestors in Massachusetts, none of them related to each other.

66

I cannot say that my father's ancestors contributed especially to obtaining the independence of the United States. Isaac Davis, a direct ancestor, joined the militia but when called on to serve in the continental army, he paid his brother-in-law to take his place. Another ancestor, John Chandler, was a probate judge in Worcester; he sided against the revolution, so strongly that he was known as "Tory John." He was one of the richest men in the colonies; his estate was appraised at 36,000 pounds. When the revolutionists were strong enough, they ran him out of Worcester; and when the British army was forced to leave Boston, he went with them, going first to Halifax and later to England, where he spent the rest of his life rather than live under a republican form of government. He salvaged enough money to live on. His family remained in Massachusetts.

Isaac Davis's son John became Governor of Massachusetts, and later served three terms in the U.S. Senate. He was known as "Honest John," but Arthur Schlesinger, Jr., of Harvard, was not fooled; he quoted Henry Clay as saying that "Honest John" should have been called "Cunning John Fox." John Davis was anti-slavery; he sponsored the Wilmot Proviso. He was strongly against the Compromise of 1850.

His son Horace went to California in the 1850's and worked at various jobs--not mining. He loaned some money to a man who hypothecated a run-down flour mill. He was unable to pay, so Uncle Horace came into possession of the mill. He reconditioned it and ran it, and my grandfather, Andrew came out to California and joined him. The business prospered,and the brothers were able to retire. Both of them had scholarly interests. Horace stayed on in California and served for many years as a trustee of Stanford University. He was also for a short time president of the University of California.

Andrew, my grandfather, purchased some rare old Chinese manuscripts and had them analyzed, thus establishing his reputation as an antiquarian. He moved back east in 1882 and settled in Cambridge, where he wrote and studied and where my father grew up. Andrew was something of a specialist on monetary history. He wrote an essay on Shays' Rebellion showing how the uprising of the farmers was caused by the state government's mismanagement of the currency. He also did a historical study for the U.S. Monetary Commission which eventually drew up the plans for the Federal Reserve System.

Andrew McFarland Davis was not all that rich, but after he came back east he became involved in a business which was to furnish a comfortable living to him and his family for many years. A man named Angier had developed a throat lozenge which he wanted to produce and put on the market. My grandfather put up the money and a factory was built and did produce the lozenges, which found a market in the British Empire. The firm was run by the Angiers and the Davises; after my grandfather retired his place on the Board of Directors was taken by my father and his brother Bancroft.

Bancroft was the oldest of Andrew McFarland's four children; he was followed by Eleanor, Fredrika and my father, Horace.

Uncle Bancroft went to Harvard and Harvard Law School and was one of the founders of the Harvard Law Review. He Practiced law in Boston and had the opportunity to make some good investments. He accumulated so much money that his son Gherardi never had to work. Gherry went to law school and settled in New York, where his intellectual capacities were much respected but little used.

Aunt Eleanor and Auntie Rica lived out their lives in Cambridge as members of the upper crust. They were Boston Brahmins. They eventually broke off relations with me because of my politics, which they for some reason attributed to my wife, Nanie. Auntie Rica had my sisters and brother, when they were in town, to a family party on Christmas evenings. She gave as her reason for not inviting my family that Nanie had not called on her. I tried to maintain the relationship, which had been quite warm, and called on Aunt Eleanor and Auntie Rica once each in later years. I tried to talk about family, but they couldn't keep off of politics. The Davis aunts were just another example of how families get divided by politics. In their case, the effort to keep up relations met with failure.

Maternal Ancestors

The parents of my mother were Quakers on both sides (the correct designation is of course Friends--the Society of Friends). The original home of most of the Quakers, our ancestors included, was of course Pennsylvania; but Quakers also came to New England in the 17th century and were persecuted there as the Quakers were in old England. However Morris Hallowell and part of the Haydock family moved to New York, from which Morris Hallowell carried on an importing business, selling goods mainly in the South and West. The firm was militantly opposed to slavery, and its agents in the South made no secret of their views. The customers did not appreciate their ceaseless propaganda and tried to get them to shut up; whereupon the head of the business issued a statement to the effect that its views were not for sale and anybody who implied that they were should be made to apologize for the insult!

The Quakers were far ahead of their times with respect to the position of women, who in their view were the equals of men and entitled to equal consideration. This part of the Quaker tradition has continued down to the present: the women speak up and when the occasion demands it, tell the men where to get off. It was no accident that the call for the first women's rights conference in the U.S . (at Seneca Falls, N.Y., in 1848) came from two Quaker ladies: Lucretia Mott and Susan B. Anthony. We have a special feeling for Lucretia Mott because the two families became connected: Lucretia Mott's grand-daughter Anna (Davis) married my mother's father's brother, William. So, the Mott Hallowells are our cousins. Many of the women's rights advocates were also abolitionists; Lucretia Mott knew Harriet Tubman and Sojourner Truth and worked with them.

The Hallowells were active abolitionists. The home of the Hallowells in Philadelphia was a station on the Underground Railroad.. An escaped slave who was being sheltered there was looking out an upper-storey window and saw his master coming down the street, looking for him. He was removed the same night by carriage.

Morris Hallowell had four sons: William, Richard, Edward and Norwood. The last named, my grandfather, started college at Haverford, but transferred to Harvard to be nearer the headquarters of the abolition movement. In the period before the Civil War, the abolitionists were the extremists, the radicals. The liberals were anti-slavery. Lincoln was not an abolitionist; that was why he got the Republican nomination in 1860 in place of Seward, who was. Very few of the abolitionists favored complete social equality for the blacks, even so; Lincoln of course did not. Harriet Beecher Stowe ended *Uncle Tom's Cabin* with an implied plea for "transportation" (removal of the Blacks to Africa).

The Quakers had to decide whether their opposition to war took precedence over their desire to fight for the freedom of the slaves. The Hallowell boys (men) elected to fight. Norwood Penrose Hallowell, who was in the Harvard class of 1861, began taking military training even before he graduated. He made speeches explaining what the war was about.

One of my grandfather's friends at Harvard was Oliver Wendell Holmes, Jr. He also joined the Union army and was wounded in the Battle of Bull Run. He was behind the rebel lines for six hours. While his father looked frantically for him on the battlefield, he was evacuated to Philadelphia, and in the hospital there he got to know Norwood's sister Emily, a high-spirited lass who had become a volunteer nurse. They got engaged, but had a misunderstanding. In later years Emily, who never married, advised her little nieces, "My dear, never have a misunderstanding."

NPH fought through the Peninsula Campaign, swam across the Potomac River with his sword in his mouth at Balls Bluff, and finally received a bullet in the arm at the Battle of Antietam and had to retire from active service.

He turned his attention to the problem of getting new recruits for the Union army. White enlistments had all but dried up. Conscription was tried and aroused great opposition. Up to this time (1863) blacks had not been accepted into the Union army. Lincoln was finally prevailed on to permit their enlistment.

The Abolitionists cast about to find somebody to lead them and hit on Robert Gould Shaw, who came from one of the First Families of Boston and was otherwise qualified. Permission had been granted to recruit blacks in Massachusetts, but not enough were forthcoming to make up a regiment. So, permission was obtained to recruit as far west as Ohio, and Shaw's regiment was rapidly rounded out and a second one organized. Norwood Hallowell took out this second regiment, the Massachusetts 55th. They marched through the streets of Boston on the way to embarkation. As they passed the fashionable Somerset Club they were hissed. Second in command in Shaw's regiment, the 54th, was Edward Needles Hallowell, Norwood's brother. He was wounded in the attack on Fort Wagner at the entrance to Charleston Harbor (S.C.). Shaw of course was killed and Uncle Ned took command of the regiment. He fought all through the war and rose to the rank of general. Brother William was also in the service, and brother Richard was very active all through the war in civilian capacities.

Although the blacks were accepted as soldiers, they were paid less than the whites. The abolitionists refused absolutely to accept this discrimination and advised the black soldiers not to take any pay until they got the whole amount, which they eventually did. Meanwhile their families had to be supported, and this became the task of the Quakers and other Abolitionists.

70

Norwood Hallowell knew Lincoln personally and went one time to see him in his office. Lincoln was writing at his desk. He perceived NPH out of the corner of his eye. He did not look up, but said, "Colonel Hallowell, is there a 'p' in empty?' and kept on writing.

The Hallowells and the Haydocks were friends, and Sarah Wharton Haydock, then a teen-age girl, attended a sendoff party for NPH when he as going into the Union army. She obtained his picture and held it in front of her on the way home so that people could see "her" soldier boy. After the war NPH remained in New York helping his father build up a new business, marketing wool. When he asked Sarah to marry him she did not think he meant it; she laughed in his face. They were married and moved to the Boston area; they built a house in West Medford which they called Noddebo. Two of NPH's brothers also settled in West Medford.

Edward built a house next to Noddebo, had two daughters, Charlotte and Emily, and died young. His widow, Aunt Willie, couldn't stand the constant racket emanating from Noddebo, and moved her house across the street. Richard had a house on the same block as Noddebo. William settled in Minneapolis.

NPH went into banking, and for many years was President of the small but successful National Bank of Commerce. He and his family were well known and highly esteemed in Boston society. He was President of the Union (League) Club; Grandmother was president of Miss Winsor's School, which she had helped to found.

Some of the abolitionists who were still around took a position against the Spanish-American War, for the right reasons. NPH did not. Yet Boston was the center of the opposition to that war and especially to the annexation of the Philippine Islands. The Anti-Imperialist League, though it lost its main campaign, still had enough influence to block the massive investment of U.S. capital in the Philippines which Governor-General W. Cameron Forbes, a Taft appointee, sought to promote. NPH was a friend of Cam Forbes. He (NPH) was integrated into the Establishment.

My mother, Anna, was the oldest of six children. The others were, in order, Robert, N.P. Jr. ("Buck", or Uncle Pen), John W., Esther Fisher and Sue. The boys all went to Harvard, where they interested themselves in athletics, and they continued active in Harvard affairs after graduation. The girls all went to Harvard Annex, later Radcliffe. My mother was the intellectual of the family. She graduated summa cum laude; Aunt Esther was magna cum laude.

My mother's three brothers each had a personal experience of the seamy side of the Boston (and New York) business community, varying all the way from lapses of judgment to false accusations and outright chicanery. They were not involved in any public scandals, but the period in question produced its share of such scandals, showing that the family experience was not untypical of the wheeling and dealing and dishonesty of the period, and of the system in general.

All of the Hallowell uncles were conservative, especially Uncle Pen, who backed an extreme right-wing periodical called *The Review*. Arthur Morse, who married Aunt Esther, was also conservative, but Lawrence Brooks, who married Aunt Sue, had pretensions to being a liberal.

My mother was not a sport, but she was in on the good times and high jinks of her brothers. When Bryan came to Boston during the campaign of 1896 Uncle Bob, then of college age, was at the Station. Bryan was put in a hansom cab with his party and Uncle Bob climbed into the carriage too. The Bryan people thought he was one of the welcoming party (he wasn't), and the welcoming party thought he was one of the Bryan entourage. So, he drove through the streets of Boston waving to his friends and the hoax was never spotted.

After college Mother was shipped off to Dresden for a year in Europe. She didn't like Dresden and went off after a few months to Italy, about which she became very enthusiastic. She read the *Divina Commedia* in Italian.

Back in West Medford, Mother had a circle of friends some of whom her children later came to know. There was Winthrop Lee, whose hobbies were walking and Esperanto. Another member of the set was Humphrey Baker, who was later the first judge of the Juvenile Court in Boston, one of the first anywhere. Also in the group was Richard Cabot, who became a doctor and pioneered in percentage diagnosis. When he retired as a doctor he was given a chair at Harvard in the field of what was called Social Ethics, and had a liberalizing influence on my college generation.

My mother's father, known as the Giant (he was tall and fat) had a theory that all courting and spooning should stop at 10 o'clock. He resorted to various stratagems to get Mother's young men to leave. The family's shoes were shined overnight by the servants, and the Giant used to throw his shoes down to the lower floor with resounding echoes. He also resorted to the childish expedient of setting the clock ahead an hour. But the young law student Horace Davis was not to be discouraged. He wooed and won the "beautiful Nannie Hallowell." Cousin Bess Walton later said that their romance was one of the hottest she had ever seen!

My father spent his early boyhood in San Francisco; then the family came east and he went to Cambridge High & Latin School and so on to Harvard, where he was something of an infant prodigy. He had literary interests and belonged to a group to which Robert Morss Lovett, later a distinguished literary critic, also belonged. Lovett said of my father, "He was the youngest of us all, and the smartest." Father followed his brother Bancroft into Harvard Law School, and eventually won an essay contest with a paper on arbitration.

II

Boyhood

My parents decided to settle in New York, and lived for a year in Manhattan; Hal was born there. By the time I arrived, two years later, they had moved out to Dongan Hills, on Staten Island, the seat of the Richmond County Country Club, which had tennis courts and a golf course.

My father was quite a sport. In college he had been on the cricket team (there was one then) and had developed proficiency at "hare and hounds" (now cross country). He participated actively in the Country Club. He was also active in the Republican Party, which had a progressive wing; in fact, he was nominated on the Republican ticket for Member of Assembly (the lower house of the New York State legislature) in 1908. He was not elected, and did not follow up his political interests.

The Angier Chemical Co. provided a steady income, and some other investments that Father made turned out well--Welcome Soap, for instance. He did not have to work. The Lawyers Title and Trust Co. would have given him a job doing legal research, but he did not want to be tied down. When he wrote a big book on *Marketability of Title in New York,* it was on his own initiative. He opened a law office in Stapleton, a nearby town on the island, but it did not get much business and was presently wound up. Father speculated a little in real estate, how successfully I never knew.

Father wrote several articles which were published in magazines. He also dabbled in one little business after another, apparently because making money was the ethic of the business community in which he moved. He played golf by himself, carrying only one club, a cleek. Eventually he found pleasure in attending ball games; he was a great Yankee fan--they could never win too many games for him. He also participated in club life, in Manhattan, while not neglecting his family. He was able to get elected to the highly exclusive Century Club. We did not realize how seriously he took his little business ventures, until one time I put on a questionnaire under "Father's Occupation" that he was a "gentleman of leisure." When I mentioned this at home he turned on me in a rage: "Thee knows perfectly well what my business is."

Mother had two more children, both girls, born on Staten Island: Sarah (Sally) and Esther Fisher. Mother's health was not too good, and for many years she had few outside interests. Running a household with two or three maids takes time and energy, even though the only housework she did was mending, and making curtains. She was on the local school board and kept up her reading. She had persuaded herself that woman's place was in the home; when she participated in public life, it was to give papers on *anti*-suffrage.

I remember the period before the First World War quite vividly, although I was then only a boy (I reached age 16 in 1914). It was a period of optimism. There was a recognition that there were problems, and the reforms then under way would, it seemed, continue and other problems would be solved as they arose. The prevalent philosophy, at least of the liberals, could be summed up in Arthur Clough's poem, "Say not the struggle naught availeth." I remember taking comfort in lines like "Far back, by creeks and inlets making, comes silent flooding in the main." I thought that progress takes place through small advances which at times are imperceptible, or nearly so; then one realizes all at once that the world has moved after all.

People with a social conscience, among whom I include my mother (probably my father too), were still not satisfied. Mother remarked on "this terrible poverty" that did not seem to go away. And neither she nor practically anybody else appreciated the evils of imperialism, the subjugation of colonial peoples, the plundering of their resources, and the perversion of their economies. In England and the U.S., colonial revolts like that of the Southwest Africans against the Germans, were attributed to the false, oppressive policies of the Germans, not to imperialism in general. There were voices against imperialism--Rosa Luxemburg, Lenin, the Little Englanders--but they were submerged. The anti-imperialists in the U.S. had waged a successful campaign against annexation of the Philippines, and that settled things for that time.

Dongan Hills turned out to be a gathering ground for sports rather than intellectuals; both Mother and Father missed the stimulus of intellectual challenge. They did not rise to the dances that the Country Club crowd was always throwing. There was also a problem with the schools. The Staten Island Academy to which Hal and I were going, got very much thinned out in the upper classes.

So in 1911, when I was 13 years old, the family, after a summer spent in France and England, moved back to the Boston area. We lived for a year in a hotel, which gave Mother a rest from housekeeping but was not a good idea. Then we moved into a rather large brick house in Brookline, which Mother bought with $25,000 that she had inherited from her Aunt Anna. The house was bigger than we needed--a reporter who came out to interview Mother later on when she had become active in public life (not in politics though) described it as "palatial." Mother and Father were proud of it, though it was not nearly as luxurious as the houses that Mother's brothers were building in Readville.

My mother, who was quite religious, found the Unitarian church in Brookline a congenial haven, and she took along as many of her children as were willing to go. I went sometimes. Nanie was quite shocked later to learn that I had served as usher there for a couple of years.

Hal and I attended the Country Day School for Boys of Boston, in Newton, a suburb of Boston at a little distance from Brookline. We commuted by street-car, or sometimes rode our bicycles in the season. School lasted all day, with athletics in the afternoon and a study period until five o'clock. The girls went to Miss Winsor's School. The family spent the summers at some seaside resort, different every year. We had all the advantages. We children took advantage of the opportunities and did well in sports and studies. With a classmate, I started a weekly newssheet at school and it became the school paper a year later.

The success of the paper was due in part to the contribution of our teacher of history and German, Mr. Eugene Hecker, who wrote humorous sketches for us. The students were much amused at the shafts that he directed at us severally and collectively. It was suggested that the school should have a motto, and he contributed three suggestions. One was, "Pro Havardiense, non pro schola, estudiamos" (not bad for a prep school). The last was "Ignorantia est felicitas", which I changed to "Ignorance is bliss" because the only time that occurred in literature (I thought) was in English, in a poem by Gray.

Mr. Hecker also gave us quite a political education in history class. He had written a history of women's rights and was well posted on current events. In 1913 and early 1914, when talk of a European war filled the air, he said several times that such a war would be impossible. He based his argument on the financial interpenetrations of the big powers. Norman Angell, a British publicist who had written a book *The Great Illusion* proving that war does not pay, fell into the same trap. When the war clouds gathered in 1914 I tried out Mr. Hecker's line at home. But Father did not buy it. He said there was a very real danger of a big war, and he was right. The war began in Europe when I had still two years to go in school.

76

III

The Calhoun School

My mother (may she rest in peace!) was born to be an administrator. Since fate decreed that she should be a wife and mother, she exercised her not inconsiderable talents in that field. She could shuffle people around like nobody's business. In the winter of 1916 she got the idea that grandmother needed a rest from keeping house in West Medford. So grandmother and the Giant came and stayed at our house in Brookline for a spell. I suppose it was a rest for grandmother, but for the Giant the strain of adjusting wore him down, and he was very tired when the two of them returned to West Medford. He used to go riding in the Fells before leaving for work, and he did this on a day of inclement weather. He caught his death of cold--died of pneumonia.

Mother also didn't notice that at the end of the winter of 1915-16, when I had one more year of secondary school ahead of me before college, I was completely tuckered out and badly needed a restful spring vacation. One of my sisters came down with a contagious disease, and the rest of us had to vacate. Even then, I might have settled into a quiet backwater, say at Grandmother's in West Medford (my grandfather having died). But no, I was sent to my cousin Dick Hallowell's for a few anything but restful days, and at the end was squeezed into brother Hal's room in the Freshman dormitories at Harvard. School resumed and I commuted for several days, adding to my later collapse by changing into a spring-weight-suit. So, I didn't make it through the spring. I came home from school one day and took to my bed, staying there for a couple of weeks, and got back to school only toward the end of the term.

That fall, instead of playing on the football team, I took riding lessons-- learned to ride horseback. Not until the winter did I get back into athletics (I was captain of the track team, and the leading schoolboy middle distance runner of the Boston area).

Our extended family, I have noted, was integrated in an unusual way. We knew what our cousins were doing, and even our mother's cousins knew what we were doing. The family knew about my taking riding lessons. Cousin Milly had been teaching for many years at a trade school for Negroes, or as we would say today Blacks, at Calhoun in Alabama. She heard that riding was good for my health. There were horses at Calhoun waiting to be ridden, so she invited me to come and visit at Calhoun in the Christmas vacation, and it was so arranged. That was a really interesting experience for me.

The Calhoun School was a pet project of a group in Boston, which included the Hallowells. After the Civil War, the abolitionists had a strong feeling of responsibility for the freed slaves, who were unable to get any economic power to go with their newly acquired political power, and who lost even that as a result. The educational system for blacks had to be built from the ground up, and several of the schools and colleges for blacks that were set up at that time were financed from the north, including the Calhoun School.

Another cousin, Louise, who had married Mott Hallowell, was the chair of the Boston committee for Calhoun. So, it was quite natural for Cousin Milly to go to teach at Calhoun and for me to visit there.

Calhoun was a small settlement in Lowndes County, 20 or 30 miles south of Montgomery. Lowndes County was deep south; it later became well known as a center of resistance to the Sharecroppers Union, and as the place where Viola Liuzzo, an activist in the civil rights agitation from Detroit, was murdered in the registration campaign. But in 1916-17 the faculty of the school was not agitating for political rights. It was seeking to prepare the black population to compete for the skilled jobs in certain trades.

Actually Lowndes County had some tradition of Negro militancy. "Uncle Isaac," a local resident who remembered the post-Civil-War days, used to tell about how the Blacks had gone to vote at Fort Deposit, the voting center for that part of the county. The whites who were conducting the election told them they couldn't vote (this must have been after the Northern troops were withdrawn, as they were in 1876). "We said, 'We'll vote or there won't be any Fort Deposit,'" related Uncle Isaac. And he concluded: "We voted!"

Negro rights in the South were at a low ebb in 1916. The Blacks had lost the vote and had not gained any economic or other power, and the new militancy (such as it was) of the NAACP had not yet taken hold. The whites in the area were not all oppressors; a few actually helped the school. One such was Mr. Chestnut. He used to take me on horseback rides into the farming area surrounding the school; we stopped and chatted with the black farmers, who were sharecroppers and small owners.

January 1 is Emancipation Day for the Blacks and is celebrated as such. There was a celebration at Calhoun School. A few of the attenders remembered slavery and told, on request, about the rather gruesome aspects. Mostly though they preferred not to talk about it. Slavery, they said, was too terrible. So, the atmosphere of the meeting was forward-looking.

It fell to my lot to give a talk of my own before I left. I had gone out with the gang to do road work, and they had smiled politely at my efforts to use a spade and pickax. So I gave them a slightly overdrawn version of how in my school we were able to have a good time, and concluded on the moral note that sooner or later we would have to learn to work. The students did not mind the preachment; they were used to it. They gave me a good hand. I decided that I was a rising public speaker. The evidence was inadequate, but from then on I never got stage fright when obliged to go before an audience. Incidentally my letters home from Calhoun had their little part in the school's money-raising efforts; they were read aloud by Cousin Louise at a meeting of the Boston committee.

Cousin Milly took a little vacation of her own at the end of my visit and brought me back North by way of Tuskegee Institute, Atlanta (where we visited Morehouse College), and Hampton Institute. So, I got a good view of the higher levels of Negro education in the South. The buildings at Tuskegee, built largely by the students themselves, were especially impressive. I seriously considered going into Negro education in the South when I finished college, so when I landed there perforce, much later, it did not seem like a terrible come-down. My sister Sal taught for two years at Hampton after she finished college.

IV

The First World War, Pacifisim and Liberalism

The period 1914 - 1917 was a time when people in the U.S. who thought at all did a lot of thinking. Mother set about to reexamine the bases of Quaker pacifism. George Fox, who founded the Society of Friends, was a pacifist, and peace has ever since been a major concern of the Quakers, as his followers were called because of their religious enthusiasm. Not all of the Quakers have been pacifists, and even those who served in the armed forces have not been expelled from the meeting. But another major concern of the Quakers came to be the abolition of slavery. The leader in this campaign was John Woolman, who lived at the time of the American Revolution. He was a Northerner who made trips to the South. He and his followers, few at first, succeeded in convincing all the others. The Quakers in the South who had slaves got rid of them. A number of Quakers left the South and came to Richmond, Indiana, which is still a Quaker stronghold.

Mother read up on George Fox; Stephen Grellett, another leader Quaker; and John Woolman. I even read John Woolman's *Journal* myself. Mother decided that she was against U.S. participation in the war, and tried unsuccessfully to sell her ideas to her brothers and sisters. Her own sons were a more receptive audience. I was studying history in my Freshman year at Harvard, and did some reading on the side. Hal, who was a junior, was Secretary of the International Polity Club, which had been organized at Harvard by the British publicist Norman Angell. Some students, including Carroll Binder, were campaigning against the war, speaking on street corners and on Boston Common. Hal got them together in a split-off from the International Polity Club which they called the Harvard Union for American Neutrality. There were about 20 of them. One was a law student named Ralph Brown, who was running the boy's club at Dennison House, a settlement house in Boston. Mother got to know him and all the others in the group. In April, sure enough, the U.S. was in the war, and my classmates flocked into the Reserve Officers Training Corps. The Freshman dormitories became like a barracks. Instead of going out for the Freshman track team as I ordinarily would have done, I coached the baseball team at

Dennison House, and incidentally struck up a friendship with Ralph Brown, under whom I worked.

In February 1917 the Tsar's government fell, and a liberal government took over. Practically everybody in the U.S. was in favor of the Revolution at that stage. Mother and Hal and I went to a meeting at Ford Hall, where an enthusiastic crowd was welcoming the takeover. The Socialist Party of the U.S. had not split at that time. Later, in November, the "October" Revolution was to bring the Bolsheviks to power, and the liberals were left far behind. We did not at that time, in February, understand the implications of what was happening. We did not wave flags and cheer with the left-wing socialists. But we were moving left-some faster than others.

Making up one's mind about the war issue was no mean task. Not even all of our immediate family was agreed. Father was a Wilsonian liberal and supported the war, for the reasons that Wilson gave. In fact he went to Washington and worked in the Committee on Public Information under George Creel. On the Fourth of July 1918 President Wilson put out two statements, one with special political importance which he presumably wrote himself, and the other written by my pa, calling on Americans to support this day as a day of independence for the peoples of the world. This noble sentiment was unfortunately mixed in with the current blather about the aggressions of the Germans, but Father was quite a hero round his office. He had the statement framed and hung it on the wall in our parlor.

In the spring of 1917 I was thrown increasingly with a man who roomed on the same floor in Gore Hall, namely John Leslie Hotson. His whole family were devout Svedenborgians; his brother became a Svedenborgian minister. Also, they were passionate members of the Socialist Labor Party. The SLP was against the war, even more so than the Socialist Party, which was on record as being opposed but was not living up to the implications of its stand. Leslie's oldest brother was a full-time organizer for the SLP. He had another elder brother who became a conscientious objector (CO) and was jailed for it. I did not become a socialist at that time, but was very susceptible to the philosophy.

I have to admit that I was influenced in the stand I was taking by my religion. Later I gave that all up and became an atheist. But at the beginning of the war I was a religious objector (at the end I had shifted my position and was a political objector. But I did not come of age for the draft until the war was nearly over, and was never drafted, so did not have to declare myself).

Half of the Quakers in England and the U.S. were against the war, and they were impressed with the need to do something. Some found ambulance work consistent with their consciences; some thought that was too military and engaged in mine sweeping in the English Channel. The U.S. Quakers at this time were divided into several groups (the 5-year meeting with headquarters at Richmond, Ind., the Hicksites, Philadelphia Yearly Meeting, Wilburites, and Primitive Friends), but they managed to develop enough unity to organize the American Friends Service Committee, which still goes on. Its first big job was to set up and finance a Reconstruction Unit, which undertook to build houses to replace houses that had been destroyed in the war. The main field of operations was France, but branches of the Mission, as it was called, did famine relief in Russia and relief of various kinds (very small scale) in some other places. I joined the Reconstruction Unit and spent 16 months in France, 1917-1919. The Americans joined up with the English Quakers, who had already been doing reconstruction work in France for two years.

The English had built some houses at Sermaize-les-Bains, in the Marne, and were running a maternity hospital at Chalons-sur-Marne. When we Americans came on the scene a rather ambitious project had been decided on: to build sections for portable housing at factories in Ornans-sur-Doubs and Dol, both in the Eastern part of France, well behind the lines. These portable houses were then to be shipped to the Somme and erected, close behind the lines.

Just why it was necessary to get so close to the lines has never been explained. Some may have thought that the Friends should show they were not afraid. In any case, the idea was not a good one. The factory at Ornans, where I spent a couple of months, was not ready to operate when I got there, so that we had to cool our heels for several weeks. And when the Germans made their last big try to break through the Western front and win the war, it was precisely at the Somme that they aimed their blow. The Quakers had to get out, but quick.

For me also, the Friends' Mission was not a good idea. My breakdown in health the year before graduation from school had left me susceptible to a recurrence of what had then been diagnosed as accumulated fatigue. I was sick for some time at Ornans, went to Samoens in the French Alps to recuperate (still under the Friends of course), then spent the last months of the war in Paris. But when I eventually did come back to the U.S., my speed as a runner was gone, and a promising athletic career was down the drain.

On the positive side, the Friends' Mission was for me an eye-opener. The religious objectors to the war were thrown in with the political objectors and got a political education. I used to argue about democracy and socialism with Owen Stephens, Carleton MacDowell, and William Bell. These arguments were recalled afterwards by Owen Stephens, who wrote a book about his experiences in the Mission. "He always hits hard," he wrote of me. But my best friend was Leslie Heath. And the man who worked me back into shape, in Paris, was Lewis Gannett, who had gone through Harvard several years ahead of me, and had got himself a job on the *New York World*. He was an earnest liberal. The mission suffered from a lack of integration; people in one area did not know what those in the other areas were doing. Lewis proposed to establish a journal, *Reconstruction,* which would go to all centers and maintain morale. He was the editor - in - chief; Francis Birrell, an art critic and son of the former British Home Secretary Augustine Birrell, was a supervising editor; and the actual job of getting out the paper fell to me. I edited the copy, read the proof, and got out the paper. Lewis was in and out, making the decisions on what would be printed.

Leslie Heath was unique in more ways than one. At Haverford College Campus, where our unit had gone for a couple of months training, he appeared from nowhere, not a member of any meeting (he was not then a Quaker), tall and raw - boned, thin and bald. His diction was so poor that some people could not understand him. But he knew the liberal movement, and especially he knew and understood people. And what was more, he did something about them.

I got to know him at Ornans. I got bronchitis and spent a couple of weeks in the makeshift infirmary (one room, with a comfortable bed). He would do his day's work and come in with an armful of wood, start the open fire and chew the fat.

His conversations did me no end of good. I had to reevaluate so many of the values I had taken for granted, and was glad to find that there was a common-sense answer to the problems I had set for myself, or at any rate to most of them. He got me to lay out the problems that had been bothering me, and set me right on a lot of things. He had the persistence to stay with the job. Later I found him doing the same kind of job with my roommate in Paris, and he continued the same practice in later life; in Germantown, where he settled, he was known as a builder of men.

This sounds as if our relationship was a one way deal, but it wasn't. He had arrived at age 30 with a frankly cynical attitude to people in general; he had decided that you couldn't trust anybody. He said I changed his attitude. Apparently I was somebody he could trust, and the discovery meant a lot to him.

He was the son of a doctor in the Berkshire Mountains. His father had become a victim of opium, and had died young, leaving Leslie to support his mother and younger brother. He never went to College, but got a job in a railroad station. This was before the days of electric lights, and the station was lit by a hanging oil lamp which was turned off by pulling it down. Little boys, to bug the station-master, would climb on the radiator and pull the lamp down, then skip. Leslie, who had electricity as his hobby, hooked up a surprise package for the young scamps, and when they reached up to the lamp from the radiator, they got a dandy shock. That cured them. A General Electric factory was near by, and a man from there heard about Leslie's exploit and offered him a job in the plant. He took it--had no choice actually.

Leslie was studying electricity, in spite of not having had a college education. He was a good mechanic, and had charge of the heating plant at a hospital run by the Mission. He gave up his job with GE when he joined the Mission, and stayed on in France for a couple of years after the war.

My social life in Paris was limited pretty much to the Mission itself. And we did have some fine young ladies: Helen Elder, already mentioned; Dorothy Walton, known as Tommy, who later married Carroll Binder; and several more, all of course older than me. I was the youngest American member of the Mission.

It might have been thought that a group of a couple of hundred young men and women in their twenties--for the most part--and single, as most of them still are, would have occasioned some problems, but I only knew of one case. Artie Collins, who had been in Samoens when I was, had an affair with a French girl, and went back to the U.S. as a consequence. For most of us, the taboo on pre-marital sex had been internalized to the point where we didn't even consider it. I remember Leslie Heath saying that he just couldn't imagine getting mixed up with a girl that way unless he loved her with all his heart and soul.

It was part the ethos of the Mission that we should undergo hardships, to show that in rejecting military service we had not opted for the soft life. This philosophy led to the deliberate imposition of hardships--"mortification of the flesh", as Leslie Heath called it. There were a few married couples in the Mission,

84

but it was not expected that they would be assigned to the same work places.

The Germans had driven to within 25 miles of Paris before they were turned back at the Battle of the Marne, and they were still there in 1918. One day Lewis Gannett and I were walking across the Place de la Concorde when we heard an explosion that made us both jump. It was a shell from Big Bertha; it had hit a wing of the Ministry of War, which was a pile of rubble when we passed it a couple of minutes later. The shelling of Paris did not pose any great risk to us civilians, although once in a while a shell did hit something--a hit on a church resulted in several dozen women and children being killed. Most of the shells sailed harmlessly by; some didn't even hit Paris.

More dangerous were actually the night air raids. We were supposed to take to the cellar. Sometimes we went down, but as it happened the night when a bomb dropped the closest, I was upstairs, watching the fragments from the anti-aircraft shells strike sparks from the cobblestones in the street. We heard a bomb hit--in the Seine River, a few hundred yards from Notre Dame cathedral. But there was no intention to hit the cathedral. The city of Reims was within shelling range of the German lines, and the city really took a beating, but the great cathedral of Reims was never hit.

More dangerous than the bombs and shells was the Asian flu, which hit in 1918. Several members of the Mission died and several more took sick and recovered. I used to go into their respective rooms and talk to them, not worrying about possibly getting contaminated. Nobody knew how it was transmitted.

The war ended in November 1918. The armistice was signed early in the morning of Nov. 11 and entered into force at 11 o'clock. My friend Larry Austin, who had visited me in Paris, was on the front at the time and was killed at a quarter past ten. At 11 every gun on the front went off, and many soldiers were killed after 11 o'clock.

The October Revolution had forced Socialists everywhere to take sides. The French Socialist Party eventually split several ways, into the reformist S.P., which retained the name, the Communist Party, which took perhaps two-thirds of the membership and the newspaper; and several splinter groups, led by people like Souvarine, Frossard and Loriot. All factions were present to hear a delegation of Russians which had arrived from Russia to present the point of view of the non-Bolshevisks, those who had been left behind when the Bolsheviks took over. The

Bolsheviks of course had their own emissaries, but these were not present at the meeting in question, which I had heard about from Lewis and was lucky enough to attend. The speakers emphasized the disastrous condition of the country, the inflation, shortage of goods, etc. The audience was not impressed. Its sentiment was expressed by one delegate who shouted, "Prove to us that it's the fault of the Bolsheviks, that's all we need!" After the three Russians had concluded, a French leader whose name I unfortunately did not catch, was given the floor to answer them, and he laid them out in good style. I was on his side in the exchange, but had not then decided to go all out for the Bolsheviks.

Lewis Gannett, returning to the U.S. after the war, worked for a time as an editor of *The Nation* under Oswald Garrison Villard, who expected him to become editor-in-chief and carry on the liberal tradition. But Lewis became instead a book reviewer for the *N.Y. Herald-Tribune* and drifted away from liberalism.

I left the Mission at the beginning of 1919, and my place as Managing Editor of *Reconstruction* was presently taken by Leslie Hotson, the friend of my Freshman year at Harvard. He had stayed on at Harvard through the academic year 1917-18 and joined the Mission after that. I was to room with him in our junior year at Harvard.

V

The Lawerence Strike of 1919

Our house at 44 Edge Hill Road, Brookline, was big enough to accommodate guests, and Carroll Binder, Bill Southworth, and Bob Dunn spent shorter or longer periods living there while I was away. From them, especially from Bob, Mother got a political education. She became interested in the movement. She sold the house to Father and used the money for worthy causes.

The Socialist Party had split and the Communist Party had still to be formed. The Left in the U.S. in early 1919 was in a state of disarray. The best known intellectual Leftist was Scott Nearing, who had been fired in 1915 from his tenured position at the University of Pennsylvania for advocating child labor legislation. He had moved rapidly to the left and was supporting the Russian Revolution. The Harvard Socialist Club had gone to pieces and there was nobody to invite Scott to come and speak, so I undertook the assignment. By way of getting a Harvard building for the meeting, and also of attracting an audience, Prof. Leo Wiener was invited to debate against Scott, and he accepted. The authorities refused to grant permission for using the Harvard Union, or any Harvard building, so we hired the basement of Brattle Hall. Everybody came. The meeting was moved upstairs into the main hall, which was packed. Scott gave his usual hard-hitting speech and Wiener answered him with the conventional unwisdom. Wiener did not pretend to know anything about socialism.

The spring of 1919 was a period of great excitement. In Russia, the Bolsheviks had taken over, and the Allies responded by invading the country from three sides. It was a question whether the revolution could be salvaged.

John Reed and his wife Louise Bryant came to Boston and addressed a mass meeting. His was indeed a novel approach. He had been in Russia during the last of the fighting against the Germans, who had penetrated far into Russia but had to withdraw when the offensive in the West failed. John Reed claimed some of the credit for undermining the German morale. He described how he and Boris Reinstein had prepared tons of propaganda leaflets, in German, which were scattered over the German lines.

The liberals were at first rather sympathetic to the Bolshevik Revolution and were generally opposed to the intervention. Pres.

Wilson was going along with the policy of the *cordon sanitaire*, developed by Clemenceau and endorsed by Lloyd George, the Allies must contain (and if possible upset) the Revolution. To mobilize public opinion against the *cordon sanitaire*, a law student named Arthur Fisher organized a mass meeting in Tremont Temple to be addressed by a panel of notables. Samuel Eliot Morrison chaired the meeting; Raymond Robbins came in from Washington: Felix Frankfurter and several other Harvard professors spoke. The meeting overflowed Tremont Temple and filled Faneuil Hall also, with the speakers shuttling back and forth. A strong resolution against the intervention was adopted. But in the end it was Russian force of arms, not U.S. pressure of public opinion, that determined the outcome.

Three anti-war ministers had lost their pulpits in 1917-18, and Mother belonged to a pacifist group with them. They were filled with enthusiasm for the movement, and even organized a group of their own, the Fellowship of the New World, from which the ministers drew their support for a time, which meant from Mother. Their names were Abraham Muste, Harold Rotzel, and Cedric Long.

The period just before the First World War was a time when reform was in the air. The long overdue personal income tax was finally passed, and the Federal Reserve System was set up. A Commission on Industrial Relations collected material foreshadowing some serious labor legislation, and social insurance was seriously discussed. But this wave of reform legislation was interrupted by the war, and by a couple of perverse decisions by the U.S. Supreme Court, and the 1920's did not see any great advances.

At the beginning of 1919 the Lawrence textile workers went on strike. Prices had been rising and the 8-hour day was being won in establishments which had never had it. The working week at Lawrence was 54 hours. The strikers demanded the 48-hour week with a pay raise enough to bring their earnings up to what they had been getting for 54 hours. The only union in the plants was a small craft union of loom-fixers, the United Textile Workers, affiliated with the AFL: it opposed the strike. The operatives formed their strike committee but had no trained leaders. Muste, Rotzel and Long went to Lawrence and offered their services. The offer was accepted. Muste became chairman of the Strike Committee. The Boston liberals were generally sympathetic to the strike. One member of the Gardner family, Mrs. Glendower Evans, was herself a large stockholder in one or more of the mills, though without influence on policy. She contributed to the strike funds.

We were back and forth to Lawrence all spring. One expedition of about twenty from Boston had been advertised in advance and was met at the railroad station by a detachment of police, who thought that most of the people on the train were from our group. They rode their horses up on the sidewalk in an evident attempt to provoke and intimidate us. The strikers were holding meetings, not all together, but each language group in a separate hall. We went from one hall to another, speaking in English with a translator. Mrs. Peabody managed to say "Grazie, signori" to the Italian group and got a big hand. At the end of the afternoon we took off for the station, stopping at the police station on the way: Rotzel protested at the way the police had acted. The question came up of how many of us there had been. The police had their idea. When Rotzel told them how many we actually were, the chief curled his lip and said, "That is a matter of opinion." Later the police told Rotzel they would hold him responsible if there was any violence that night.

Actually violence was the last thing the strike leaders wanted. Periodically Muste would give speeches on the "violence of folded arms." In Lawrence, people remembered the strike of 1912, which had also begun without leadership; the IWW had stepped into the vacuum, and Wobblies Ettor and Giovanitti became the spokesmen for the strike. There was a persistent campaign in the commercial press against the IWW, which was accused, correctly, of believing in violent revolution, although the conception was rather of a revolutionary general strike than of an armed uprising. So, in the Lawrence strike of 1912, a bomb had exploded, under a bridge; and the IWW had been blamed. This frameup backfired when it was shown that the bomb was planted under the directions of the head of the American Woollen Co.

Among the intellectuals who had offered their services to the strike committee was one who said he had training in several European universities and knew something of finance. They made him treasurer of the strike committee. He went by the name of Mack. Every evening he made a written report to the mill owners on what had taken place in the strike committee. Late in the spring he decided to give himself up. I drove Muste to an address he had given in Roxbury. I rang the bell and asked for Mr. Reichauer, and Mack came down. He let on to have had qualms of conscience about what he was doing. But it is also possible that he had discovered that he was under suspicion, or that his bosses had decided that what he was reporting was not worth their money.

The family had never before had a car, but it got a Ford model-T that spring, and it was used for trips to Lawrence. One day in Cambridge I ran into Harry Dana, who had been on a trip to Lawrence with Mother. He said she had been injured in an accident. I went right home and it was true enough. Hood van den Arend, a Harvard Freshman, had been driving the car when it locked with a car that was trying to pass it. Mother was thrown over the driver and suffered a painful injury to the coccyx. She was laid up for weeks.

The Lawrence strike attracted national attention. John Fitch, a liberal reporting on it for the *Survey,* wrote that it was "unconsciously class conscious." The Boston press gave it plenty of space, featuring the United Textile Workers (in big black headlines across the front page) when they came out against the strike. Perhaps the nastiest bit of reporting was a one-paragraph writeup of the meeting in Boston when Muste, Rotzel and Long summed up the results of the strike. Quotes were taken out of context in a final, futile effort to make it appear that the strike was violent, perhaps revolutionary.

The fact that Mrs. Evans was supporting the strike was a sticker. *The Boston Evening Transcript* noted the fact of her position, but even then did not attack her. She was (said the *Transcript*) a member of the Boston Gardner family, and could have anything that Boston had to offer, even, it seemed, a favorable press--for her, not for the strike. The Gardner family was one of the wealthiest families in town. The strikers appreciated Mrs. Evans's support, which was financial as well as moral, but they still felt that they had created the wealth that she was dispensing-- and a lot more too.

The strike ended in June. The economic demands were granted but the union was not recognized; there was no signed agreement. it was decided to continue the union, which took the name of the Amalgamated Textile Workers. Muste was the Secretary, and wanted me to become an organizer for the union, but I ducked. I wanted to finish my college course, and did so.

VI

Organising Farmers, The Nonpartisan Leauge

Arthur Fisher, when I saw him later that spring (1919), was all set to do organizing for the National Nonpartisan League in Wisconsin that summer, and he did do so. He suggested that I might like to do the same in Minnesota. I knew about the League. It had begun in North Dakota in 1916, the product of many years of domination of the state's politics by the special interests--the banks, the railroads, the grain elevator operators, and Eastern capitalists. A Socialist named A.C. Townley saw that all the farmers needed was organization, and he and a group including William Lemke talked up the idea, meeting a favorable reception. The political complexion of the founding group was leftist; one of the group, Clarence Sharp, later became a Communist Party leader. But most of them were just farmers. The plan they worked out was to form a farmers' political organization, the Nonpartisan League, and to get the League's members to vote together at the primaries of one of the two major parties and get their man nominated, and later, if possible, elected. Starting in 1916, the League had managed to take over the Republican organization, elect a governor and a majority of both houses of the legislature, and put through its whole program, which consisted mostly of having the state go into the businesses in question. There was a state bank, a state grain elevator, a state hail insurance plan, and a state home loan association. The League favored government ownership of the railroads, but this of course was a federal matter.

I was in favor of the League's (liberal) program and was eager to get some ideas on organization. I did go out to Minnesota and offered my services to the League, which by that time had set up organizations in 16 states. It had already fought two campaigns in Minnesota, and the county I was assigned to work in (Murray County, in the southwestern corner of the state) had elected a League leader to the legislature. I signed up 114 farmers, mostly renewals. It was a great experience, giving me, the city slicker, a taste of what farming was like, and also some ideas on organization.

Many years later, the story of the Nonpartisan League was revived in a movie, *Northern Lights*. It looked at things from the point of view of the exploited farmer, and in general showed what the League was all about. But it was defective in that the producers

91

did not understand organization. The hero was represented as going out and visiting farms one by one, alone, and convincing the farmers individually to join the League. This was originally my conception too, and probably that of other inexperienced observers. Maybe it was the idea of the original Nonpartisan League organizers. If so, they soon outgrew that approach. Each farmer was very unwilling to be the first to take a stand. For the league to get established in a community, there were three steps, (1) prepare the ground by house-to-house visiting: (2) call a meeting in the local school house, where the League would be explained by an organizer, and where a local leader or two who had been lined up in advance would come forward and join, whereupon most of the others would join too: (3) follow up with more house-to-house visiting by the organizer, not alone, but accompanied by a local leader or booster. Once the organization was established in a community, the schoolhouse meeting did not have to be repeated, but the booster remained an essential ingredient.

As to whether a given farmer would sign up with the Nonpartisan League, it is clear that that depended on a number of things: whether the League was already established in the area, the presence and quality of the booster, and the farmer's own personal feelings at the moment. A very important element not often mentioned was the personal presence and feelings of the organizer. On my breaking in trip, the man who was showing me how it was done arrived with me about lunch time at the farm of one Hjort, who was sitting outside his house. The organizer did not spend much time with his sales talk; he knew that Hjort knew what the League was. He just sat there and fixed Hjort with his stare.

"Well," he said, "are you going to join?"

Hjort hesitated, then said. "Well, I guess it's the only way you'll leave me alone."

The organizer said later, "I couldn't have put Hjort on if I hadn't been feeling just right."

Incidentally in that two-week breaking-in period we did not have a booster along; we were working territory where the organizer was known.

I did stick to the job, was still there at the end of the day, and earned the respect of my mentor. If I had thought it was really important, I could have made a passable organizer. But as a way of life, organizing did not appeal to me. I was not like my daughter Terry, who is an extrovert, likes to talk, and did become a union organizer. So although I had a real interest in the labor movement,

I later turned down two opportunities to become a full-time organizer.

I went to a big farmers' rally that was addressed by Thomas van Lear, former Socialist mayor of Minneapolis. I was interested to see what issues the urban workers, who were not especially interested in grain elevators and problems of credit, would have in common with the farmers. Van Lear had plenty to talk about-- largely in terms of how such progressive legislation as there was, was being emasculated by lax enforcement. The organized farmers (the Non-Partisan League) and the organized city workers eventually got together and formed the Farmer-Labor Party, which was strong enough to elect some Congressional Representatives and two United States Senators, first Henrik Shipstead and later Magnus Johnson. They even took a progressive point of view on foreign policy for a while, criticizing the U.S. for landing marines in Nicaragua.

After attending the Van Lear meeting I continued on to Minneapolis and heard President Wilson on his last tour, making his pitch for the League of Nations. I was interested to hear what he would say about the Russian Revolution. He was totally unsympathetic. Russia, he said, had been seized by a little clique-- "I think there are about 34 of them"-and in the good intentions of this clique he had no faith at all. He left Minneapolis for Wichita, and collapsed on the way. From then on the battle for the League of Nations was carried on by others.

My side trip to Bismarck gave me an impression of the country (North Dakota) and the leaders. I saw Townley only for a minute: Tall, personable, very busy, the typical organizer, a promoter type. Lemke was personally just the opposite of Townley: short, homely, with a bad eye, but a fluent talker. He talked about Mexico, as, it seems, he always did whenever he got a chance. He had been elected to state office and remained active in North Dakota politics for years. But in the end he defected, and in the presidential campaign of 1936 he ran as an independent against Landon and FDR, with the purpose of attracting liberal votes away from FDR (It didn't work).

Actually the League in North Dakota had accomplished its aims very early. It had enacted its whole program in the first session of the legislature after its surprise victory. The governor was a dirt farmer, Lynn Frazier: he was out plowing his field when the delegation came to tell him he had been nominated for Governor--a modern Cincinnatus. The League used to claim that the legislature in question was the only one in history in any state that had carried out all its campaign promises. But with the legislative part of the program achieved, there remained the problem of administering it, and that was another story. I did not participate, but my father did. He had got interested in the League about the time that I did, and had come out to North Dakota and met the leaders too.

The political education that we gave the farmers did not result in the adoption of the whole program of the League as in North Dakota, but a liberal party, the Farmer-Labor Party, was set up, and presently merged with the Democrats. We had concentrated on domestic issues, but the U.S. Congressmen and Senators took a good position on Latin-American affairs. Henrik Shipstead of Minnesota was the only Sandinista in the U.S. Senate. Even as late as the 1930's, the lone vote in the House against boycotting the Spanish Loyalists was cast by John Bernard from the Minnesota Iron Range.

VII

Liberalism at Harvard

While I was in Bismarck, Boston was making national headlines. The police were on strike. I hurried back but arrived after the strike had been broken. Some of my college mates had been strikebreaking and had been chased home by pickets. The excitement was, or had been, intense. The liberals generally sympathized with the police. Working hours were excessively long at a time when the 8-hour day was being widely introduced, their pay had not been raised to correspond to the big increase in living costs, and working conditions were appalling.

At this time in my career I was an eager reformer, and went along with the liberals who also wanted to see things improved. It was only later, when the limitations of the reformist point of view became evident, that I became critical of liberalism as a philosophy and eventually ditched it altogether. The man furthest left on the Harvard faculty at this time was undoubtedly Harold J. Laski. Although still in his twenties he had written a book and several articles espousing a distinctive political theory: he was a pluralist. As such, he was interested in the anarcho-syndicalist theory of the IWW. He sympathized with the police strike. He was attacked in the public press in the most immoderate terms: some of his strongest critics were members of the Harvard faculty. The president, A. Lawrence Lowell, was under much pressure to get rid of him. The fact that Harvard was then conducting a drive to increase its endowment was a factor in the situation.

At this time Laski is supposed to have come to Lowell and said, "I understand that I have been a source of some embarrassment to you."

Lowell is supposed to have answered,

"You have, you have. I expect that you have cost me a million dollars." [That was real money in those days]

Laski is then supposed to have offered to resign, to which Lowell is said to have replied,

"You are perfectly free to resign any time you want, but it is only fair to tell you that if you resign, I resign too."

As a trusting liberal, I repeated this story many times, and the truth of it was never called in question. If today it seems hard to believe, I still quote it as an illustration of how things ought to be and how for many years I more or less believed they were.

Laski was an entertaining talker and lecturer, and his classes were well attended. He was a popular teacher. He invited students to come to his house, and many did, including me. He came down to the student dormitories and stood on the street corner thumbing through a book, and students came by and talked to him there. But the conservative element in the student body remained hostile. The *Lampoon* published a whole number devoted to attacking him as a Bolshevik.

Laski was brought to Harvard by Felix Frankfurter, who was then a professor in the Law School, and the highly respected C.J. Haskins, a historian and Dean of the Graduate School. They presumably stood by him when he was under fire. When Laski left Harvard a few years later, it was widely supposed that he had been forced out, but that was not the case. He left voluntarily. He was highly regarded at Yale, and had been invited to lecture there, which he had done on various visits. Meanwhile he had built up an imposing publication record, add Yale offered him a full professorship. Laski then tried to get Harvard to match the offer, but it couldn't be done, not so much because of his politics (he had backed way down from his pluralistic ideas) but because it would have involved jumping over too many heads and violating the unwritten rule about advanced degrees being necessary. When it became evident that Harvard had no future for him, he accepted an offer from the London School of Economics, which he evidently preferred to Yale, and became an informal adviser to the Labor Party. He even wrote on Communism when it was fashionable to do so, in the 1930's, but showed no understanding whatever of Marx, whom he did not pretend to have read. He was a consistent liberal (so far as that is not a contradiction in terms) and I felt obliged to take him apart in my last book, for his inadequate treatment of nationalism.

I went out for the *Crimson* editorial competition in the fall of 1919. The editor was Fifield Workum; in charge of the editorials was Alexander Kirk. The man who quickly forged to the front in the competition was named Gavit; his father was an editor of the *Survey*, and the son was a fluent and capable writer. He was not following the competition very closely and was on the point of dropping out because so few of his editorials had been published. He did not realize that all the others had had even fewer. I was running second in the competition and continued to do so. I envisioned a senior year when Gavit and I would be writing the editorials. I thought we would be a good team. I persuaded him to come back in. Of course, I was cutting my own throat but I didn't know that then.

Midway through the fall I wrote a slashing editorial calling on President Wilson to withdraw U.S. troops from Russia and institute a policy of economic and political aid to the Soviet Union. I brought it in and handed it to Alec Kirk. To my great surprise, he said, "Yes, that's fine," made a few editorial directions, and walked off down the hall to give it to the printer.

The editorial caused quite a stir. But Alec Kirk stood by it all the way. Two weeks before the end of the competition, when I was running second to Gavit, with two to be selected, Fi Workum called me in and said that it had been decided--on a split vote-not to take me onto the board.

Powers Hapgood was on the Board of the Crimson, having been taken on in the business end. When he heard about my purging he was furious. He brought the matter up at the next meeting of the Board, which had not been consulted theretofore; the purging was the work of three men, Workum, Kirk (who stood up for me), and the incoming editor Bill Lowderback. But although Powers put up a strong case for me, the rest of the Board could not be bothered. It was past history, for them. The decision stood.

Powers Hapgood was not a radical exactly. He came of a liberal family. His grandfather had built up a canning business on the outskirts of Indianapolis. Powers' father William P. Hapgood, continued the family business, the Columbia Conserve Co., and set about to reorganize it as a worker-owned cooperative. When the reorganization was complete, William P. Hapgood was still the manager; so, the change was in form only. But the idea of workers' control was in the air; so, when Powers wrote an honors' thesis about the form of organization of the Columbia Conserve Co., Prof. Taussig, chairman of the Economics Department, was much interested.

Powers went through college in three years. He started after me and finished before me, so I really only knew him for one year, but came to like him a lot. He used to go down to Socialist Party headquarters in Boston. This was at the time when the S.P. was splitting into three factions: the continuation of the old S.P.; the group that became the Communist Party, which went underground; and the so-called Communist Labor Party. The Palmer raids were intended to break up the radical movement so far as it depended-- as it did quite largely by that time-on foreign-born workers for membership and leadership. Powers made contact with one of the victims of the raids who had managed to get free, and he came out to Harvard and described the raids--which were illegal--to an attentive audience in Phillips Brooks House. It was suggested that the *Crimson* might participate in a campaign against the raids; but "wiser" counsels, led by John Cowles, prevailed, and the *Crimson* did nothing.

The raids, conducted under the direction of A. Mitchell Palmer, the Attorney-General, by one J. Edgar Hoover, were reviewed by Judge Anderson and found to be an abuse of executive discretion. Richard Cabot, an old friend of my mother's, had made his mark in medicine and taken a chair at Harvard in the new field of Social Ethics. He had the students read the Anderson Report. Here was Harvard liberalism again. What made it so difficult to size Harvard up was these outbursts of liberalism alternating with acts of repression.

It was in the spring of 1919 that the Harvard Liberal Club took the initiative in setting up a student Liberal Club. The Harvard Liberal Club was composed of liberal graduates of Harvard who took a stand on public questions and tried to influence Harvard itself in a liberal direction. The student Liberal Club, under John Rothschild's leadership, arranged a series of lectures on the Russian Revolution, importing such authorities as Isaac Hourwich and Col. Rustam-Bek. I was not admitted to the student Liberal Club at first, Workum having blocked me, but did join a little later, and John Rothschild and I alternated in the leadership of the club, Workum having lost interest.

Part of the technique used at Harvard at that time in the name of liberalism--hearing both sides--was to permit representatives of left-wing groups to speak in Harvard buildings provided a speaker was on hand to refute their fallacies. Thus the meeting at which spokesmen for several Left parties presented their respective cases in the Harvard Union under the auspices of the student Liberal Club in the spring of 1920 was chaired by Richard Merriam, a conservative instructor in the economics department and a self-appointed socialist-baiter from his undergraduate days. Harry Laidler presented the case for the Socialist Party, Dr. Antoinette Konikow for the Communist Labor Party, and the final speaker was J. T.Doran of the I.W.W. In rising to introduce him, Merriam raised the question, Why should Harvard students who have every opportunity to be members of the privileged strata be interested in socialism? Doran undertook to answer that one. He said to the Harvard students, "Circumstances will make you socialists." He went on to tell the story of the Everett massacre in 1913 and the framing of the IWW leaders during the war, and made a big hit. Merriam was discomfited: the Harvard strategy had backfired.

The years 1919 and 1920 were a period of great union activity, and the employers were fighting back with the traditional method of spies in the movement. One project of the Student Liberal Club was to expose labor spies, and Norman Himes, who was entrusted with this assignment, actually did expose one; the story was given a whole page in the Sunday *American*.

Liberalism at this time meant for many, including me, an interest in and sympathy for labor, and a mistrust of employers as such. We hoped to eliminate the employer by gradual means. I mentioned William P. Hapgood, who was an employer and eliminated himself by reorganizing the company as a workers' cooperative. Carter Goodrich, a liberal who later was to give the labor courses at Columbia, wrote a book *The Frontier of Control*. In England, a man named Unwin was attempting to bypass the employer by forming what were known as building guilds. When I went to England in the summer of 1920, I looked up Unwin and took note of his plans. Later, in 1927, I was to go to England again, and found that nothing had come of them.

But in 1920 guilds were the talk of the town, and a movement called guild socialism was being backed in England by an influential group of liberals including G.D.H. Cole.

In the concept of Cole and his group, industries were to be organized into guilds, having a certain resemblance to medieval guilds, which had no employers, only masters and apprentices. The guild was thought of as similar to the revolutionary industrial unions contemplated by the I.W.W., but were not revolutionary; the guilds were to be introduced peacefully. This idyllic perspective was of course anathema to the employing class as a class, but Cole had a certain following. I was carried along and started calling myself a guild socialist.

Originally I had planned to go to England in the summer of 1920 in company with Bob Dunn, who was more to the left than I was. Unfortunately this did not work out, and his influence had to be exerted on me over the years in my visits to the Labor Research Association.

My time in England was spent largely at the Labour Research Department, where I had volunteered my services at Laski's suggestion. The Department was an adjunct of the Labour Party, and was run by R. Page Arnot: on the staff was R. Palme Dutt, of (East) Indian extraction but domiciled in Britain. Both Dutt and Arnot were strong supporters of the Russian Revolution and presently gravitated into the Communist Party, which was actually formed that summer. The Department dug up research material which the Labour Party M.P.'s used in their speeches in Parliament. It also did economic research, and was then engaged in a study of minimum wages and prices. I was assigned to dig out the minimum wage rates over a period of years from the files of the periodical put out by the government's Labour Department. Much to the surprise of the management, I showed up for work every day and my material was later incorporated in a pamphlet. Later in the summer, I made a swing around the industrial district of Lancashire and Yorkshire, talking to employers and union leaders. The employers talked like American open-shop employers. The greater reasonableness of British employers, I concluded, was due to the greater solidarity and outright strength of the British union movement.

This solidarity was indeed very noticeable in the course of that summer, which was a momentous one for the history of the Russian Revolution and of Western Europe generally. The union movement had grown strong during the war; the Labour Party was passing the Liberal Party and becoming the second party, expecting to take power in a few years. Business was booming, prices were rising, and strikes were being won. The miners were leading the way; one of their demands was for nationalization of the mines.

I attended two Congresses of the Trades Union Congress. a regular one and a special one. The Russian Revolution, fighting for its life, had repulsed the invasions from the North, South, and East and was engaged in a war with Poland on its western front. A lot of war materiel had remained in the hands of the Allies at the end of the First World War, and it no doubt seemed natural to Lloyd George, the British Prime Minister, that this should be put at the disposal of the Poles to carry on the policy of the *cordon sanitaire*. The British Labour Movement did not go along with the revolutionary philosophy of the Bolsheviks, but neither did it fancy seeing the Revolution strangled so to speak in the cradle. The Trades Union Congress adopted a very strong resolution opposing the turning over of any munitions of war to the Poles. The government replied that it had had no such intention, and that danger was averted. The Poles won the war anyway and annexed a large slice of Russian territory, but the Revolution survived and remained grateful for the moral support it had received in the West. I can testify that the resolution was no paper resolution; when it was adopted, there were cries of "down tools" from the floor of the hall.

One of my assignments was to attend an international Friends' conference, which I did. The Friends were generally respected though not much of a factor in public life. They adopted resolutions against war (surprise!) but an attempt by George Hallett, an American liberal Quaker, to introduce an amendment deploring also the blockade of the Russians, was quickly shouted down.

The high point of the summer for me was a week at a conference called by the Guild Socialists and attended by left-wingers of all descriptions. They discussed the future of socialism in England and climaxed the week with a show including some lyrics written for the occasion. The right-wing socialists like Sidney Webb took quite a beating . Of course, they were not there, but G.D.H. Cole, the leader of the Guild Socialists, was, and a revolutionary named Ellen Wilkinson. In the show, the revolutionaries won and chopped off the heads of all the others, including mine (I was Bill Haywood), whereupon Ellen Wilkinson remarked, "Now we can have a real revolution!"

Back at Harvard during the fall of 1920 I used to go with a friend and swim in the Charles River after dark. I continued this practice through the warm weather and into the cold. The last time was four days before Christmas. The temperature was below freezing. I knew that it was risky to swim in icy water; John Rothschild's father had died that way. However I broke the ice without misgivings, had my swim and broke a little film of ice that had formed while I was in the water, to get out.

The course on Marxism at Harvard was given by Prof. Thomas Nixon Carver, the leading anti-Marxist on the faculty. I did not take the course on Marxism, and indeed shared the prevalent opinion that Marx was probably out of date. But I still used to argue with Prof. Carver, whom I encountered many times. I heard a lot about the virtues of the free contract. Finally I asked Prof. Carver whether the bargain in which Esau sold his birthright to Jacob was a free contract. He answered, "Yes, but--". I came to learn that he was wrong at law: a contract made under duress is not a free contract.

I really enjoyed my college courses, and got a lot out of them--some more than others, naturally. The problem was that if one took all the preliminary courses the advanced courses, with the men I had been hearing about, like Prof. Turner in history, Laski and others, would have been squeezed out. So I tried taking the advanced courses without the preliminaries. This worked badly in some cases; but in anthropology it was just right. My social anthropology course was one that I still look back on with gratitude. Another course that I enjoyed was one on the drama, from Aeschylus to Bernard Shaw, with George Pierce Baker.

Having come out of the Friends' Mission with a pro-labor orientation, and intending to make my career as an intellectual in the labor movement, I changed my major from English to economics. In my senior year I found myself in three courses intended primarily for graduates: theory with Taussig and Allyn A. Young, and labor with William Z. Ripley. My favorite was Young, an underestimated economist and a fine teacher. Taussig used the Socratic method, and I adopted that as my standard procedure when I became a teacher of economics. Ripley's labor course was a washout. He did not know the subject, did not prepare for the classes, and altogether scamped the job. Labor was my major, and I was furious, but there was nothing I could do about it.

The fall of my senior year was a presidential campaign year, and the Student Liberal Club organized a forum in which the Republicans and Democrats shared the platform with the Socialist (Norman Thomas) and a speaker from the Farmer-Labor Party. At Radcliffe, and to some extent at Harvard, this last man stole the show.

Harvard had the most active student Liberal Club in the college community. We contacted other colleges and organized a conference at which was born the Intercollegiate Liberal League, a federation of Liberal Clubs. The women's colleges showed a lot of interest and sent delegates; the President of Vassar (a man) even came to the conference. The men's colleges were not so much interested, but the event, and the organization, did not pass unnoticed in the academic community.

The Harvard Student Liberal Club worked that spring quite closely with the Radcliffe Liberal Club. At Harvard the leaders, beside John Rothschild and me, included an ardent youth named Bob Wormser. At Radcliffe the leaders were Edna Cers and Mary Switzer. At a certain point it became evident that a leader for the following year would have to be chosen, and Mary chose John, who took over and ran the Intercollegiate Liberal League after the college year was over.

The form that the new organization was to take was discussed in a meeting that John and I had with the editors of the *New Republic*. Walter Lippmann, who had gone through Harvard ten years before us and was riding high as a liberal, thought that the organization should take a modest role and operate on a limited budget. This was just my way of looking at it. John, seeing things big as usual, rented an office on Morningside Heights (near Columbia), hired a couple of secretaries, and proceeded to put out literature which went to a mailing list that he worked up. He had access to funds that we didn't know anything about. In the course of the year the name of the organization was changed to the National Student Forum, and it concentrated on bringing over leaders of the youth movement from Europe and circulating them to American colleges--not a bad idea actually, since the youth movement in places like Germany was more advanced than anything the American colleges had to offer. Some of the European youth leaders stayed on in the U.S. One who did was Achim Friedrich, who became a Harvard professor.

Mary Switzer took a job in a government office in Washington and stayed in Washington the rest of her active life. She made a distinguished career. The last job she held was chief of the Bureau of Vocational Rehabilitation. Edna continued in the academic field, and married a Columbia Professor. They had two children. Gone were the pert remarks and sly digs which had made Edna such a joy in her college years. She raised her children to be highly respectable citizens.

VIII

On the Bum

I set out at the end of the summer to get a job in the steel industry in Pittsburgh.

In college my friends, who were thinking big about what they would be doing after graduation, used to ask me what line I was going into, and I would say, "labor research." They would look stunned and say, "What does that lead to?" to which I would answer, "More of the same." It would not have occurred to them that anyone would want to do research for a labor organization, but that was what I had in mind. I would get a job in the labor movement if possible; if not, then an academic career was not ruled out.

It was not unusual at that time for college graduates with leftist tendencies to go into industry. I have mentioned Powers Hapgood. There were also Justine Wise, who got a job in a textile mill in Passaic; Dorothy Walton, who came back from the Mission and worked in several different industries, writing each one up for the *New Majority*, a left-wing labor paper published in Chicago; and several others.

In Europe there would have been no problem about working for labor--in the Labour Party in England, or some branch of the movement on the continent--there were lots of intellectuals in the labor movement. Not so in the U.S. In Boston, there had been a struggling labor paper, edited by Paul Harris Drake, and I had written a couple of articles for it; but it had gone under.

Anyway, I headed for Pittsburgh and the steel industry. This was in spite of the fact that I knew there was a depression on--a mini-depression, to be sure, nothing like what happened after 1929. And in fact I got a couple of jobs on the way to Pittsburgh--one as agricultural laborer, another in the building industry at Jeanette (Pa.) which would have lasted all winter; and still another, also in construction, in Steelton, right next to Three Mile Island. But the steel industry was not hiring in Steelton, nor in Pittsburgh when I got there; so I hit South along the Monongahela River, headed for Clarksburg, W.Va.

I passed through a couple of towns that specialized in making glassware, with a nucleus of workers who had come over from Belgium. In Charleroi at the end of the day I saw the Salvation

Army in action, standing on the street corner and singing hymns, with a cornetist. I passed a remark about them to a man standing next to me, and he said, "They're doing a great work," and looked at me accusingly. I put him down as a member of the local Establishment, boosting the Salvation Army as a means of keeping the workers' minds off their real grievances; and indeed the S.A. sometimes did go to bat for the local businessmen in other places. They knew where their money came from.

I had read in the paper that a plate mill in Clarksburg was starting up again after a period of idleness. I did work for a couple of days in the plate mill, replacing somebody who was out sick; then left town before payday (I had to write for my pay, and finally got it around Christmas, wondering all the time how many unfortunate hoboes not so used to pencil and paper and with no continuing address had lost how much in unpaid wages).

I was traveling with a knapsack and had learned how to ride "blind baggage"--on the front platform of the front passenger car, just behind the tender of the locomotive. I sneaked onto that perch on a passenger train bound east some time in the evening. But at Piedmont, W.Va., I was hauled off by a station cop and marched off to jail. He almost apologized for arresting me. There were a good many hoboes on the road at the time, and he realized that locking one of them up would do no special good. He said that with my knapsack I looked like two boys who had just escaped from a nearby reformatory and whom they were really anxious to catch.

I stayed in jail the rest of that night and all the next day. My wallet with $11 and some odd cents in it was confiscated. At the end of the afternoon the guard who had arrested me said that the company had decided to prosecute me for trespass and that the lawyer was on his way over from Kaiser, some miles distant. I said what did that mean? and he said maybe 30 days of road work, and went out.

He was gone only a couple of minutes, then came back, handed me my wallet, and instructed me how to go--across the bridge into the next state where I would be safe. I noticed that the $11 were gone and asked him about that. He said that $10 had been taken out for "bail money". I said, Did that mean I would have to come back and stand trial? He said No, and kept pushing me out. I was glad enough to go. As I neared the far side of the bridge an auto came up behind me. I lost no time covering the extra distance.

I slept in a barn and took to the highway at 7:30 A.M., a poor time for lifts ordinarily, especially on a Sunday morning. I had discovered that trucks were the things to depend on. Not that they actually gave you more lifts than passenger cars or covered more mileage for you, but that they would stop when passenger cars wouldn't. The rules have been tightened up some since then, and truck drivers are not supposed to pick up hitch-hikers, but they still do. So, keep to the truck routes is my motto. Unlikely as it seemed, I was picked up by a passenger car that took me all the way in to Baltimore. A single man was the driver; he had been going all night because he had just the weekend to visit with his fiancee. I cashed a traveler's cheque in Baltimore and came along in to New York by train that same night. In the morning I registered for graduate work at Columbia.

IX

In New York, 1921-22

I was taking advice at this time from Robert Bruere of the *Survey*, who was rather contemptuous of the academic establishment, and I did not take the graduate work at Columbia all that seriously. I was more interested in a labor seminar at the New School for Social Research with Leo Wolman, then an economist for the Amalgamated Clothing Workers. I was fascinated by his accounts of the work he was doing--of how he had got the transcripts of the hearings in England on amendments for the Unemployment Insurance Acts, and worked out a basis for taking care of unemployed workers in the clothing industry; of statistics he had collected to win a wage arbitration in Chicago; and other constructive contributions to the workers' cause. For many years I thought I might find myself a job comparable to his. I was not especially oriented on writing a Ph.D. thesis, but I did intend to write a book, and on Wolman's advice I set out to study the New York building trades, which had just been investigated by a committee of the New York legislature, the Lockwood Committee.

Thorstein Veblen was on the faculty of the New School for Social Research, and I signed up for a course with him. The students, about 12 in number, would assemble around a table in a room which was connected with Veblen's lodgings by a short arbored walk. Precisely at the hour for starting the class, the door would open and the Professor would shuffle along the walk and take his place at the head of the table. He would lecture for an hour, then get up and retreat once more into his lodgings. He could not be detained for personal conversation. He was the timidest man I ever saw; it seemed he was allergic to people. I was really surprised when I learned that his affair with a colleague's wife had cost him one academic post.

Occasionally we would push him to clarify his position on some point of theory. He was an opponent of the "great man" theory of history. Speaking of Trotsky, he said:

"A few years ago there was a man in the Bronx whose only occupation was that of an unsuccessful writer of inflammatory pamphlets. Now, he is considered perhaps the greatest military genius that the 20th century has produced. I wouldn't say, 'There's a leader born every minute', but--pretty near."

The course was a washout; I stopped attending it before Christmas. This had been the story of his courses at other institutions. Yet he was one of the big names in the history of U.S., and world, economic thought, and was recognized as such (though not by Nanie, who did not consider him to be an economist). An effort to make him President of the American Economic Association--an honorary post, lasting for one year--broke down because he would not agree to anything that involved any administrative work.

The New School for Social Research was started just after the war, when several top professors were available through having been fired from Columbia for opposing the war. James Harvey Robinson and Charles A. Beard were the nucleus of the faculty, which also included Horace M. Kallen; with Veblen and Wolman, they made up a distinguished group. The money for the School was put up by Mrs. Willard Straight, who gave away millions of the money left her by her late husband. She was also in back of the *New Republic*, and gave a big hall to Cornell, as we discovered when we went there.

Columbia's faculty had lost others too. Henry Wadsworth Longfellow Dana, Professor of English, had been fired along with Robinson and Beard. He did not join the faculty of the New School however.

Harry Dana was one of the blue-bloods of Boston society. He lived in the Longfellow House in Cambridge known to tourists as the residence of his distinguished grandfather. He was a booster for the Russian Revolution, and interested in the Soviet drama (English literature was his field). We thought he might develop a specialty and become known as an authority, even in the absence of a university chair, as Beard and Cattell were to do. (Beard eventually was invited back to Columbia as a visiting lecturer!) But no, Harry lived along on the fringes of the radical movement, never deeply in it. He did go to Lawrence to support the strikers in 1919; in fact he was in our car when it turned over, throwing mother to the ground. He made the acquaintance of Sacco and Vanzetti.

But whereas some people know all the gossip and use it to help people and make them feel good, Harry seemed to delight in making people feel bad. It must have given him a feeling of power. So when my aunts Eleanor and Fredrika attacked the radical movement by attacking Harry Dana, I had nothing to say.

Of the graduate students among whom I found myself at Columbia, the one that I liked best was one George Stocking of

Texas. He was older than I was, in his late twenties, and had been around; for a year he had been in the oil business in the Ranger field in the Panhandle of Texas, a new field just opening up. The code of ethics was low--so low that one could not be decent and stay in it, so he quit. The material that he collected in that year became the basis of his Ph.D. thesis. He reported some of his findings in the graduate seminar and the others were impressed, both by the revelations on business and by the appalling waste of natural resources that was disclosed.

In private conversation George had expressed the belief that socialism was the only cure for the ills he saw. But this conclusion somehow got left out of his report to the seminar. I remarked on this omission after the meeting, and he like an honorable man asked for the floor at the beginning of the next session and stated his conclusion. Prof. Seligman did not much like that, and that made it all the more noteworthy for George to have done it.

George became a leading anti-trust advocate, and with Myron Watkins wrote several books about combinations; but their remedy was the atavistic one of busting the trusts and restoring free competition--not quite the same as the remedy he had supposedly supported in 1921. One might have thought he would be leery of unrestricted competition after his experience in the Panhandle. Morris Copeland considered him a dangerous reactionary masquerading as a liberal.

The year 1921-22 was a good one for me. My father had a standing date to take me to the theater once a week, to a show of my own choosing, which I much enjoyed. Perhaps the high point was "A Bill of Divorcement," because it was Katherine Cornell's debut on Broadway, and she made the most of it. We also appreciated the revival of *Lysistrata*, and the ad: "2381st year."

I also had a circle of friends around Columbia, although not many of them were connected with Columbia. Gardner Murphy was. He was Professor of Psychology, and during the year there was a short strike of students, which he supported by not showing up for classes. Whether for this or other reasons, he was not appreciated at Columbia. They let him go to CCNY, the College of the City of New York, where he stayed for many years and wrote texts on psychology jointly with his wife Lois, who was not in evidence when I knew him.

Another member of the group, which we called "the gang", was Karl Llewellyn, then a prof at Yale Law School, and recognized then and since as a big brain. At 34 he was the country's leading authority on negotiable instruments, but his interests were much more catholic; he eventually wrote books on sociology as well as law. He gave a paper before the American Economic Association. He also wrote, and sang for us, several highly intelligent jingles such as "Jonathan Smith."

The gang had a seminar to discuss current affairs, with reports and discussion. I am afraid I monopolized too much of the debate, but the others let on not to mind. The general tone of the group was liberal-to-radical, and all of them that I had contact with later retained their progressive points of view, except Brownie.

One time when the gang debates seemed to be getting repetitious, Bill Simpson was invited in. He was a young anarchist who had rather extreme ideas. He would not use money, for one thing (I remember after I had lunch with him, and paid my check and walked out in the usual Dutch-treat style, I had to be called back to pay his check). Bill put forward his idea, which was to follow your ideals wherever that might lead. The more practical-minded members of the gang, like Brownie, were not influenced; but some, like Bunch (Margaret Alexander), who had an underlying rebelliousness, were moved, even deeply. Bill married my friend Eloise, and when they traveled together Eloise carried the purse-- also in domestic arrangements.

The Sandinistas having triumphed after all these years in Nicaragua, it is not out of place to recall how people in the U.S. reacted to Sandino when he was in opposition in the 1920's, fighting a civil war to get rid of the U.S. marines. Liberal opinion was on Sandino's side. Scott Nearing wrote a piece, "Bravo, Sandino", which I am sure was widely reprinted in Latin America. The U.S. marines left Nicaragua, Sandino did lay down his arms, after which he was promptly assassinated, and Somoza, who had been trained by the U.S., seized power. He and his family held it for 40-odd years.

I was finally influenced by the academic environment and decided to go for the Ph.D. In my senior year at Harvard I had had as much advanced economics as a graduate student would get in his first year. So I was able to come up for the generals after only one year of graduate study instead of the usual two, and did surprisingly well in them. My study of the New York building trades became my Ph.D. thesis, but eventually it ran into difficulties, or rather I did, and the Ph.D. was a long time coming.

For exercise in the winter I did some wrestling, and my opponent pulled a leg a little sideways, tearing loose a ligament on the outer edge of the knee joint. I limped around for a week or so and finally saw a doctor who immobilized me for a short spell.

Thereafter I thought I was cured and resumed violent exercise; but on a beach party in the spring something snapped again. I went to a doctor who thought it was a semilunar cartilage that had got broken, but it wasn't. So, I again resumed going about.

The gang went on a weekend hiking trip to New Jersey, then at the end of the year had a 3-day camping trip in the Ramapo mountains, also in northern New Jersey. A rattlesnake came into camp, but Karl socked him on the back of the neck and he died; so we boiled him and ate him. Later we read in the paper about a hotel in the Adirondacks that put rattlesnakes on the menu, and reported that they couldn't keep the supply equal to the demand. We found ours rather tough.

In New York I got to know Caroline Whitney, who as an undergraduate at Vassar had made the news a couple of years before by refusing to be inducted in Phi Beta Kappa--she didn't believe in honorary scholastic societies. In New York she had become a member of Our Cooperative, which was renting an apartment house where the members lived cooperatively. They mostly wanted milk and the question came up whether they should get Grade A or Grade B milk. Nobody seemed to know just what the difference was, except that Grade A cost more. People more or less assumed that Grade A milk had a higher butter-fat content. Nanie's Uncle Charlie in New Jersey got Grade A milk because he thought it was better for the kids. On investigation it developed that the difference was that Grade A milk had been raised to a higher temperature in the process of Pasteurization. But was that necessary or even desirable? Grade B milk was safe enough. Our Cooperative brought the matter to the attention of Mayor LaGuardia, who then abolished Grade A milk.

I also met Justine Wise, the daughter of Rabbi Stephen S. Wise. The Rabbi, her father, was well known in liberal circles. I had heard him speak at Ford Hall in Boston, and while I had decided reservations about his talk--he had not prepared a speech, but made an evening out of kidding the chairman and shouting against the vulgarity of the theater--I was bound to be impressed by his eloquence and personal charm. Like Rowland Allen in Indianapolis, he was in back of most of the constructive reform movements. He had a Ph.D. from Columbia, and attempted to keep up his interest in research. He could no doubt have made good at college teaching, but his volcanic energy would have prevented his staying out of the battles that needed to be fought.

Justine when she finished college took a job in a mill in the Passaic textile industry, known as a stronghold of the open shop.

As noted, it had defeated a unionization move just before, led by Bob Dunn and Even Thomas for the Amalgamated Textile Workers. Justine got a job under the name of Waterman (her mother's family name) but the employers were not fooled. They called her in and told her they knew she was there, and in effect dared her to do her worst. Justine left industry for law school, at Yale.

The top leadership of the American Federation of Labor at this time was conservative. But liberals had high hopes for left-wing leadership from the Amalgamated Clothing Workers, led by Sidney Hillman. Shortly before the First World War they had won a strike in Chicago at the plant of Hart, Schaffner & Marx, the biggest men's clothing factory in the country, and greatly improved the condition of the workers there and in New York, where they established headquarters and won many agreements.

Hillman did retain his image as a progressive trade union leader and as such had the ear later of President Franklin D. Roosevelt. Not many people realized how thoroughly the Amalgamated leaders had become Americanized. A graduate student told us in Germany in 1927 that they had speculated on the stock market in the 1920's and built up personal fortunes. In 1927-28 I went into Wolman's office and found it set up like a broker's office, keeping track of the stocks. This was not in connection with wage negotiations.

Wolman left the Amalgamated in 1930-31 and went to teach at Columbia. I had been working on the New York building trades unions and had produced a thesis which was presented to him and two other members of the faculty. I was told that the subject was not satisfactory, although it had been approved at Columbia. Theses had been written and accepted on the buildings trades unions of Chicago and San Francisco. I was outraged. Wolman was by this time anti-labor and used to write weekly pieces for the *New York Times*.

X

Roger Baldwin and Scott Nearing

Two men to whom I looked up during this year in New York, and later for many years, were Roger Baldwin and Scott Nearing.

Roger came from St. Louis, and had begun life as a social worker. He founded the American Civil Liberties Union in 1920. He remained at the helm of the organization but the actual work was apt to be in the hands of some other person. Roger was in a key position in that he was not affiliated with either the Communists or the anti-Communists but was still known as a radical, or liberal. He served as father confessor to the young radicals who were confused by the battles of the right and left. I went to him with my troubles right through the 1930's. He and Scott were not of my generation, but not of the older generation either; they were in between generations, with all the prestige that that position has to young people who have developed a healthy disrespect for the "old folks".

Roger knew the family and came to Cousin Bess Walton's house while I was there. He was rather high-strung, with lots of nervous energy. He and Scott had reserves of vitality that enabled them to outlast people much younger. I became impressed with the fact that vitality is a prime element in what is called success; those who forge to the leadership are not necessarily the smartest (although that helps) but those who keep on when others faint and falter.

Roger was married to Madeleine Doty, the feminist leader. When Nanie and I got married, we spent the summer in a cabin on the Hackensack River which was right next to Roger's cabin. Nanie got to know Madeleine, who was shocked when she learned that Nanie was taking my name. "What will you do when you leave him?" Madeleine did leave Roger soon after. She found that he was rather inconsiderate in his personal relations.

When the ACLU was set up, the F.B.I. in its present form had still not been organized. It was set up in 1924. Harlan Stone as Attorney-General called on J. Edgar Hoover to head the new Bureau. Hoover's part in the Palmer raids was of course well known and might have been expected to give pause to Stone, who had been against the raids. He put Hoover on notice that nothing like that was to characterize the new Bureau.

The ACLU was perturbed at the prospect of having Hoover in the position. Roger was sent to Washington to check on whether Hoover would abuse his power and carry out red hunts. Roger talked at length with both Hoover and Stone, and came away convinced of the good faith of both. Hoover even persuaded him that in carrying out the raids under Palmer he had acted unwillingly. Roger wrote to his colleagues in the ACLU,

"We were wrong in our estimate of [Hoover's] attitude. That estimate was based upon some of the unfortunate performances of the Bureau in a previous administration in which Mr. Hoover doubtless played an unwilling part. What he told me of the details and changes made in the administration of the Bureau all indicate that the reorganization meets every suggestion any of us could possibly make, and that it has already carried out faithfully in accordance with Stone's stated policy."

Actually red-hunting was quite in accordance with Hoover's personal inclinations, as was indicated by the fact that he had continued it on his own after the Palmer raids were stopped. Roger may not have known about this. Roger always remained a defender of the F.B.I., even when the Radical Bureau was revived in 1936 (under FDR!) and during the years when FBI persecution of radicals had become notorious. As Hoover's biographer notes:

"For the rest of his career [Hoover] could count on endorsement from ACLU luminaries like Roger Baldwin and Morris Ernst when he was attacked by civil libertarians, even when the attackers were other members of the ACLU."

Ernst, who was general counsel of the ACLU for many years, had indeed a very special relationship with Hoover and corresponded with him at length.

The ACLU worked with the Communists during the 1920's and 1930's, and even had Communists on its Board, although it later tried to pretend that it had not known they were Communists. In 1940 Elizabeth Gurley Flynn was removed from the Board of the ACLU on the ground that she was a Communist.

The lady in question had a hearing, the notes of which were preserved, and were published somewhat later by Corliss Lamont, who led the fight against her expulsion. They were also studied with care by Dr. Jesse Lemisch, who came to the surprising conclusion that Richard Nixon, who parlayed his anti-Communism into the presidency of the U.S., had learned red-baiting from the ACLU!

The ACLU has never understood the real meaning of free speech.

114

I remember attending a meeting in Boston while I was in college, which a group of right-wingers from Harvard attempted to disrupt. At a certain point one of the group walked up on the stage and said he had heard a lot about free speech and he wanted to say a few words about what the United States had done in the war. The audience shouted him down, and when he refused to leave a policeman was summoned and escorted him from the stage. The ACLU might have been embarrassed by the incident, because it (the ACLU) sometimes seemed to be upholding the position that free speech meant that anybody is entitled to talk any time, anywhere.

The ACLU in the 1920's was maintaining the "right" of the Ku Klux Klan to hold provocative meetings in black districts. In a great show of "impartiality" it even offered to defend the Klan, and lost the support of some liberals as a result. As late as 1978, when Roger Baldwin was 95 years old, it was still upholding the same position, with Roger's approval. The American Nazis were planning to stage a parade through a predominantly Jewish neighborhood in Skokie, Ill., and the ACLU supported their "right" to do so. But the Klan in the 1920's and the Nazis in the 1970's were not being denied the opportunity to get their position before the public. Many ACLU members dropped out at this display of wrongheadedness by the national office.

It should be added for the record that some of the regional branches did not go along with the national office's shift of position on the rights of Communists. Los Angeles and Boston, specifically, repudiated the new policy. But they were not in a position to fight cases at the national level. So, the witch hunt in the 1950's drew only mild protests from the ACLU, which waged a campaign against the jailing of people for their opinions.

What we did not know, and what the regional branches probably did not know either, was that the national office of the ACLU was cooperating in its red-baiting with the FBI.

It was while I was in school that *The Birth of a Nation* with its frankly racist message was produced, and shown in Boston. The black community had been alerted and attended the first showing in force, hissing at the many objectionable features. I was there and could not agree that showing the film was a proper exercise of the right of free speech. It does make a difference whether the point of view that is in question is against public policy. After all these years people are coming to recognize that racism is anti-social and the public showing of a film like *The Birth of a Nation* (even with the chase sequence deleted, as it was in later Boston showings) is anti-social too. This line of thought was foreign to the ACLU.

Roger did not write out his political philosophy, but if he had it would have been some variety of anarchism; he edited a book of anarchist essays. The Communists found it possible to work with him--for example, in the Garland Fund--through the 1920's and 1930's; until the case of Elizabeth Gurley Flynn and her expulsion from the Board of the ACLU in 1940. During this period Roger was the man to whom leftward-moving students went for advice, as Joe Dallet did. His case is discussed below.

An independent radical who influenced many leftward-moving young people of my generation was Scott Nearing, who as I have mentioned spoke at Harvard at my invitation in 1919. Students, and others, were impressed with his indictment of capitalism, and they asked him what he advised them to do. He answered sometimes, "Stand up and be counted!" or simply, "Rebel! Rebel! Rebel!" But since during most of his career he did not himself belong to any organization of a narrowly political nature, this advice came close to meaning, "Stick out your neck (and get it chopped off!)." This advice I proceeded to take.

Scott himself had an annuity on which he could live, though sparingly. Thus he was able to do what he wanted to do. He even went around the world for $1000! He traveled third class and got a picture of life from a point of view different from that of most tourists.

After he was fired from his professorship at the University of Pennsylvania in 1915 (for advocating legislation against child labor!), he lived in Montclair, N.J., where he raised his own vegetables and two boys, one his own by his first wife Nellie, and the other adopted.

Scott was religious, and used to read the Bible. After he and Nellie got divorced, he met a young violinist named Helen at a New Thought conference, and they hit it off so well that she came to live with him and stayed with him the rest of his life.

Scott had moved to Jamaica, Vermont, where he tended a stand of sugar maples; he later wrote the definitive book on maple-sugaring. From this base he went on annual speaking tours. He had groups of non-Party radicals who came to hear him in the larger cities. These groups were largely the lineal descendants of the language groups which had made up the left wing of the Socialist Party in the period just before and during the First World War, but had left the S.P. in the 1919 split, and had not stayed in the C.P. either. He spoke also to liberals as such; he gave the anniversary address at the Boston Community Church every year from its foundation until the 1980's. And he especially enjoyed talking at colleges.

In private conversation he used the method of the Socratic dialogue, leading unsuspecting liberals into radical positions and getting unsuspecting radicals into defending untenable positions, usually defending the indefensible actions of the Soviet Union. I refused to be drawn into that trap, but Nanie swallowed the bait and got shown up. I couldn't stand this and after a few tries when we were visiting at Jamaica, it was agreed that we would not talk politics any more.

Scott and Helen moved to a seaside residence in Maine, and set out to breed blueberries an inch in diameter (They didn't quite make it). Scott was a great builder, first at Jamaica and then in Maine; he built a house and then built another one, presumably to retire into in his old age (!). When he was over 90 I went to see him on a Sunday afternoon. He was down on the beach getting a truckload of gravel to build a cement wall. He finished loading the truck, drove it up to the house and unloaded it, then sat down for a 1/2 hour conversation. When we left, at 6 o'clock, he went down to the beach to get another load of gravel.

He and Helen were advocates of the simple life, back to nature, and when that approach to life was fashionable among the young, in the 1960's, a steady line of visitors hunted him out to ask him how he did it. He did not pretend it was easy; in fact he tried to scare them by telling them how hard they would have to work. For himself, he thrived on work. He was a compulsive worker. If he had put into his writing the energy that he put into other kinds of work, he could have been a scholar of some stature. His books on maple sugar and the simple life met with deserved success. But his scholarly writing was not of high quality. Scott wrote too many books. They were not carefully researched and contained too many errors. Although the approach was Marxist, they were not models of Marxist theory either.

Scott applied for membership in the Communist Party in 1927, and was accepted after some delay. In 1929 he submitted to the Party the MS of a book which he proposed to publish with the title *The Twilight of Empire*. The MS was duly forwarded to Moscow, which turned it down; apparently the last word on imperialism had been spoken by Lenin. Scott went ahead and published it anyway, thereby terminating his connection with the Party.

In his autobiography Scott expresses scorn for the "minor reforms" sponsored by the "great liberal" Woodrow Wilson, and likewise for the reforms of the FDR era. He describes these as "crumbs thrown from the table of the rich", "sucker bait, &c." He adds:

"I consider liberalism a broken reed. Reform only provides justification and ammunition for the robbers and exploiters."
But in his day he worked hard for such reforms. One wonders if he then considered himself a liberal.

XI

The Abolition of Inheritance

Around 1920, while I was still in college, Charles Garland created something of a sensation by refusing a million-dollar inheritance. His brother, following Charles's lead, did likewise. The administrators of the estate were taken aback, to put it mildly, and continued to hold the money, or rather the stock (in the First National Bank of New York), thinking that he might change his mind, and presently he did, to the extent that he accepted the fortune and decided to give it away to worthy causes. This was done on the advice of Roger Baldwin, who was no doubt instrumental in choosing the board to administer the Garland Fund. It included him and Scott Nearing, Lewis Gannett, Bob Dunn, Elizabeth Gurley Flynn, and several others.

During the 1920's this Fund gave away the million dollars, plus another $400,000 that represented the accrued value of the stock, which went way up in value. Scott said afterwards that the donations might have done more harm than good. There was a paucity of worthy causes in that period, when capitalism was riding high and radicals were baffled (liberals too, but they are always baffled).

Charles Garland, known as Barley, had a little country place southwest of Boston, which was visited by a number of my friends. It was known as a freelove colony. Barley himself had a wife and three, later four, children; the wife was a beautiful girl who did not share his radical views but would have remained loyal to him. She did not go to the place in the country. Barley took up with a jolly, not very intelligent young lady, Bettina, and she had a child by him (whom they called Mowgli), then another. Finally Barley's wife divorced him. Barley's four children by his (first) wife and Barley himself were taken care of by a trust fund that had been set up independently of the main fortune. Barley's brother eventually took his share of the inheritance. Barley was no manager--at the camp, nobody took responsibility for meals, and it was said that they once had nothing to eat but turnips for three straight days. They were not trying to emulate the Germans during World War I-- it just happened that way.

I should mention at this time another Fund to give away a (much smaller) part of the Garland millions: the Personal Service Fund, of which my mother and A.J. Muste were administrators. The applicants used to come trooping to our Brookline home, and I saw them and had a chance to estimate them. Some were fine people, others not so impressive. The reasons for making particular donations were also not always impressive, to me. One woman got a grant because she had married her husband to reform him. I made a mental note that I could do better than that if I got the chance.

But it is difficult for even the best-intentioned individuals to make the right donations to the right people. Ida Guggenheimer, whom we knew, gave away money, so freely that the family had to take charge of her donations. At one time she was interested in a woman comrade who hit her up for $20,000, supposedly so she could work in the movement. She took the money and disappeared. Jessie Lloyd and Harvey O'Connor, trying to put their money to good use, financed the education of a lad called Jacinto Steinhardt, later known as Adrian Recht. But his political development disappointed his patrons.--Dorothy Douglas also financed worthy individuals, like Toni Grose, who had been so active in radical work that she had not managed to complete her musical education. Dorothy was very grateful when the Marian Davis Scholarship Fund was set up, and contributed liberally to it during her lifetime, and after.

The abolition of inheritance was my favorite reform at this time. I circulated a book with that title, *The Abolition of Inheritance*, by Harlan E. Read, to my friends, and when it went out of print, I even got Macmillan to get out a new printing, with the understanding that I would buy 100 copies and they would mail them out to names that I would give them (They soon reneged on the deal). I met Harlan E. Read in New York and we had a talk. He was a St. Louis businessman and writer, not a socialist--in fact one advantage that he claimed for his reform was that it would put capitalism on a more secure basis. In this he was like the single taxers. I sent a copy of Harlan E. Read's book to the CP, with the remark that I might try to do something along the same lines, but with more of a Marxist orientation. I received in return a blast from Israel Amter, who pointed out that you were either a Marxist or you weren't. Harlan E. Read, we both agreed, was not.

There was some discussion about the inheritance tax in that period, and the law on the subject took its present form, with the federal government setting the pace so that the states would not compete with each other to attract millionaires by abolishing their respective inheritance taxes, as was actually happening in the early 1920's. The most active Congressman in getting a decent

120

estate tax was Ramseyer of Iowa, and I sent him $100 for his campaign, but he sent the money back. There was no organization for the abolition of inheritance.

In the presidential campaign of 1924 I tried to get La Follette to come out for a serious estate tax, and had Boris Stern write up a short history of the subject, which uncovered some interesting facts. But the La Follette campaign manager was not interested, and the study by Boris Stern was never even published. As for me, I got more interested in another approach and eventually accepted the money that was coming to me on my mother's death ($25,000). That made me more able to fight city hall. I noted that Scott Nearing had an annuity that kept him going when his books weren't selling. Further back, the abolition of inheritance was part of the platform in the *Communist Manifesto* but was later abandoned by Marx. I asked Norman Thomas what he thought about the subject and he said that you have to live in the world as it is, but acceptance of inheritance money puts a special obligation on you to fight for the abolition of special privilege of all kinds.

XII

A Disaster Year, 1922-23

I had always intended to make the labor movement a prime object of study, and when Wert (Mildred Wertheimer) suggested during the spring of 1922 that I apply for a job in the International Labor Office in Geneva, I decided that might be a good idea. It would be an appropriate base from which I could make side trips in my spare time and get to know the European labor movement. I assembled my letters of recommendation and applied for the job, and got it. Thus began a year (1922-23) which was a real disaster.

I took ship on the Italian line, in the steerage, bought myself an Italian grammar, and for the two weeks of the trip mixed with the Italians in the steerage and studied Italian. I already knew French, had had a year of Spanish at Harvard and 5 years of Latin in school, so Italian came easy. I found I had a reading knowledge of the language; much later, I even translated an Italian book into English for *Monthly Review* Press. (It was not published)--The steerage passengers were all immigrants to the United States who were going home for one reason or another. One had a teenage daughter and did not want her to go to an American high school-- "they getta the big belly." Many were going for a visit to the old country, planning to return to the U.S.

It was on that liner, New York to Genoa, that I first met a real anti-Semite: passionate, totally unreasonable, but convinced of the accuracy of his diatribes against the Jews. The Italians had not had a mobilization of anti-Semitic opinion like what France had had in the 1890's, in the Dreyfus case. They were relaxed in their approach to race relations--could not understand the attitude of white Americans to Afro-Americans. So, when Mussolini adopted anti-Semitism as part of the Fascist creed at Hitler's urging, in 1938, some thought that Hitler had imposed his creed on the Italians. I can testify that there was at least one Italian who was just as much of an anti-Semite as Hitler himself.

While getting up from a sitting position on the deck, I snapped something in my knee once again, and arrived at Geneva with water on the knee. This immobilized me for a long period, which was added to quite unnecessarily by my own folly. At first I was in a *pension* or boarding house, and shared a room with a man my own age who was just out of Oxford; later I was moved to a

122

public hospital. When I finally went to my job at the I.L.O. I was in poor shape physically from having had no exercise for so long. My job consisted largely of reading newspapers to cull out the labor news for the I.L.O. information service. My office was poorly lighted, and toward the end of one afternoon my eyes went out on me. They never came back. Since that time I have not been able to do more than three hours a day of straightforward reading, or five hours a day for a week at a time.

I stayed on in Geneva for some weeks, having my work read to me in the hope that my eyes would come around. I had gone to live at the home of a German-Swiss music teacher, hoping to learn German better than I had done in school. They described how Geneva had been split by the First World War; they had been largely ostracized by their former friends, most of whom were French-speaking. After the war the ones who had participated in the boycott wanted to resume as before, but this family would not: a friend in need is a friend indeed, and those who duck out are not friends any more at all. Now you know why I can never feel the same about my own brother, who cut me off during the period of Nixon-McCarthyism.

There was a daughter in the family, and she earnestly desired to have an affair with me, but I repelled her advances.

When they discovered that I was leaving my job in Geneva for a period of recuperation and possible return, two cousins, Charlotte and Emily, invited me to come with them to the Balearic Islands and recuperate there. Having a wealthy extended family does add to one's resources.

I joined them at Florence in January 1923. This was about the time of Mussolini's takeover, and the street corners were packed with men eagerly discussing politics. A little later, when Mussolini's power was consolidated, political discussion went out of fashion for 20 years.

The cousins took me to an oculist in Florence. He was a real expert. He diagnosed my trouble as eye cramp. Of course most people don't get eye cramp, but I was a special case. From birth my eyes had had a tendency to diverge, which the doctors like to call by fancy Latin names, exaphoria or strabismus. My parents had discovered that I was getting two images instead of one, and had me take exercises with a stereoscope, learning to bring the two images together. I did this, and could read all right, but at rest the eyes still tended to drift apart. My accumulated fatigue which caused me to crack up in 1916 was probably associated with eye strain. So eventually the eyes just quit on the job, as indicated.

The oculist recommended exercises to train the muscles to work together. But it didn't help. In the Balearic Islands, I strained my knee again and spent days in bed, unable to read to myself. I learned the touch system on my portable typewriter, and the cousins took turns reading to me. They read Meredith's *Egoist* and went all the way through *The Brothers Karamazov*, by Dostoyevski, which was a real treat (reading out loud was a family habit with us. Mother used to read to us at meals. Sal kept it up with her boys. I read Cynthia Quentin *The Pilot* and *Swiss Family Robinson* in the bedtime hour. Nanie never rose to the idea).

XIII

Brother Hal and His Problems

My brother Hal had finished medical school, but since he was headed for research, not medical practice, he went for a year to study under Dr. Adrian at Cambridge University in England. He had stopped by Geneva, where I was in the hospital, and he and a friend, Gregg Bemis, came down to the Balearic Islands in their spring vacation.

This was a dramatic period in Hal's life. He had been engaged to Pauline Allen, Rowland's sister, known as Pud. The previous summer, they had had a series of misunderstandings and she had gone off to Constantinople to work for the Near East Relief. While she was there and he was in Cambridge (England), they got things straightened out by correspondence, and it was arranged that they would be married when they got back to the U.S. Then she got typhus fever. When Hal and Gregg arrived in Soller de Majorca she was desperately ill. For a week Hal could not think about anything else. Then he got a cable, "Fine now."

Hal and Gregg went back to the University of Cambridge, and Pud recovered in Constantinople. In June Hal went to Constantinople and they were married on a hill outside the city.

Shortly before that, Pud had been at a hospital fire. One of the women patients who had to leave the hospital was transferred to another one, and Pud volunteered to go in the cab with her. On the way the woman had an attack of nausea and threw up on everything around. Pud took it stoically, and won the admiration of the commanding officer, whose account of the fire included the information that Miss Allen had been very helpful and "did not flinch when vomited upon."

Apparently the final clause did not get through to the American press, and when the story was written up, the reporter drew on his imagination. How would one be "very helpful" in a hospital fire? He had her conducting the firemen to remote parts of the building and saving the lives of patients--why not? So, Miss Allen was a heroine.

The Near East Relief was conducting a drive for funds just at the time when Hal and Pud arrived back in Boston, and the fund-raisers saw to it that the newspapers had ample advance notice.

Their pictures were on the front pages--the heroine who had so romantically concluded her stay in the Near East.

I won't say she didn't deserve the encomiums. After all, she had gone to the area when she knew there was plenty of typhus around, and had worked well on that visit as on a previous one.

The romance wore off and she emerged in a very different light. Mother was anxious to be relieved of the burden of housekeeping and in one of her less happy decisions she arranged for Pud to move into the home at Brookline and run the household.

She and Mother clashed continually. The friction developed, on Pud's side, into bitter hatred. It must have torn Hal apart. But he did not at that time see that Pud's inability to get along with Mother was part of a character defect which was eventually to wreck their marriage.

XIV

My Father Takes Up Labor Banking

My knee had not healed up completely when the cousins and I took ship from Barcelona in 1923.

Arriving at New York on crutches, I was treated with great deference, even obsequiousness, by the customs officials, who put me at the head of the line. I appreciated not having to stand in line, but was revolted by the bootlicking, which I was at first unable to account for. Then I remembered that during my absence my father had become vice-president of the Empire Trust Co., one of New York's leading banks.

This extraordinary development had resulted from Father's connection with the Nonpartisan League, a connection which was established during the summer of 1919 when I was organizing for the League in Minnesota. Father, who had been interested in the League on his own account, had gone out to North Dakota and made friends with some of the leaders. The North Dakota State administration, controlled by the League, had run short of capital for its various enterprises and sought to float a bond issue. Ordinarily there is no trouble in finding a broker to market an issue of state bonds, but this time no broker came forward. The job of marketing the bond issue was put in the hands of George Webb, a man with considerable experience in various kinds of business who at the moment did not have any occupation. He came to Wall Street, and Father was the only connection the League had there, so Webb looked him up and invited him to work with him, and this Father was glad enough to do. They rented an office and set out to sell the bonds, either through a broker or directly to customers that they would find. This was in 1921.

Some of the farmers whom I had organized into the Nonpartisan League had paid their dues with postdated checks, maturing in periods up to a year. When these checks were accepted for deposit by the bank, it was in effect granting credit to the farmer. Naturally the country banks sought to dispose of the checks as soon as possible, and in North Dakota the State Bank was under heavy pressure to rediscount them, which at first it did without much question. The farmers who had been prosperous during the war and immediate postwar years found after 1920 that the going was not so easy. Production of wheat had been greatly expanded during the war, the U.S. wheat replacing wheat that was not being grown in Western Europe because of the war. After the war the West European belligerent countries came back into production on the previous scale, and the price of wheat fell. The decade of the 'twenties was one of worldwide agricultural depression, anteceding the industrial-commercial depression of the 'thirties. The State Bank of North Dakota found its portfolio choked up with farmers' checks that could not be collected. The floating of the bond issue was only a temporary palliative for a much deeper seated problem.

Webb went to Cleveland and eventually it was a Cleveland firm of brokers, Spitzer-Rorig, that marketed the bond issue. There had evidently been a sort of boycott in Wall Street against the North Dakota bonds because of Wall Street's prejudice against any kind of socialistic experiments, although the modest ventures into state ownership in Dakota could hardly be called socialism.

There was nothing wrong with the bonds, which in fact were a good buy at the price.

In Cleveland Webb consorted with the liberal-labor crowd and met the leaders of the Brotherhood of Locomotive Engineers, including its president Warren Stone. The Brotherhood had not had a major strike since the 1870's. It ran an insurance system for the members, whose occupation was dangerous enough so that they had had trouble getting life insurance from the commercial companies. It also charged high dues, its individuals being among the highest paid wage-earners in the country. So there was a lot of capital looking for opportunities of investment.

At this time labor banking was a much-discussed subject. The International Association of Machinists had broken new ground when it bought a savings bank in Washington, D.C. The Amalgamated Clothing Workers, darling of the pro-labor liberals, started banks of its own in New York and Chicago--not cooperative banks or credit unions, but conventional commercial banks. Several other unions went into banking as a side occupation, using funds from the union treasury.

The Brotherhood of Locomotive Engineers decided to go into banking, and called on Webb to arrange something. The Brotherhood bought a controlling interest in the Empire Trust Co. The existing management continued, under the direction of the president, one Baldwin; but Webb was the super-manager and representative of the controlling interest. Father became a vice-president of the bank and sat on the Board of Directors as representing the same majority interest. So, Father was a big shot. The obsequiousness of the customs officials was explained.

I went back to Brookline and spent several months recovering my health. The outcome of my months in bed on account of my water on the knee was that the knee was completely cured. So, I was able to revive my project of going to work in a steel mill.

I was able to see the Communist Party in operation in Boston at this time (1923-24)--small but active, with delegates in the Central Labor Union trying to interest people in worthy causes. Harrison George, a Party stalwart who had done time in federal prisons during the war, came by and stayed at our house in Brookline, and we had some talks, which were continued in a correspondence that lasted some months. He wanted me to join the Party and Nanie later thought I should have, but I had reservations, pacifist and otherwise. I was not then prepared to accept the idea that socialism was what the United States needed.

XV

The Steel Industry
Hours of Work, The Safety Movement

In the fall of 1924 I set out for Pittsburgh, as I had done three years earlier. I arranged to meet Powers Hapgood on the way.

Powers had entered college after I did and finished before I did; he went through in three years. When he graduated he went on an extended bumming trip out to the Pacific Coast and back. He got jobs along the way in different industries, but gravitated to coal mining; he learned the job of coal cutting, which was a skilled job and highly paid, at least in union mines. He joined the union, the United Mine Workers, which then (1920) controlled maybe two thirds of the country's tonnage.

It was recognized that the union mines could not pay high wages without being undercut by the coal from the nonunion mines. So, the union sought to unionize the nonunion fields, especially those in West Virginia and Central Pennsylvania. Powers was hired by some liberal organization to do an investigation of the mines in the latter field, and did produce a report, "In Nonunion Mines." Soon afterwards there was a national strike in the industry, and Powers was taken on as a union organizer in that same field, Central Pennsylvania. He made good, and union organizing became his chosen occupation.

In 1924, when I started my second bumming trip from New York to Pittsburgh, Powers was making a swing from North to South in the coal mining area of Central Pennsylvania, where he had been organizing a couple of years previously. I was in touch with him and we arranged a rendezvous, where I heard his story of the strike. I even applied for a job at the mine that was nearby, but they were not hiring. I kept on to Pittsburgh, and got myself a job as a steel worker in the Edgar Thomson works of the Carnegie Steel Co., in Braddock, Pa. Carnegie Steel was a constituent part of the U.S. Steel Corporation.

The Edgar Thomson works were the first in the U.S. where the Bessemer process of converting pig iron to steel was used on a large scale. It was an integrated mill, taking the iron ore direct from the mines in Northern Minnesota, making it into pig iron in the blast furnaces, then into steel in the open hearth and Bessemer departments, and finally rolling the steel into rails and other

130

shapes, ready to be further processed in various specialized mills up the Monongahela Valley.

The year 1919 had seen a nationwide strike in the steel industry, led by William Z. Foster for the AFL; but it had ended without securing either union recognition or the 8-hour day. The two-shift system in the continuous processes persisted down to 1923, when the companies finally decided to go over to three shifts of eight hours each. The timing was really bad from a business point of view. If they had made the changeover, which could have been seen as inevitable, in (say) 1921, there would have been no problem in securing the extra manpower needed. As it was, the company was obliged to recruit labor in the South. There were a number of workers, some black and some white, who came to the mill from Petersburg, Va.

At the time before the changeover to three shifts took place, the going rate for unskilled labor was 40 cents an hour, for a daily wage of $4.80. When there were only eight hours of work per day, the hourly rate was raised to 50 cents. There were a few workers, especially among the immigrants who had no idea but to get as much money as they possibly could before going home, who preferred the $4.80 for a day of 12 hours, but most of the men were well satisfied with the change although they were perfectly aware that wages in steel were below the going rate in outside labor.

The shifts were rotated every week. The day shift, 7 a.m. to 3 p.m., went to the night shift, 11 to 7, with an interval of 8 hours. The night shift, getting off work at 7 a.m., went back to work that afternoon at 3 p.m. and worked till 11. Each shift thus was able to get 32 consecutive hours off every third week. The management was telling its friends in the middle class that the 7-day week had been abolished!

The men in the labor gang were a miscellaneous lot. Beside the newly recruited arrivals from the South of the U.S., there were still some European immigrants, from Italy and other countries. The semiskilled jobs were largely held by immigrants who had come before the war. If you asked them where they came from, they were quite likely to say "Owstria", meaning some part of the old Austro-Hungarian Empire. Some men from "Owstria" remembered the country they had come from and professed loyalty to it even after it was broken up. One said that he still treasured a picture of Emperor Franz-Joseph, who had died during the war.

After a short spell on the labor gang, cleaning up around the yard, I was called to the furnace front, where I formed one of a

131

gang of six whose job was to tap the blast furnace every so often. In the early days of blast furnaces, the iron had been run out into sand molds in a branching pattern. A central mold received the iron and distributed it out to half a dozen smaller molds on each side. This pattern bore some slight resemblance to a sow suckling her pigs, whence the terms "sow iron" and "pig iron". But in modern mills the pig iron is kept in a molten state until it is ready to be turned into steel in the open hearth furnaces and Bessemer converters.

I had been accustomed to think of the steel industry with its 12-hour shifts as an exhausting industry, in which people were always tired. This was the burden of the *Pittsburgh Survey*, conducted before the war by the Russell Sage Foundation. If the men had actually worked the whole 12 hours they would have been plenty fagged. But after the heat had been tapped--maybe 40 minutes' work--and the runnels got ready for the next heat, there was nothing much to do for a couple of hours. The men went into the shack and went to sleep, if they felt like it.

I came on the job soon enough after the changeover so that the pace of work was still what it had been under the two shifts. The pace was being speeded up, gradually. The company found some things for the men on the furnace front to do while they were waiting for the next heat. But I had plenty of time to go out into the rest of the mill and get a look at some of the other furnaces and the other processes.

Walking home from work along the railroad track where some empty freight cars were parked, my attention was attracted by a call, "Buy some grapefruit!" A couple of young fellows about my age had got permission to use an empty box car to hawk their wares. I bought some fruit, and others did too. After a few weeks this team had enough money to rent a store on the main street, and they sold their fruit there, in a room completely devoid of fixtures. They had apparently started from scratch, without capital, and had already made enough to contemplate setting up a continuing business. Horatio Alger please take notice.

I had rented a room from a steel worker named Will Watt. He and his wife were decent people and I got along fine with them. He had been a rail straightener in his day, an arduous, well-paid job; his picture had appeared in one of the volumes of the *Pittsburgh Survey*. He was now working at a much less exacting job, inspecting molds and marking those that were cracked and had to be retired from service.

He had been a steel worker all his life, except for a period when he had quit the mill and got a job as policeman. He was approaching retirement age, but without the prospect of a pension. The company did have a pension plan of a kind, but the pensions were payable only to those with 20 years of continuous service, and his stint as a policeman had broken the continuity, although he had indeed worked 20 years with the company.

His wife was a woman with some spirit. When she was first married she went to the butcher shop to buy some liver. They asked her, "Do you want the bones taken out?" and she said, "If you please." So, the joke was on her. But she had the last laugh. She transferred her custom to the rival butcher shop from that time on.

Will Watt was of old American stock. He had seen the immigrants come in and take the unskilled jobs. They lived in the poorest quarter of town and had large families. This incensed Will Watt. "They just breed down there," he used to say. At first I couldn't figure out why he was so bitter about it, but finally I realized that in his economics those who increased the labor supply were bringing pressure for decreased wages. He used to rail against the Catholics and other immigrants. His wife always called him on it, asking him if he didn't esteem such and such a family whom he knew personally. He always admitted the point. But he still was anti-immigrant enough to join the Ku Klux Klan. He was perhaps influenced in this surprising decision by the fact that the Klan was a middle-class organization and he was pathetically eager to be a member of that class.

The fact that Will Watt belonged to the Ku Klux Klan struck some readers of my manuscript so forcibly that I was driven to reexamine his psychology as I came to know it. I was struck at this time with a statement on working-class psychology as follows: "Full membership in the national community is what most workers aspire to." (William E. Cain, *Monthly Review*, Feb. 1990, p. 62.) For Will Watt, membership in the middle Class (not formulated as such by him) was the equivalent of membership in the national community. So, he was willing to participate in the electoral process, even to stay up all all night counting the votes in the primary, and considered himself confirmed as an American by doing so.

The Klan in the Northern cities like Pittsburgh was primarily anti-immigrant and only incidentally anti-Black. Will Watt used to talk about it: "a certain-organization"--he probably was not allowed to mention the Klan by name. His account of it contained some surprises, as for instance that the organization was anti-alcohol--at a convention all the drinks were soft. The Klan was riding high at the time (1924). It burned a fiery cross on the hill above the town while I was there. But it was hurt by the exposure of corruption at the top levels of the Indiana Klan and declined in the later '20s.

Of course, Will Watt's economics were defective. He did not take into account the fact that the Central European immigrants when they had moved up into the semiskilled jobs and adopted an American scale of living began to limit their families and stopped flooding the labor market.

Will Watt remembered the time when Charles M. Schwab was assistant engineer at Braddock, and introduced a scheme to keep the molten iron hot while awaiting processing in the open hearth. The open hearth furnaces were on the second-story level, so to speak, because when they were tapped the metal had to run down into the molds. Schwab had them build a trestle so that the dinky engines could carry the vats with the molten iron in them up to that level. There the molten iron was transferred to a huge container (mixer) where it was kept in a liquid state until the time came to run it into the furnaces and get it cooked.

Schwab was a great talker, and it fell to his lot to talk the men out of their grievances. Even in a nonunion plant, the men get up delegations from time to time to air their gripes. There may even have been a union at the Edgar Thomson plant in Schwab's day. Schwab would talk until he had you half persuaded that the moon was made of green cheese; but when you came out of the conference you suddenly realized that he had given you exactly nothing.

Schwab went from his job as assistant engineer at Braddock to superintendent of the mill at Homestead, across the river, and continued on up to the very top. As President of Bethlehem Steel Corp., he used to receive encomiums and bonuses regularly at the annual meetings of stockholders, and as regularly he used to deplore the practice of paying him extra. Bethlehem had a system of bonuses by which amounts up to a million dollars were paid to each of the top officers, including in years when the stockholders were not getting any dividends. The stockholders finally called Schwab's bluff; whereupon he fought back and said he was entitled to the money. But the bonus system was modified in the depression.   Will Watt's son-in-law John had the job of assistant engineer at the Edgar Thomson works. But he was not promoted to be superintendent at Homestead. In fact he was not promoted, period. He got discouraged and took to drink. This was after I left.

134

The company encouraged the men to learn more about the process of steel making. It had a works course after hours. Sam, who worked in the rolling mill, was ambitious and waited his turn to get into the works course. The company tried to pass him over when his turn came, and give the opportunity to some friend or relative of a boss. But Sam raised so much hell that he did get into the works course.

This was not a full engineering course. But there was a young fellow in the course who did take a full engineering course in the evenings, at the same time supporting his aged mother by his wages at the mill.

I was not seriously considering staying in the industry, but I thought I would see what the prospects of advancement were. I asked the engineer about it. His answer really surprised me. He said, "Have you got any folks in the steel industry?" I said no.

Favoritism was the rule in promotions. The story was that Catholics had the better chance at the Edgar Thomson plant, other things being equal, while Protestants were more likely to get the nod at the big Westinghouse plant in Turtle Creek.

The U.S. Public Health Service made a study about this time that showed that respiratory diseases were more prevalent among steel workers than in the general population. When we finished a shift all sweaty from the hot, heavy work, and walked home in the biting cold, we understood why. Will's son Sam, a rolling mill worker, got pneumonia and almost died; the doctor did not think he would pull through. He never went to a hospital. I tried to get a trained nurse for him, and one did agree to come, but later reneged. There was a lot of sickness that winter.

I dropped a piece of iron on my foot and had to take three days off work. The blow boss was outdone with me. I think if he had known I was planning to take time away from work he would have urged me to come to the plant and draw my pay, even if I had to sit around the whole shift. I later saw a man in another part of the plant who had sprained his ankle but still came to work and dragged around after his crew until it healed up--if it did. The fact was, the company policy was to hold lost-time accidents to a minimum, and this policy was enforced by putting constant pressure on the top-level bosses, who put the pressure on the lower-level bosses, who put the pressure on the men.

Later I investigated the history of this safety drive in the steel industry. It dated from a time when the companies were completely hard-boiled about accidents. One story, no doubt apocryphal, was that a man fell clear to the bottom of a complicated machine structure. It would have been possible to get him out, but that would have involved dismantling the whole machine, so they ran over his legs, severing them, and paid him $10,000, which in those days was real money.--When a man applied for work and was told there was no job available, a friend was always ready to tell him to sit down and wait a while and somebody would be carried out; he might get his job.

In 1907 William Hard wrote an article for a popular magazine called, *"Making Steel and Killing Men."* He had the facts. The steel companies were really alarmed. They were getting a bad public image. They adopted a completely new policy--of cutting down the accident rate by whatever means. They put on a major campaign throughout the industry, and extended it outside. They set up the National Safety Council as a kind of clearing house of information on the subject. They even adopted a policy of paying the men who were injured, using the compensation principle in force in workmen's compensation abroad. But they fought workmen's compensation in the U.S., and when it was adopted over their opposition they abolished their own system of compensation. They were also not especially generous in recommending candidates for compensation under the public system, as I was to discover.

The old-timers on the blast furnace used to talk about the old days when a furnace might blow out. The blow boss said that had happened one time and had taken the head right off of one of the men. "He was standing right where you're standing now." I was not too much worried. I knew the furnaces were built more sturdily than in the early days.

"Socks" Carney was being broken in--to take the place of the old blow boss. He talked about the strike of 1919. The Slavs in the furnace crew had walked off in a body, saying that the hole would not be opened again until it was a union hole. Six hours later it was tapped by Carney and a makeshift crew.

"I'm in favor of unions," he said, rather surprisingly. "I would have joined the union but nobody asked me." When I told Bill Foster about this later, he hit the ceiling. "Didn't he know there was a strike going on? Couldn't he have--" and so on. Which was all true enough, but it was also true that a little more effort spent in reaching the skilled workers, instead of depending on the semiskilled who had actually formed the backbone of the strike, would have paid big dividends. In a few cases, as in McKeesport, the skilled men made the strike their own, but not in Braddock. Will Watt I believe had also worked through the strike.

I tried to join the union. There was no union office in town, so I visited the headquarters of the Amalgamated Association of Iron, Steel, and Tin Workers in Pittsburgh and talked to Mike Tighe, the president. He argued against strikes, just as he had all through the strike of 1919. He wouldn't accept me as a member. The Mine, Mill & Smelter Workers had jurisdiction over the blast furnaces. I gave up.

The crew on the furnace front consisted of six men, one of whom was the keeper; that was a senior job. Then there was the monkey boss, also known as cinder snapper, who tended the back of the furnace, running off slag into the ladles on the railroad track below. The job I had set my sights on was hotblast man, tending the stoves in which the producer gas was stored while waiting to be fed into the furnace. The temperature had to be kept up to a certain level, and it was the hot-blast man's job to regulate the level. I worked as laborer for a couple of months, then took a turn at monkey boss, but the hot blast job seemed as far away as ever. At Christmas time I quit and came home for the holiday, then reported back for work and passed myself off as a hot blast man. There was an opening at one of the other furnaces and I was given the job there.

Before quitting the job on the first furnace, I had got myself a job on the ore dumper, so that I briefly held two jobs. This was deliberate; I wanted to do 16 hours consecutively to get some slight idea what the 24-hour shift had been like. My 16-hour shift was not eventful; I got through it all right, but was impressed with the danger of men working in an overtired condition when they were in constant contact with hot metal.

Working with the molten metal was always dangerous potentially; you had to keep your wits about you. It was at this time, or shortly after, that I got acquainted with Kipling's poem which had this stanza:

"They finger death at their gloves' end where they piece and repiece the living wires.
He rears against the gates they tend; they feed him hungry behind their fires.
Early at dawn, ere men see clear, they stumble into his terrible stall.
And hale him forth like a haltered steer, and goad and turn him till even-fall."(Emphasis added)

(From *"The Sons of Martha and the Sons of Mary"*)

From the blast furnace and the ore dumper I went to the open hearth department and worked for a while on the labor gang, waiting for a chance at the furnace front. My fellow workers were Italians, Slavs, and blacks. One day we were unloading sacks of lime in a shed. The air was full of dust. The labor boss came by and summoned me out. He said, "That's not a job for a white man," and transferred me to another gang. I was interested in his use of the word "white" to mean old American stock, also at his obviously discriminatory attitude.

There was a whole vocabulary in use to define the particular ethnic group that a man belonged to. The foreign-born were likely to call a Yankee "John" but the Yankees called each other "Mac." An Italian would be "Tony"; a Slav might be "Steve". To call a Slav "Hunky-boy" was of course an insult, and intended as such, the same as addressing a black worker as "boy". The Italians called each other "Walyo," if they came from the Naples area.

The companies that made such a fuss about their safety program had continued the 12-hour shift, with 24 hours every other weekend, for many years. And when they went over to the 3-shift system on continuous processes, they continued a tradition of driving for record production every March, even when they did not have the orders ahead. It was during such a drive that I strained my back. Having broken the record, the company began laying off men and a fairly long period of relatively slack production set in.

I always thought that the insane drive for production record in March was the immediate cause of my back strain. I was working as third helper on the open hearth at the time. I had had no instructions on how to lift heavy loads, and my inclination was to do it with my back, whereas the correct way is to bend your legs and then straighten them up. I was not likely to find this out by myself, because I was coming off a year of trouble with my knee, and while it had healed up solid, I was still not going to put extra pressure on it. The job I was on was reputed to be the toughest in the mill. But I could do the work. Ordinarily there is time to rest up after one furnace is tapped before it is time to go to another (the crew of third helpers serves several furnaces in turn). Of the six furnaces on our half of the charging floor, one was usually down for repairs. But not in this crazy record-breaking March. All six furnaces were in operation. So toward the end of the shift I felt something go in the small of my back. I was told much later that I had rotated a vertebra.

I did not realize at first that there was anything seriously wrong, and did not quit work for a couple of weeks. When I did, I applied for workmen's compensation. The company doctor said they did not pay compensation for back strain, so I appealed to the

State Workmen's Compensation Board. This was an almost unprecedented thing for a wage worker to do. The company had a staff of investigators which it turned loose on me. It learned all about my background, and even discovered that I had gone to Brockton for the American Civil Liberties Union.

The State Workmen's Compensation Board processed my application and set a date for a hearing. But by that time I had left Pennsylvania and did not think the prospects of getting compensation were good enough to warrant a trip back to Braddock.--Much later, after many years, compensation for back strain began to be paid, but not to me.

Before I left Braddock I had got to know a worker in the sheet mill, whose job was even harder than that of third helper on the open hearth. He had to grab an unfinished sheet with a pair of tongs from the front of a terrifically hot furnace, drag it across the floor to a pair of rolls, one above the other. He and his mate had to lift up the sheet to go through the top pair of rolls, catch it and feed it back into the bottom pair of rolls, then grab it again and quench it in a vat. Their work was twenty minutes on and 40 minutes off, to rest up.

I came to visit him in his room and was amazed to see an exercising apparatus on the wall. He said he used it to keep his muscles evenly developed; the job in the plate mill only called for certain ones and he was afraid they would get overdeveloped in relation to the others.

It might be remarked in passing that in 1924 the American Rolling Mill Co. was just perfecting the continuous sheet mill, which has since taken over altogether the job that my friend had been on. A good thing too. The sheet mill workers were liable to get the hot mill cramps from their exposure to the excessive heat. These cramps were very painful at best and fatal at worst.

That spring I attended a Young Friends Conference at Westtown, Pa., and conducted a workshop on industrial relations. From this experience two important conclusions emerged: (1) the Friends could not be counted on to do any work useful to the movement, in which I was now seriously interested; and (2) teaching was my dish of tea; I liked it and could do it. Religion, which had meant something to me at the time I joined the Friends Mission, was now a back number. At the same time I was not totally committed to teaching, although I saw that it would obviously be a good meal ticket if I was unable to find a full-time job in labor research, as I was unable.

XVI

Marian Rubins Davis

I went to Columbia and walked right into a job teaching economics, to start in the fall. I also ran into Marian Rubins.

Our meeting was not accidental. We were introduced by the secretary of the Economics Department at Columbia, but we were moving in the same circles and were bound to meet. When I got myself a table to do research in the Economics Room of the N.Y. Public Library, who should I find across the table but Marian Rubins! I had just been hearing about her from Edna Cers, who came to our house in Brookline direct from a vacation on Martha's Vineyard with Haggott & Margaret Beckhart and Marian Rubins. MR had come to do graduate work in economics at Columbia the year after I had been there. We were both going for the Ph.D. in economics. No accident at all. It was only unfortunate that I had not stayed for a second year of graduate work instead of going off to Cornell and Geneva. We might have been married much earlier. It didn't take us long to discover the similarity of our tastes. We got engaged on a ferryboat 17 days after we had met.

I was asked much later how I knew she was the right one for me. I had indeed a list of qualifications more or less explicitly drawn up. I would hope to marry--and I did intend to get married--someone who was smart, a leader, a woman of spirit, and politically sympathetic, which meant at that time, a liberal. Marian (or Nanie, as she was called) was smart (she had graduated from Smith *summa cum laude*); she was a leader (the leading woman graduate student in economics). She was part of the group of liberals with whom I had been associating, including Edna Cers, who had just been singing her praises to me. As for her spirit, I was to have evidence of that in later life when she took to making important decisions on her own. It took only a short acquaintance to become aware that she was no clinging vine. So, I was attracted to her, and she to me. I was never attracted seriously to any other woman. "Age [did] not wither her, nor custom stale her infinite variety." I never had sexual intercourse with any other woman, either before or after marriage.

When we had been acquainted about a week, we went for a weekend at Brookwood, and on the train returning we had a long talk, including discussions of people we both knew. Her reaction to them was almost exactly mine. I still didn't propose marriage, but she wrote her family that it was all but settled between us. And shortly thereafter, it was.

When we decided to get married Nanie and I did not have any well-defined social philosophy. We had both opposed the First World War, and were both against oppression and injustice, with reserves of idealism waiting to be tapped. We were not interested in making a lot of money; we figured our life style as somewhere near the middle, while working to improve the lot of the underdogs.

In 1924-25 Nanie was teaching at Smith and I was teaching at Columbia, and we got together weekends. I had thought she was a career gal, and pushed her to take her generals for the Ph.D., which she did; she passed, but not as well as people had expected from her. It turned out that she was more interested in family than in career. She was by nature a happy person. She fitted into whatever situation she found herself in, and found ways to interest people in doing worthwhile things.

I was going for the Ph.D., but when I tried to pick up where I had left off with my book (thesis) on the building trades, I could not find my notes! The family had moved from Brookline to New York, but the notes had not been left in Brookline. I finally remembered that I had left them in the Library of Industrial Relations, a private undertaking; but the librarian to whom I had entrusted them, Frank Anderson, had shot himself and the library had been wound up in my absence. The notes were long gone.

XVII

Why College Teachers are not Radicals

On becoming a member of the Columbia faculty, I was inducted into some of the trade secrets. I learned that while the custom was for a university to recommend its Ph.D.'s for positions, this did not apply to Russian Jews. At Columbia this was especially disgraceful because the chairman of the Economics Department, E.R.A. Seligman, was himself a Jew, but a German Jew of the old immigration. Harvard was the same way. The leading graduate student of economics, with whom I took a couple of courses in my senior year, was a man named Bober. He was highly qualified in every way, but was a member of a minority group. He wound up teaching not at some large university as he deserved but at Lawrence College in Appleton, Wisconsin. Cornell was the same way, as I discovered the following year. They were quite open about their anti-Semitism-among themselves of course.

Radicals were also discriminated against. A man had to be "safe". This was long before the days of Nixon and McCarthy. Boris Stern, who was a contemporary of ours and got his Ph.D. from Columbia in 1924, was a Russian Jew and supposedly a Marxist; he spoke English with an accent. He despaired quite early of getting a teaching job and went to work for the U.S. Bureau of Labor Statistics. He became a conservative, even a red-baiter. As a teacher he would have been quite "safe".

The young teachers who were still, or had become radical could still be weeded out when the time came to put them on tenure, usually when they were due to be promoted from Asst. Prof. to Associate Prof. At Harvard in the mid-'30's there was a vacancy at the higher levels in the Economics Department, and the aspirants included Raymond Walsh, Alan Sweezy, and John Cassells. The choice fell on Cassells, whereat there was a great outcry; Walsh and Sweezy were to the left of Cassells, a decent sort of man actually with an interest in consumers' problems. Alan Sweezy took a post at Williams College, and Walsh became an economist for the CIO.

Young radicals who made a good record as students might be and frequently were given teaching posts at the lower levels; they might even be invited in on temporary assignments, as Granville Hicks was invited to Harvard in the late 'thirties after he had come out as a Communist. The long period of apprenticeship in a conservative environment, with the preference always being shown to the "safe" men, was enough to weed out most of the radical aspirants to a teaching chair. The "safe" men were those who could be counted on not to antagonize the big-money men, or the politicians who had to grant the money to the public institutions. Not all the college administrators were as frank as the head of the Univ. of North Carolina Social Science Department who once interviewed me for a possible job there. The conversation drifted onto what I would be doing in my spare time, and I dropped the word "organizing"(Actually what I had in mind was some innocent sort of community organization). He jumped as if I had hit him, or bit him. When I expressed surprise at such a strong reaction, he said,

"Oh, you must realize, there is an acquisitive interest--"the rest was left unsaid. He satisfied himself that I did not have in mind a textile workers' union, and dropped a hint in his turn as to the kind of subject that might suitably be studied; something like workmen's compensation. I did not get the job.

Professors who campaign for worthy causes and attract the attention of graduates and the public may find themselves in trouble even if they are not Communists and even if the cause is not very radical. Scott Nearing's case has already been noted. Jerome Davis was a Socialist, not a Communist, but he too carried on campaigns in the early '30s while on the faculty of the Yale Divinity School, and lost his job.

It is the fear of being disciplined or not promoted that holds academic people back when they are tempted to take a public stand. That, or the fear of incurring the hostility of their conservative colleagues, which means most of their colleagues.

The long and trying period of celibacy imposed on Nanie and me by the moral code in which we were raised was continued for another year, quite unnecessarily. We were not married until the summer of 1925. The wait had one good effect: the families had a chance to get used to each other. My family came out to Minneapolis en masse for the wedding. The Morris Hallowell family was already there, and right in the middle of things.

Although we both came from families that would be rated happy, we were fashionably cynical about marriage as an institution. We did not have a minister for the wedding. We married ourselves, in a pseudo-Quaker ceremony. But the marriage was duly registered, and we found out later that it was legal under Minnesota law, and hence recognized as legal throughout the U.S..

In any case it would not have been long before it would have been recognized as legal under common law. We used to joke about whether we were legally married or not. But we found out later that is not considered a joke for college professors.

I taught for a year at Columbia, and was reappointed. However I had other options. I was awarded an Amherst Memorial Fellowship for study abroad. I was also invited to join the faculty of the University of California (Berkeley) with the perspective of being promoted eventually to professor. I did not have my Ph.D. but it was assumed that I would get it within a few years at most. And Cornell University, seeking a man to give the labor course while Professor Slichter was on leave, offered me a one-year job, which I took. Slichter left Cornell shortly after, and if I had fitted in there, I could have stayed on. But I did not, and I also did not go to California. I did however accept the Amherst Scholarship, which was renewed twice (1926-1929).

Even though the Cornell appointment was an interim appointment, for one year, I had been screened as carefully as if it had been for a permanent appointment. So, if I had played the game I might have been invited to replace Slichter when he moved on, as he presently did (to the Harvard Business School faculty). But I had not played the game; I had been too ostentatiously pro-labor. So the only constructive result of that year was the birth of Chan in August. Then we left for Europe on the Amherst Fellowship which was to extend in the end over a period of three years.

My back strain at Braddock had left me with an interest in the problem of accidents and safety, also occupational diseases, in the steel industry. I looked up the history of the safety movement which had begun in the steel industry and spread from there. I interviewed the head of the National Safety Council in Chicago; my writeup was published in the *Reichsarbeitsblatt* of the German Ministry of Labor, but not in the U.S. I had safety in mind when I went to England.

The image of the steel industry as a dangerous one was fixed in the public mind there as in the U.S. There had been a contest for steel workers to write a piece for a book that was to be published on what it was like to be a worker in each of a number of industries. There were many entries, but the man who won the contest, and whose piece was indeed published, had given a graphic description of an industrial accident--made up, no doubt, out of his fertile imagination (but Mike Gold's poem "A Strange American Funeral"--about Braddock--was founded on fact).

144

The British approach was nevertheless different from the American, as was illustrated by this story. After the rails had gone through the rolls, they had to be turned over and processed further. To handle this process, one of the steel companies had installed a mechanism consisting of a pair of huge tongs that rose up out of the floor and grabbed the rail. A man dropped his pipe and leaned out over the rail bank to get it. The tongs rose up just at that moment, caught the man and squeezed the guts out of him. It was a terrible accident. "He was one of our oldest employees," said the plant guide who was showing me the works.

"So, what did you do?" I asked.

"We took out the machine," he replied.

I was sure that a U.S. plant in the position of the British one described would have tinkered with the machine, put up a safety guard, but surely not abandon it because of one accident, even in the era of "Safety First."

The British were willing to work a furnace long after it had got so worn that it was liable to break out any time. The blow boss at a blast furnace I visited in Skinningrove, making specialty steels, said that his furnace had not been relined in 34 years! It was not worked very hard, to be sure--not like the Jones & Laughlin mass-production furnace in the U.S. that was scheduled for relining after only one year.

On the Amherst Fellowship in Europe, we had hoped to supply some statistical measure of the differences in scales of living among the several countries studied, but this undertaking proved too difficult. We were advised to that effect early, and it proved to be correct.

For countries quite far apart in levels of living, it is no doubt quite feasible to calculate the percentage of the family budget that goes for food, just as in comparing the levels of living within one country--the higher the percentage spent on food, the less is left for other things. The consumption of food does not vary all that much between one country and another in calories and nutritional value; even the unskilled laborer has to eat and be nourished.

For clothing, much of course depends on the weather. But where the real difference appears between countries is in housing.

In England, the whole working class apparently lives in brick row houses, consisting of two stories, with a kitchen and scullery and a spare room on the ground floor and two or three bedrooms upstairs. The spare room, facing on the street with an aspidistra in the window, stands empty in most of the houses. It may be pressed into service when the family is unusually large, or when visitors come (we lived in such a room for weeks at a time), or when the young lady of the family has visitors. In our room there was a piano. Bathrooms are no doubt quite general now, but the house we lived in did not have one; the family used a washtub in the kitchen for baths, and the toilet was in the back yard, which was called the garden, although there were no flowers there.

In Germany, the housing of the working class was a scandal. The typical working class dwelling was one or two large rooms in an apartment house, called a "renting barracks" (*Mietskaserne*). There was no bathroom; toilet facilities were shared with several other families. Each family supplied its own cookstove, which served also for heating and was transported when the family moved. This was quite a contrast with the British system of open fireplaces, used for heating and cooking. The open fireplace gave good ventilation and was healthier all round.

I could have written a book about the differences observed in the several countries. I had the opportunity to get out a series of articles for publication in a social science review. But the years slipped by and in the end all I had to show was an article on the labor courts (in *Political Science Quarterly*) and some fugitive articles in the U.S. and Germany. Our visit in Europe gave us a view of the poverty there and started us on the way to joining the Communist Party.

146

XVIII

Pittsburg and the Fight Against the Coal Companies, 1928-29

When the Amherst Fellowship was renewed for a third year, we decided to spend the year in Pittsburgh, a logical enough place to study the steel industry. I was in touch with Powers Hapgood and also knew that the coal industry was in a state of crisis, although the general economic crisis was not to begin until a year later The United Mine Workers was on the ropes. John L. Lewis, the president, had been reelected over a mounting wave of opposition; it was said that he stole the elections. Finally in 1928 the dissidents in the union, finding it impossible to make progress through constitutional channels, decided to withdraw and form a coal miners' union of their own. A convention was called and met in Pittsburgh, where we had just arrived. I was in the meeting hall when the convention was due to start. Powers was there too, an observer like me, or rather a potential but not actual member of the secession movement. The secession was led by the Communists in the union, and Powers was not a Communist nor even a fellow traveler.

The Communist leadership was no secret, and this was all the excuse the police needed to break up the convention. The thugs from the U.M.W. were there too. I saw a group of them beat up one of the delegates in front of the hall. The police went through the hall, from which the delegates were now scattering; the police were crying, "We want leaders"; but of the two dozen or so that they arrested, only one could be called a leader; the others were getting into automobiles that were parked beside the street and taking off for an unknown destination. I went in one of the cars, and found myself in Wilmerding, a suburb outside the limits of the city of Pittsburgh and thus beyond the jurisdiction of the Pittsburgh police. A fraternal order of Lithuanians had put its hall at the disposal of the delegates and they met there and founded the National Miners Union. The motion to form the union was made by Veazey, a delegate from Indiana. Watt of Illinois was the President, Veazey was the Treasurer, and the Secretary was Pat Toohey of Canonsburg, Pa. Powers might have been elected secretary, the most important position, but he declined the nomination. The convention met all afternoon and was scheduled to meet the following day. Meanwhile the sheriff of Allegheny County had been alerted to the Communist plot that was being hatched within his jurisdiction, and he set out with an auto load of deputies to find it and break it up. But he had no clues to go on.

The following morning the prisoners, who had spent the night in jail, came before the magistrate, who was set to discharge them; but first they had to take the non-Communist oath. I was there and heard the local leader of a Communist branch and writer for the *Daily Worker*, Tony Minerich, solemnly give the "right" answers. It went like this:

Judge: Are you a Communist?--A. No.
Judge: Ever go to any of their meetings?--A. No.
Judge: You're discharged.

All answered "right" except one, a real outsider like me. His name was Jasper Deeter, and he was a drama student and teacher from the New York area. He made difficulties about the questions, which he said he would not answer, and indeed they were irrelevant and unconstitutional. He was held after the others but eventually he made his point and was released without answering the inquisitorial questions.

Actually it was not necessary for the defendants to have spent the night in jail. It was conveyed to them that all they had to do was to slip a little baksheesh to certain specified persons and the whole thing would be dropped. The decision was against playing that kind of game.

When I worked in Braddock, there was nobody on the faculty of the University of Pittsburgh that I knew except a liberal prof of economics named Frank Tyson, and with him I had struck up a friendship. His wife was a social worker and an outstanding woman.

In the years that had followed, a group of young faculty members had appeared, determined to fight the injustice and company domination that they saw all round them. There was Colston Warne, in economics; William Ellison Chalmers and Bill Nunn, also in Economics, and Fred Woltman, a young philosophy instructor. They had organized a Western Pennsylvania branch of the ACLU, and were taking advice from Roger Baldwin and from Forrest Bailey, who was actually running the New York (national) office of the ACLU (Roger was in and out). I had contacted this group on first arriving in Pittsburgh. When the founding convention of the NMU was broken up, they knew about it immediately and quickly arranged a conference with Mayor Kline. They took along a highly respected lawyer, a well known fighter for civil liberties and the rights of labor by the name of Louis Kossuth

Porter--named after the Hungarian Nationalist leader of 1848. They added me to the party. The chief of police was called in to hear the protests and make his response.

Kline was a grafter like so many others (he was actually indicted during the ensuing year) but he was anxious not to antagonize the liberals, and he heard the protests against the violation of the right of assembly. However at a certain point he started calling for more concrete evidence concerning what had happened. I told my story. Porter was furious and berated the mayor and police. The ACLU men brought up a rumor they had heard, that the police had been ordered to intercept the leaders of the NMU on their way out of town and arrest them. The mayor asked the chief of police what about that, and he said,

"There was no such order."

"Any patrolman who does anything like that will answer for it within 24 hours," said Porter.

The action of the convention, as indicated, had moved out of the jurisdiction of the city authorities. The sheriff and his deputies finally located the convention in the middle of the second day and came busting into the hall, as I was informed later. The chairman declined to be flustered, and merely said,

"Oh, yes, gentlemen, have a seat; we'll be with you in just a minute."

The sheriff was hesitating when someone in his party recognized one of the miners, who he said was a member of his American Legion post: "Hi, Bill!" The sheriff and his party sat on the stage and waited while the convention did half an hour's business, then adjourned. Nobody was arrested.

We were allowed to conclude that anyone who spoke for an appreciable number of voters, as a miners' union representative obviously did, could do business with the establishment, no matter what his politics.

In the course of the academic year the local ACLU men had several brushes with the authorities, meaning not only the city police but the State police and the coal and iron police. The last named were a unique Pennsylvania institution. They served as guards for the coal and steel companies, and were innocuous enough most of the time. One with whom I got into conversation had heard Scott Nearing talk once, and said that what Nearing said made a lot of sense. But they did have commissions from the State, and in time of crisis, like a strike, they were empowered to make arrests. Their salaries were paid by the companies, of course. It was an intolerable situation, and in the end there was a major confrontation on this issue.

I had an occasion to see the system in operation. One of the coal and iron police had got into an altercation with one of the miners and had beat him up. It fell to my lot to visit the "patch" (company town) where the miner lived and if possible get an account of the incident from neighbors. The town was actually not too far from Pittsburgh, and I arrived outside the patch at the end of the day and talked to the cop who had been complained of. Afterwards I walked out toward the company patch. The road ran under a railroad track, and standing on the track was a guard, another of the coal and iron police, silhouetted against the sky. He wanted to know what I wanted in the town, I said I wanted to talk to someone there. "Who?" "Oh, just anybody."

That wasn't good enough for him, and I didn't get to go into the town. We checked and found that as the law then was, it was quite possible, even legal, for the company to keep out anyone who was not actually delivering goods that had been ordered. The idea obviously was to keep out union organizers--also no doubt ACLU investigators.

When a union drive was in progress, ACLU lawyer Arthur Garfield Hays was able to get a judge in Central Penna. to issue, however unwillingly, an injunction against stopping Hays and a UMW organizer from entering the company town of Vintondale. They did go in. The company took the injunction to a friendly judge of the State Supreme Court and had it vacated within 24 hours, but they were too late; the miners in the town had all joined the union. When the union has come in, the closed company town ceases to be closed.

We were reading the *Daily Worker* and had become aware of the arrest of two Slavic radicals in Aliquippa, a small city on the Ohio River dominated by the Jones & Laughlin Steel Corp. Their names were Pete Muselin and Milan Resetar. I went out and looked them up, and wrote up their case for the ACLU. The two, who had been out on bail when I saw them, were afterward given prison terms and Resetar died in prison. The ACLU branch was much interested and circulated my report. It was after that that they took me onto the committee. They had held back because of my friendship with Prof. Tyson, who it turned out was not only not a part of their group but had actually opposed them on some issues.

The repeated violations of civil liberties by government agents led to one confrontation after another, with Fred Woltman usually carrying the ball. Finally an innocent coal miner named

John Barkoski got into an argument one night in a private home that got so heated that somebody called the police. They came and took him to the headquarters of the State Police, who were not allowed to marry and lived in a kind of barracks. The Captain remarked, "I feel like a good workout," picked up a poker and began to beat Barkoski, accompanied by other State Policemen. Barkoski died of his injuries.

The coal and iron police were not involved, but the campaign against them rose to fever heat after the Barkoski incident. The demand was for the abolition of this corps. Bills to that effect were introduced in the State legislature. The bills did not pass, but the incoming Governor, Gifford Pinchot, with pretensions as a liberal, did not renew the commissions of the coal and iron police and the whole system was eventually dropped.

The students knew about the campaign of the ACLU branch and many offered their services, which were gratefully accepted. The University administration and the President, one Bowman, did not like the activities of the civil libertarians. At one point an emissary of the administration, some kind of Dean, came and sat in Bill Nunn's office where the students were coming to volunteer their services. Bill, not to be flustered, introduced the Dean to each one of the students.

Warne was the senior member of the group, but he played it cool and did not appear in public. One time, though, he very nearly had to.

The Communist Party was fighting for the right to hold street-corner meetings, and they had a particular street corner in mind. One night they collected there and tried to start a meeting, but the police arrested the whole crowd. Warne and I were not there, but arrived soon after and stood on the disputed corner until a cop ordered us to move on. Warne, instead of moving, attempted to argue: "Say, buddy, I wonder if you know who I am?" The cop was not impressed and repeated the order. I had moved to a little distance, not defying the cop, but when he decided to arrest Warne he took me along too. We found ourselves in the jail with the Party crowd.

A reporter presently appeared with a camera and wanted to take Pictures, but Warne remained quietly seated in the rear of the cell and was not spotted. The next morning the whole crowd appeared in court, and a press photographer was there too. He tried to photograph Warne, who protected himself by raising his arm in front of his face. In the end his picture did not appear in the paper.

The judge that morning was in a good mood. One of the younger party members, a man from out of town, tried to get political; "Why don't you arrest them Teapot Dome grafters?" But Pat Devine, the District Organizer, played up to the judge. He talked to him as one Irishman to another, and got him laughing. In the end all cases were dismissed and Warne kept his job.

Around the turn of the year I went to Birmingham, Ala., where I met up with Art Shields and Esther Lowell, and their young son Allen. They had decided that the South was newsworthy, and were writing it up for Federated Press, a labor news service started during World War I by Carl Haessler. It was a tough year for them; both Art and Esther had health problems, but they did a pioneer job of reporting on a little-known field.

Together we walked past a "Keep Out" sign and into a company town of the U.S. Steel Corp. subsidiary in the area. It was an all-colored town. I had to talk to a man for three quarters of an hour before he came up with the information that a black mechanic in the Fairfield mill, Matt Lucas, had been taken out and put to death for sassing the foreman. The Negro press had heard nothing of this, so completely cut off was the company town from the social life of the area.

Since three men had been in the party that killed Matt Lucas, it was technically a lynching. Tuskegee was keeping a list of lynchings, but even after we had sent them all the data they refused to list Matt Lucas' case as a lynching. If the story had appeared in the *New York Times*, no doubt they would have accepted it as true.

I saw to it that the head office of U.S. Steel learned of the lynching. I was interested to see what they would do. I got to see the man who apparently was delegated to handle labor matters nationally, one Charles L. Close. He did not deny the facts, which he described as regrettable. But the men who had done the job on Matt Lucas continued to work for the company. No attempt was made to prosecute them, as far as I ever heard, although the company eventually, after court actions, paid $700 to the Lucas family. The coroner had described the killing as "justifiable homicide", and that remained the official verdict. The liberal weekly *The Nation* published my article "A Substitute for Lynching", in which I cited the decline in the number of lynchings and tried to couple it with the increase in the homicide rate; but the statistics, which I had taken from Frederick L. Hoffman, were poorly compiled, and the point could not be substantiated.

The year at Pittsburgh ended in a blaze of excitement. Harry Elmer Barnes, a liberal professor from Smith, had been invited to speak on campus, but permission was refused at the last minute. He spoke anyway, in a parking lot adjoining the campus. At the same time a Tom Mooney protest meeting, organized by MRD, was meeting not far away. Both meetings were in deliberate defiance of the academic authorities, who responded by firing Fred Woltman and withholding degrees from the two students mainly responsible for organizing the Barnes meeting.

Warne and the others did not take any action in response to the firing of Woltman, who they said had repeatedly had been carrying the ball in the brushes with the authorities, some of which had resulted in outstanding victories. Legally and academically, there was no action that could be taken; the firing was legal, although it was plainly a political act; Fred was not on tenure. But some mark of appreciation could have been given. It was not. Woltman was furious. He went to New York and got a job with the *World-Telegram*, then supposed to be the most liberal paper in town. A couple of years later he had turned violently against the whole movement, and continued for many years as a red-baiting reporter.

I had written up the episode of the banned meetings for the *New Republic* (which had earlier published as an editorial a piece I had written on the coal and iron police). I had been approached by John Cover, for whom Nanie had worked that year on a research job, about doing a study on unemployment. Only, it was to be under the auspices of the University of Pittsburgh, and the Dean, who was personally not unsympathetic, said with regard to my qualifications that even if I was the Angel Gabriel my appointment "would never get by with the Chancellor--and Mrs. Davis would be even worse!" Nanie treasured that remark.

XIX

Memphis, 1929-30

I accepted a teaching job at Southwestern College, in Memphis, and we moved there in the fall of 1929. Memphis was a city of contrasts. Tennessee was a border state, and the Negroes voted. But the atmosphere was that of the backward South, in everything touching race relations. Memphis was the commercial center for the Mississippi Delta, so-called: the rich bottom-land of the big river, where the cotton plantations were still conducted on a large scale and in much the same spirit as in slavery days. Technically the plantations were divided up and leased out to share-croppers; but the overseer had everything to say about the sharecroppers' operations, and they could be made to move on at a moment's notice.

I learned from my students that race relations were tense in proportion to the ratio of blacks to whites; so, in the Delta, where that ratio was four or five to one, the tension was as great as anywhere in the South. White people going out into the cotton area usually carried a gun.

The cotton planter's idea of the way things should work in cotton raising went something like this. At the beginning of the calendar year the share cropper had spent his money from the previous crop and began drawing supplies from the company store or commissary. The advances continued, at 25% interest, until the crop was made, at which time the share cropper paid off his debt to the commissary (plus accrued interest) and had enough money to live on the rest of the year, when the cycle started again. I had heard that the commissary sometimes cheated the share croppers, and I asked a planter whether the blacks kept accounts of their own. He said they did, even those who were not literate. I asked what happened when the cropper's accounts did not agree with the commissary's. He answered with unexpected candor, "They lose." Education for the blacks was not on the landlords' agenda.

The blacks in Memphis voted, but they had no rights that a white man was bound to respect. In the patriarchal spirit that prevailed, a black man (or woman) coming into court had to have a white man to speak for him if he was to have a chance. We were initiated into this system when the mother of the girl who did housework for us got into an altercation with a neighbor and was fined $20, as was the daughter, Willie Mae. I was asked to go and plead for them before the magistrate, to reduce the fine, which amounted to a week's wages--too much for them to stand. The mother worked for Southwestern and Willie Mae worked for us. So, I had standing before the magistrate. He cut the fines in half.

Willie Mae and her mother had relatives in the country, and we went out and spent a day with them. Willie Mae ate with us, but our hosts ate in the kitchen. The farmer had mentioned that he used to go hunting with the white man who had the next farm, so at my suggestion he took me over and introduced me. The white farmer and I talked about this and that, but the black farmer carefully stayed outside. For him to have stayed and conversed would have implied a degree of equality, but hunting together apparently did not.

The contradictions in the community were paralleled in the college. The amount of education that went on at Southwestern far exceeded that in northern schools, for the student's whole outlook on life had to be reconsidered. Also, the white schools in the area from which the students came, though vastly better than the black schools, were indeed primitive. Many of the students came in as fundamentalists. Yet four years later they not only had jacked up their spelling and punctuation to acceptable college levels, they had come to accept evolution as a matter of course.

I did not understand at first how this was done--how Southwestern graduates were accepted for advanced standing at any university in the country. At the beginning of the school year, entering students came with such a variety of preparation that they frequently found themselves in classes that were over their heads. Rather than have them waste their time for the rest of the semester, the college had adopted the policy of collecting them into a class which would give them something worthwhile that they could handle, but which did not duplicate the work in any other course. This course was assigned to me. I was somewhat perplexed, and for a time thought of using as a text a book called *Introduction to Reflective Thinking*, which began with how Copernicus came to be preferred to Ptolemy, went on to Darwin and evolution, and included a chapter on the higher criticism of the Bible. The President intercepted this text, and I eventually settled for anthropology, giving them a dose of Franz Boas with his heretical ideas on racial equality.

I still didn't know how the students came to accept evolution. The biology prof explained that in biology the sophomores (not the first-year men) were introduced to the idea, and accepted it as logical without anyone making an issue of it.

The curriculum at Southwestern was varied, and contained a reasonable amount of science, but the emphasis was reminiscent of the 19th century. The most popular professor, and the one with the largest classes was the professor of Greek.

The standards at Southwestern were high, and were kept high, but not without exception. The faculty could be persuaded to grant degrees to students who had not met the requirements. One such was a student named Raspberry, who had come to Southwestern as a transfer and whose English was inadequate by any standard. He had been in one of my classes and had made 63 mistakes in English on his final exam. So, when the question of granting him a degree came up in faculty meeting I moved that the degree not be granted. In the debate that followed, the President, who had visited Raspberry's family and for some reason was sympathetic to him, made his attitude quite clear, and many of the faculty went along with him. One such was Prof. Cooper of the History Department, who was heard to remark off the record: "Might as well do what the President says; it'll come out that way in the end anyway." He was so right. The chairman of the English Department said, also off the record: "I hope the English Department will not be held responsible for granting this joke degree." The faculty did in fact vote to refuse the degree. But the President went around later and got a majority of the English profs to agree to the degree being granted, and it was. Neither the President nor any of his supporters contended at any time that Raspberry's English was adequate.

Just how backward my students were on race relations did not emerge at first. But in the course of a class discussion I took a vote on whether it was ever justified to burn a man to death. The class divided about equally. On the question whether lynching was ever justified, it was no contest; the affirmative won 26 to 3.

The students soon discovered, of course, that I did not share their point of view, but they stayed by and learned what they could, even ended the year with friendly feelings all round. It was not student objections that would have made it impossible for me to stay on at Southwestern. It was chapel. The profs took turns leading chapel. When it came my turn I took as my text one of the egalitarian passages, protesting against interest and unearned income in general. I also didn't say, "Amen." The students laughed at me: "Where would this institution be without unearned income?" The President was much concerned because I didn't say "Amen." (He was a former minister himself) But what took

156

everybody's breath away was that I got them to invite a Unitarian to speak about labor relations in the South. An atheist they could take, but a Unitarian--!

One fine day early in 1930, we drove South into the Delta and stopped for a conversation with a share cropper near the highway. The house he was living in was rather run down, and he himself was in a combative mood. I mentioned something about organizing a protest and he picked the idea right up: "Where do you reckon I could join an organization like that--in Memphis?"

I wrote up the conversation for the Federated Press, for which I had been writing as a correspondent since Pittsburgh. The *Daily Worker* picked up the story and printed it on the front page, with my concluding remark, that the sharecroppers were "ripe for organization--rotten ripe."

The Party had not had any organization in the South, but the area had been much written about in the 1920's, not only by Art Shields and Esther Lowell, and that spring the Party sent an organizer, Tom Johnson, a former Wobbly, to Birmingham. (The only contact he had was an FP correspondent who later turned out to be a stool pigeon!) Also a small group including Ann Burlak went to Atlanta to try to organize for the left-wing National Textile Workers. They were promptly picked up and charged with sedition, under a law passed just after the Civil War.

Nanie had been in the Party since Pittsburgh. She was now called on to organize a protest meeting in Memphis about the Atlanta arrests. I also went around to the *Commercial Appeal* and talked to an editorial writer about the arrests, which were pretty raw by any standard. Somewhat to my surprise, he responded, and his editorial "Down in Atlanta", appeared a couple of days later.

Tom Johnson was to speak at the meeting, and he sent the copy of a leaflet to announce the meeting, which we had printed and distributed. Then things began to happen.

A reporter came out to the house and interviewed Nanie; the story appeared with her picture, labeled "Communist leader." The day of the proposed meeting, the police, who had seen the leaflet, decided that the meeting would not be held. That morning a radical lawyer named Goldberger called up and offered his services, which we were glad enough to accept; we hadn't known him before. The Police commissioner called up and asked if we were going ahead with the meeting; we said, "Yes." Tom Johnson had arrived by that time and we both went down to the Commissioner's office. The Commissioner objected to our advocating social equality for Negroes, and asked again whether we were going on with the meeting; Tom Johnson, not wishing to appear yellow, said Yes. The police arrested him. I said if they were going to arrest people for advocating social equality they should arrest me too as I believed in social equality. He obliged, and we were both marched off to be finger-printed, which actually they had no right to do, and locked us up so that the meeting should not be held. Police also went out to our house and arrested Nanie, who managed to call Goldberger; she had had the foresight to dump the kids on friends.

They held us overnight, then put Tom Johnson on the train for New York. (He was going actually to Chattanooga, to meet with an ILD group; he telegraphed ahead for them to hold the meeting "underground.") We took a train to Chicago a few days later.

We were flattered by the amount of attention we were attracting in Memphis, but we had no intention of having an equal amount of attention attracted to Mata and Pitar in Minneapolis, our next stop. So, our first order of business on arriving in Chicago was to shake the cops. We had two contacts who we thought might be of service. I left Nanie and the kids (Chan and Bursha) in the park east of Michigan Avenue, opposite Randolph St., and went to call the contacts. I went by a circuitous route and was pretty sure I was not followed.

Arthur Fisher, the liberal, was not interested, but Carl Haessler rose to the occasion. He invited us out to his home in Highland Park, and said if any dicks came nosing around out there he would sic his friend The Highland Park chief of police onto them. I went back to get the rest of the family and found they had disappeared; only the dick who had been following us was there, and he wouldn't tell what had become of them. I hotfooted it back to Carl's office, and the others were already there. The kids had had a call of nature and they walked the whole length of the loop, to the museum, to find a place where they could relieve themselves.

We went to the station to take the train to Highland Park, and had the happy sensation of not being followed. But we still had a typewriter in the parcel room at the Illinois Central Station. Carl said;, "Leave that to me." The next day, while we were resting up, he took the claim check and went to the I.C. station. As he had expected, when he got the typewriter a man who had been standing there followed him up to the el platform. Carl made as if to get into one end of a car, and this man got into the other end, whereon Carl stepped back off and the train went on without him. He went over to the other platform and took the train to Highland Park.

It was too bad that the revolution didn't come to the U.S. in our generation. Carl and Nanie would have made fine revolutionary leaders.

Our lawyer in Memphis had been, not the lawyer who was the local representative of the ACLU (he issued a statement attacking us after we were arrested) but a man named Goldberger, as noted. He continued active in defense of radicals and we later learned that he was killed in an auto accident. His car had gone off the road. Nanie thought it had been forced off the road, as Karen Silkwood's was later.

Another man who had come forward to help us was the proprietor of a little meat store, a former Party organizer. He lost business on our account.

For a time, the Memphis Police Department reacted hysterically at any mention of Communism. Henry Fuller, a book salesman who was just getting interested in left-wing causes, came to Memphis and asked, perhaps naively, where the Communist Party headquarters were. They told him, "In this city, at the Police Station," and he was taken there and held for investigation. While there he saw an officer take a swing at a black woman and knock out several teeth. He wrote up his experiences for the Federated Press. (But later he became violently anti-Communist) As it turned out, the C.P. did establish a branch in Memphis only three years later.

X X

Sunnyside, 1930-33: Radicalism on the Rise and the Spy System Concealed

The H. A. Davis family finances survived the crash, and Mother was able to keep financing our family. We went to Sunnyside, on Long Island, and stayed there three years, the first two in an apartment and the third in a separate house. Sunnyside was a special development built by a limited dividend housing corporation amid considerable publicity. Many liberals and radicals had moved there. So, we had interesting neighbors.

My mother and father had both visited us in Memphis, and they were aware of my interest in Federated Press. Mother worked out with Harvey O'Connor, who was running the New York office of FP, an arrangement by which I would work 1/2 time for FP, the other 1/2 to be devoted to finishing up my thesis for the Ph.D. She put up the money for both halves of my time. This did not work out very well. I had to rewrite the manuscript that I had produced in the early 'twenties.

After 1 1/2 years I attempted to present the rewritten thesis to a committee of three: a Mrs. Burns, who had supervised the rewriting without showing any enthusiasm for it; Carter Goodrich, and Leo Wolman, who had just joined the Columbia faculty. They turned it down. This was of course a bitter blow; but what made me furious was their statement that the topic was wrong--this although I had been working on it for ten years off and on! Degrees were then being granted at other institutions for theses on labor in the Building trades (in Chicago and San Francisco respectively).

I shelved the New York building trades and concentrated on *Labor and Steel,* not as a thesis at all, at first; but when the manuscript was completed after another 1 1/2 years, I decided that the quality was of doctors' thesis calibre and approached Columbia about offering that.

First though, I had a real scare. The first chapter, which had proved to be a stickler, was finished, and was in my brief case when I went Christmas shopping with Chan, then six years old, on a Saturday afternoon. Snow began falling, and the taxi we were in was making slow progress. I paid off the taxi driver, grabbed Chan and the presents, and set out to beat the taxi on foot. Later I remembered the brief case--but too late; the taxi was gone. I had made a carbon copy, but that was in the brief case too.

The taxi driver of course found the brief case, and when he knocked off for the day a little later, he took it with him to the saloon where he came for a drink with his cronies before going home. He tossed the brief case on the table and remarking, "Look! I got a Communist brief case!" went off to the john. Present in the room was a Communist sympathizer who, fearing that the next stop for the brief case might be the police station, gathered it up when nobody was looking and made off with it. The address of the Labor Research Association was all over the MS, so he had no trouble dropping it off at 80 E. llth St. when the offices opened on Monday. I got it back later that day.

I presented only the first half of *Labor and Steel* as my thesis. This was done on advice of Carter Goodrich, who acted as my sponsor for this second effort (he was quite friendly, having apparently forgotten the circumstances under which I had been turned down the first time). He said that he had found the second half, dealing among other things with recent efforts at unionisation, more tendentious than the first half, which was taken up with the condition of living of the steel workers. He was not alarmed at the tendentiousness, but thought that other members of the committee might be. So, since the thesis was plenty long even when thus truncated, I took his advice. While I waited outside, the committee took some time debating on the thesis but it turned out that the debate was entirely on the question why the thesis was cut. Carter Goodrich said it had been done on his advice and eventually the committee accepted his explanation and the degree was granted.

Nanie abandoned pacificism quite readily, as Grace Hutchins, Anna Rochester, and Scott Nearing had done a little earlier when forced to choose between pacifism and Communism. For me it was a real wrench that took me years to overcome. I was finally forced to agree with William Golding, author of *Lord of the Flies*, that there is more evil in human nature than can be explained by environment. This evil is not merely an individual matter but may be a mass phenomenon, as in Fascism. Willingness to sacrifice oneself to advance the power of the group must have been a characteristic making for survival of the group in the many millennia of pre-history. Whether human beings so constituted can survive under present conditions is a problem of the 21st century.

Nanie threw herself into the Communist movement in the New York area, going to late evening meetings on organization in

Manhattan, speaking on street corners, and marching in May Day parades, a pastime in which I presently participated. I also helped organize a branch of the International Labor Defense (ILD) in Sunnyside, and it grew immediately. As illustrating the quality of life in Sunnyside, I went house to house one evening canvassing for support for the ILD, which was known for its defense of the Scottsboro Boys. A Sunnyside housewife was sitting by the window reading when I rang the doorbell. She let me in and I explained my mission, to which she was sympathetic. She and her husband had been active in a cooperative in Nova Scotia. She joined the ILD and became secretary of the branch!

There was a swing to the left in the U.S., and the prestige of the ILD was growing. It grew especially among the black population when the Scottsboro campaign got rolling. I went all the way to Washington to give a speech at a Scottsboro rally. Janie Patterson, the mother of Heywood Patterson, one of the nine, was traveling from one city to another and giving speeches at such meetings. She stayed with us in Sunnyside. The defense had originally been in the hands of the NAACP, and they had selected a lawyer named Roddy who turned out to be a bust. Everybody thought the NAACP had paid him, but Janie Patterson said that was not the case--the families of the boys had put up the money.

The ILD got into the case on the appeal, and the NAACP, thus goaded, also hired an appeal lawyer. So, with Samuel Leibowitz and Clarence Darrow both participating, the case went to the U.S. Supreme Court, which gave two highly important decisions favorable to the boys. Several of them got off, but it was many years before Heywood Patterson was finally released.

I was on the city committee of the ILD. I went as a delegate to the national convention, spoke another time at a meeting for Tom Mooney's release; and prepared an abstract of the Angelo Herndon case for use by speakers.

It was while we were in New York that the campaign for the Scottsboro boys reached its height, around 1931. An enormous mass meeting was held in Harlem, and a number of branches of the ILD were organized. We on Long Island were able to observe how the black community had been stirred. The nearest black settlement was in Jackson Heights, a little farther out on the Island than Sunnyside. A little group of blacks there had heard of the case and we were assigned to help them organize. There was a dance, with a speaker. The conservatives were there, trying to find something wrong with the movement. The event passed off smoothly, although the speaker was white, and misjudged the psychology of the group;

he had as his opening remark the news that Tom Mooney was to get a new trial. The people there did not know about the Mooney case. But they knew about the Scottsboro case, and felt honored to be part of the defense.

We spent a couple of summers at Croton-on-Hudson, and a branch of the ILD was functioning there. It arranged a meeting at which the principal speaker was Ruby Bates, one of the two girls who had supposedly been raped. She had recanted and confessed (to Harry Emerson Fosdick) that the whole case was a frameup. But the other of the two girls, Victoria Price, stuck to her story, and the boys, whose convictions had twice been upset by the U.S. Supreme Court, were convicted again. Judge Horton threw out the conviction as being contrary to the weight of the evidence--and was defeated for reelection.

People got more and more disenchanted with the capitalist system in the early 1930's, and it was not hard to work up interest in the consumers' cooperative movement. We were part of the group that decided to start a cooperative bakeshop, getting the baked goods from a Finnish cooperative bakery in Brooklyn. The people wanted me to be president of the society, but I ducked; I became vice-president.

The consumers' cooperatives, called Rochdale co-ops after the city in England where the viable combination was first worked out, are non-capitalist but not anti-capitalist. They perform a useful service for their members and protect them from the exploitation inherent in the system of private property and from deliberate adulteration. They do form a worldwide movement, which has entered many fields, not only retailing. Credit unions are a favorite form of consumers' co-ops in the U.S. Farmers and Scandinavians are great cooperators.

However the movement has shown a certain lack of imagination in appealing to the public. Also its non-political nature makes it too slow-going for those seriously interested in replacing capitalism. I remember how the head of the Russian consumer co-ops showed up in the U.S. not long after the Russian Revolution. I heard him speak in Boston. One of his proudest boasts was that the movement had functioned under both the Bolsheviks and Kolchak (one of the reactionary leaders who had invaded the S.U. and tried to upset the Communist-led government)!

Dr. James P. Warbasse was the leader of the cooperative movement in the U.S. After Cedric Long died, the Cooperative League of the U.S.A., under Dr. Warbasse's guidance, was looking

163

for a new secretary. The functions were chiefly educational and arbitrational, ironing out disputes between member organizations and promoting the movement with the public. Dr. Warbasse told me that I had been considered for the job but was passed over because I was considered insufficiently diplomatic.

The organization in Sunnyside held together, and when we left it had set up a green grocery, which also did not last; and a milk route, which did. Indeed the Sunnyside cooperative became a kind of consumer spokesman; Meyer Parodnek, a young lawyer who took my place on the board, went to Washington and appeared before the N.R.A., on behalf of consumers.

Labor and Steel was written under the auspices of the Labor Research Association, whose resources were put at my disposal for the collection of material. Volunteer workers went through the files of the *Iron Age* and some other periodicals looking for material with a labor angle. Anna Rochester was clipping the *Wall Street Journal* in connection with her big book *Rulers of America*, and she found data there. The LRA was working with the left-wing unions which were sponsored by the Trade Union Unity League, during the period (1928-34) when it was Party policy to set up (dual) left-wing unions. One of these unions was the Steel & Metal Workers Industrial Union, and we got to know John Meldon, the General Secretary of that union.

The steel companies seemed to be well informed about the doings of the union, and Johnnie finally became suspicious. He had had considerable correspondence with a man in Pittsburgh who said he had a group that was interested in the union, so John sent him the union constitution and even the constitution of the left-wing International Metalworkers Federation. But the man never gave a street address and all efforts to get him to present himself personally failed.

The Labor Research Association was appealed to and unleashed its private detective John Spivak, who went to Pittsburgh. The mystery man had a P.O. box number, and John S. was writing postcards in the P.O. when someone came to pick up the mail from that box. When the emissary went to the Carnegie Building and entered his office (which was unmarked), John S. was right behind him. He found himself in the headquarters of the U.S. Steel Corporation's spy system. A staff of clerks were methodically clipping and filing the items in the *Daily Worker* and other publications having to do with steel.

The head spy was rather startled at Jack's entry, but Jack had a press card from the Hearst press and said he was investigating the

164

explosion that had recently taken place in the post office at Easton, Pa., which had been attributed in the commercial press to Communists. The head spy eventually decided to put a good front on the situation and had Jack sit down and have a drink. They talked for a couple of hours. When Jack came away he had a picture of a Left-wing dinner, with code numbers over the leading functionaries. In the foreground was an elderly black man whose number was given with an "a" after it. The head spy would not tell him who that was. But when John Meldon saw it he recognized him immediately. He said the old man had a regular assignment (volunteer) to sell the *Daily Worker* on the street. He would come back to the union office and sit in the corner of the room counting his change and if there was a committee meeting going on he might get in on 1/2-hour of it.

John Meldon then recalled how a couple of young photographers had offered to photograph the national convention, which they did at little or no cost to the union. John and the others did not know that the photographers were in the pay of the companies.

Jack Spivak's data were conclusive proof of a point I had wanted to establish for *Labor and Steel*, namely the continued existence of the spy system which had been uncovered by the Interchurch World Movement in its report on the steel strike of 1919. In the hearings for the steel industry on setting up a code authority for steel under the NRA, John Meldon appeared for the Steel & Metal Workers Industrial Union and mentioned the spy system, but he did not have the material well enough in hand and the opportunity for a big press story was missed.

When I first started working 1/2-time for the Federated Press in the New York office, Harvey O'Connor had been in charge, and he and I developed a lifelong friendship, not lessened when he divorced his first wife and married Jessie Lloyd, who had been a favorite student of Nanie's when MR taught at Smith. But by 1933 Harvey was out of the FP office, which was being run by Frank Palmer. Frank had a personal feeling about Spies in Steel; had in fact written a booklet with that title dealing with the spy system in the iron range of northern Minnesota. He felt that an opportunity had been missed, and he went to Pittsburgh and invaded the spy office and came away with a story that made the daily capitalist press. After about a year a young left-wing journalist ran a story in the *Daily Worker* using Jack Spivak's material, including the picture with the numbers over the individuals. U.S. Steel was getting a bad press, and it is allergic to a bad press.

It announced that it was abolishing its spy system, and nobody believed it. But nothing has been heard of that system from that day to this. The company signed with the union after the big auto companies had been brought to terms and after the Little Steel companies (Republic, Jones & Laughlin) had fought and apparently won a bitter strike--but the National Labor Relations Board forced the companies to reinstate the men fired for union activity with back pay, and the steel industry, like the auto industry, became unionized.

What became of the file of radicals which the head spy had told Jack Spivak was more complete than any other except that of the Pinkerton Detective Agency? Nobody knows for sure; but the FBI, which had not even been in existence when the steel strike of 1919 took place, turned up later with a very complete file.

During the three years that we spent in New York while I was writing my thesis, I used to attend the meetings of the Teachers Union, local 6 of the American Federation of Teachers (AFT). I had kept up my membership and was considered eligible although I was not actually teaching. The witch hunt was already on, and the CP had a considerable following in local 6. The conservatives were led by the President, Henry R. Linville, and Abraham Lefkowitz, both of whom later became principals. A third faction was led by Bertram Wolfe and his floor leader, one Davidson. The three factions were fairly evenly balanced. The meetings of the union were a kind of forum where international issues were threshed out.

At a certain point the conservatives sought to amend the constitution so as to center more power in the executive. The attendance at the meeting where this issue was to come up was not the usual 30 or 40 but a couple of hundred, and the amendments were pushed through with the aid of unparliamentary rulings by the chairman. The conservatives moved to expel from the union Isidor Begun, a leader of the Left; and Prof. John Dewey, America's foremost philosopher, came down from Columbia to lead the attack. Two-thirds majority was required, and the motion just failed, although a majority did vote for expulsion. The authorities were gunning for Begun, and he was later dismissed from the public school system; Williana Burroughs, who had protested his treatment too vociferously, was also let go.

In the last local election in the union before we left for Brazil (1934) I ran for vice-president on the Left slate. I got more votes than anyone else on the slate, but none of us was elected. Later, in the period of the United Front, with the CP slate and the Wolfe-Davidson forces joined, the conservatives lost control of the local and withdrew, forming the Teachers' Guild. The Establishment's attack on the left-wing teachers intensified, and over a hundred were forced out of the system. The leadership of the AFT had always been sympathetic to the Teachers' Guild, and the Teachers' Union lost its charter, which was given to the Guild.

The condition of the coal-mining industry had got rapidly worse after the formation of the National Miners Union in 1928, and by 1931 the miners were feeling desperate. Harlan County, Kentucky, was a battleground, where union organizers were being kept out by a sheriff eager to do the coal companies' bidding. The CP organized a writers' committee including Sherwood Anderson and Waldo Frank among others, and they attempted to drive into Harlan County, but were turned back at the border, thus focusing public attention on the situation. Shortly afterward, the miners in Western Pennsylvania revolted and went on a hopeless strike under the leadership of the National Miners' Union. The CP rallied support for the strike, and a national campaign for funds was staged under the leadership of Alfred Wagenknecht. The Party also attempted to organize a writers' committee to invade Western Pennsylvania; the "committee" boiled down to Theodore Dreiser and HBD. We arrived in Pittsburgh at the same time.

Dreiser was well known in Pittsburgh, where he had spent some time as a young newspaperman. So, the papers ran special stories about him, and a reporter even got up and went out with him to the picket line, where a State policeman threatened to arrest Dreiser. "I don't think you will," said Dreiser, and he didn't. The energy of the man was incredible. It took most of the energy that I had to make it to the picket line (a different one) in time for the early morning shift. I will never forget the sight of that line in the early morning grayness, walking round in a circle at the mine entrance in what they knew by now was a hopeless cause. A Pittsburgh newspaperman was there and gave me the pitch. He pointed out the officers of the local one by one, going to work, breaking the strike, which collapsed soon after.

Yet it was only two years later, after the 1932 election, that John L. Lewis, using the credit of the United Mine Workers, took advantage of the new climate, borrowed money from the banks, and signed up the whole mining industry before the operators could catch their breath. From the UMW organizers were sent far and wide, into autos, into steel, into shoes among others, and the CIO was built in spite of the AFL in the mass-production and other industries.

XXI

Year in Brazil, 1933-34

After I got my degree at Columbia, I had planned to continue living in New York for a while, publish my study on the New York building trades, give a course at the New School for Social Research and work as fact-checker (or possibly co-editor) for the *Encyclopaedia of the Social Sciences* that was then in preparation under the direction of Alvin Johnson. Then on Sep.1 I got a call from the Brazilian consul in New York, a Mr. Sampaio, asking if I would be interested in going to São Paulo for a year to help launch an adult evening school, the Escola Livre de Sociologia e Politica de São Paulo. The faculty was to consist, at first, of me and a sociologist named Lowrie who had also just got his Ph.D. at Columbia. We would be leaving in two weeks! We talked it over and accepted.

The adult evening school was the brain child of Roberto Simonsen, a rich contractor of São Paulo. Brazilian political leadership had been shared for many years by three leading states of which São Paulo was one, with the presidency rotating among the three. São Paulo was the richest state by quite a margin, with its coffee production and a blossoming manufacturing industry, and when the rotation was broken and the presidency assumed by Getulio Vargas of Rio Grande do Sul, São Paulo felt left out. It even declared war on the central government. The war failed to develop; Vargas bought off the Paulistas, for that time, even assuming their war debts. But the Paulistas came to the realization that if they had taken over the conduct of Brazil's affairs, they did not have a corps of trained leaders to put in the top (and other) positions. So, the School of Sociology and Politics was to fill this gap. Simonsen, the school's "angel", had intellectual pretensions himself; he had written a couple of papers and conducted a small research project on the prevalence of venereal disease among his employees.

The prospect of learning Portuguese did not alarm me. I had a working knowledge of three other romance languages and could lecture in French while I was learning Portuguese. Lowrie, the sociologist, had more trouble with the language, but the translation had been arranged and presented no problem.

168

I might have stayed on for a while in Brazil, which the family loved. But I was put on the spot immediately and forced to declare my political position when instead of giving a course on Social Economy as I was presently to do, I was directed to give three lectures on each of three topics: the National Recovery Act (FDR reformism), Fascism, and Communism!

This was before the nature of the Stalin administration in Soviet Russia had become evident. The Soviet Union was apparently escaping the crisis that had developed in earnest in all the capitalist countries, and interest in Marxism was high--with good reason. My lectures left little doubt where I stood. They cost me a renewal of my contract. They were published in paper-back by a young immigrant lawyer in São Paulo, and had some sale. I heard afterwards that the vote on retaining me was divided. Simonsen did not vote, and the other directors of the school split four to three.

There was then no University of São Paulo, only a number of specialized schools (Law, Medicine, Engineering). The University was in the process of being organized while we were there, and the School of Sociology and Politics, although very modest in size, could and ordinarily would have been taken in as the social science department. But it was not. Its Marxist prof was still the talk of the town years later. My friend Melville Herskovitz, the anthropologist, visiting the city in 1946, found that "the repercussions were still repercussing."

I finished out the year, and in the spring conducted a research into the scale of living of São Paulo workers, which was published in the *Arquivo Municipal de São Paulo*; a summary, prepared by Nanie and me, appeared in the *Monthly Labor Review* of the U.S. Bureau of Labor Statistics. Lowrie, who did stay on, produced a couple of monographs under the auspices of the School of Sociology and Politics, which continued independently of the University, and the School developed into a recognized center of research in the Social Sciences--for a time it was considered the best one in South America, or so I was informed.

The school year at the School of Sociology and Politics ran from September to May as in the U.S., but the school year in Brazil coincided with the calendar year. So, Chan, who was 7 and had half a year of school in the U.S., had to wait three months before we could enroll him in a Brazilian school. He got hold of a Portuguese grammar and learned to read and write Portuguese. He made friends with the neighboring boys and in play with them learned to speak the language quite well. He also read *The Outline of Science* and understood a lot of it.

One of his friends was Paulo, whose father had been a railroad worker. The father was an ardent Communist and was out distributing leaflets one evening when the cops got wise to him. He threw the leaflets down the sewer, but the company heard about it and discharged him. He picked up work as a gardener. The family was sadly short of money, and when the children (there were six) got old enough they knew they would have to work. Chan's contemporary Paulo used to go to the market in a nearby town and shine shoes.

One day he was shining the shoes of an agent of the secret police and overheard him tell a friend that when he got through here he was going to the next town to raid a bookstore which was selling left-wing literature. Paulo succeeded in getting the word to the bookstore and when the raiders arrived the place was "clean," the subversive literature had been removed. The friend who had acted as intermediary for Paulo wanted to give him money, but Paulo refused. He said, "I also am a Communist."

As you have gathered, the Party was illegal in Brazil. Immigrant Party people were subject to deportation and all Party people were subject to arrest and torture.

The Party leaders did not know at first what to make of us. They had not approved the book, which did not toe the line exactly. They considered it "very bad." For some months we had no Party contacts except through Chan's friends. Then a young intellectual was assigned to interview me. He reported unfavorably: I was an "imperialist maneuver." Finally around Christmas time the American Party sent word that we were O.K. Thereafter when the Party needed money they used to hit us up. Also contributing to the Party treasury were the leading butter dealer and the leading coffee merchant. But operating under conditions of illegality, the Party was very severely hampered. It took a month for communications to get from Rio de Janeiro to São Paulo.

São Paulo was growing at a terrific rate. When we were there (1933-34) the population was pushing 1,000,000; forty years later it was over 6,000,000. The social services did not keep pace. The health services were a case in point.

One day I was out in an auto with a party which included the very clever wife of one of my academic friends. We passed a medical school, a hospital, and a graveyard, all under the same management. She remarked that this was an example of the vertical integration of an industry. The last stage was no joke, even a grim one, to our neighbors the workers. They did what they could to avoid going to the hospital, which was so overcrowded that the patients were put in cots three high. One had to pay the nurses to get attention.

Walking in the street one day I saw a woman who was having difficulty stepping up from the street to the curb. Was she on the way to the hospital? No, she said, she had just come from the hospital, which did not have room to keep her. She was supposed to take the bus to the suburb where she lived. Another woman who lived in a distant part of the city could not even take the bus. She walked home and died two days later.

Yet there was a big building, the Institute of Health, built with Rockefeller money to carry on research. Nobody questioned the need for health research. But Rockefeller had not provided funds to carry on the research. That was good fortune for me in a way. The director, who was a very decent sort, was interested in my study and helped compile the data in the nearly empty Institute rooms.

The director had had a corps of health educators whose job had been to go into the neighborhoods and show people how to live according to ordinary rules of sanitation. This service had been abolished. Again, that was my good fortune. The Sanitary Educators were out of a job, and two of them fitted perfectly into my plans for collection of data on living scales.

If the health services were chaotic, so were the economic institutions. The Brazilian government had been buying "surplus" coffee for years, which of course tended to keep the price up so that still more coffee was produced. When the depression hit, the government was left with a huge stock of unsalable coffee on hand. They tried dumping it at sea, but the "dumped" coffee had a way of reappearing on the market. So, they had to burn it. Ovens were set up all along the Tiete River. For that whole year, the smell of burning coffee was never out of our nostrils. No wonder people were interested in the Russian economic system.

One who had become interested even before the depression was Luis Carlos Prestes, who as a lieutenant in the army had led a revolt of the minor officers against the firmly entrenched big brass. He was warmly welcomed in the back country, where the peasants saw in him a spokesman for their long-smoldering grievances. For two years he and his followers marched back and forth in the interior, never able to challenge the regular army in a showdown, but keeping alive the spirit of popular revolt. He was the "Knight of Hope." When he was finally forced across the border into Bolivia, he made his way to the Soviet Union, and came back a convinced Communist.

He had much popular following but it was unorganized, and people did not join the Communist Party in great numbers, especially in view of the illegality. The Party was always afraid that Prestes would try to cash in on his popularity and stage a coup; this philosophy of the coup was even called Prestismo. They had Prestes himself writing pamphlets against Prestismo. Finally, after we had returned to the U.S., the Party changed its position and tried to stage a coup, which was immediately defeated.

At Christmas time, when it was still thought that we might be in Brazil for some time, it was arranged that Lowrie and I should go to Piracicaba, a town in the interior, in the coffee-raising area; and Nanie was added to the party. We had an interesting three days visiting coffee plantations and talking to the people. One day on the street the folks were telling me about a Southerner from the U.S. who had come with a group after the Civil War, had settled and raised a family. Somebody said, "Here he comes now." And here he was, a scion of the old South, still able to get around and still speaking with his distinctive Southern accent. Only he didn't know the English words for all the things he wanted to say. "My son-in-law's a *chefe*--don't know what you call it in English--". The original group had become dispersed and by now were pretty well absorbed.

It was Faith Williams, a member of our old "gang" in New York and now working for the Bureau of Labor Statistics, who arranged the publication of our summary article in the *Monthly Labor Review*. Another member of the gang, Mildred Wertheimer ("Wert"), was now working for the Foreign Policy Association, and she arranged for me to write a research report on Brazil. I wrote it on the boat coming back to the U.S., finishing at 2:45 A.M. the day before docking.

To anticipate a little, it sat in the office of the F.P.A. all fall, then was sent to me in Bradford, Mass. (where I had gone to work in a junior college), with various suggestions for change. I made the changes the same afternoon and got the revision in the mail actually the same day. I was called the most cooperative writer they had ever had. The study appeared under the title *"Brazil's Political and Economic Problems"*.

What I had not realized was the way those studies were passed around for comment before publication. The State Department had seen it, and had passed it to the Brazilian Ambassador. He objected to Brazil being described as a country two-thirds of whose people lived on the land (although they did). Brazil, he said, was a modern industrial country, blah, blah, blah. He informed the State Department that I was a Communist.

The manuscript was also shown to the National City Bank, although I was not supposed to know this. The bank objected mildly to a passage dealing with banks, which however remained as I had written it. The Foreign Policy Association, nominally an independent research body, was actually part of the Establishment.

In 1935, after we had returned to the U.S., the Brazilian president Getulio Vargas staged a coup, allegedly to forestall a right-wing coup by the Fascists, who had some organization in Brazil at the time. Prestes, under whose leadership the Party had attempted a coup of its own, was discovered and arrested and nobody knew what had happened to him, or to the other left-wing prisoners.

Feeling the need for some foreign support for the Brazilian Left, we worked up a committee to protest the dictatorial rule. The Socialists were asked to join but absolutely refused to have anything to do with us. The committee was formed anyway, and was called the Joint Committee although in the end it was just the Party sympathizers; but these made a fairly impressive list.

Nanie wanted a more active political life and with her mother "Mata" in residence, she could and did take a leave for a month. She went to New York and ran the Committee with the aid of a woman comrade who was assigned to help with the work. We (they) got out a news letter which was sent to a list of sympathizers. The big effort came in organizing a delegation to the Brazilian Ambassador in Washington, and another to Brazil. The envoys to Brazil were Rockwell Kent, the artist who had just been in the news for a stand he had taken for Latin American freedom in a different connection; and Jerome Davis. The latter had been on the faculty of the Yale Divinity School, from which he was fired at just about this time. He was a well known Socialist and had been elected President of the American Federation of Teachers with Left-wing support.

The two went to Brazil and made inquiries about the treatment of the political prisoners. They did not get to see Prestes, perhaps because they did not ask to, but their visit did not go unnoticed; visits by high-level Americans, even from the Left Wing, commonly cause a considerable commotion. They came back and spoke at a mass meeting in Boston, which was well attended.

The envoys wrote up their findings, but Rockwell Kent's was too long and diffuse, and he objected so strongly to cutting it down that in the end nothing could be published. The money was not adequate anyway, and the Committee folded soon after.

XXII

Politics Split Families

Nanie's parents were liberals: they liked to say they were "middle-of-the-road." Nanie's father ("Pitar") ran a furniture business, including the manufacture of selected articles. This was skilled work, and the men in the shop were organized: Pitar dealt with the union, even though his business associates tried to get him into the "open shop" camp. He resisted such attempts, and he and Mata rejoiced when the striking truckers in their turn resisted a furious onslaught by the police (the "Battle of Deputy Run", which made labor history).

Pitar's business failed in 1928; he died in 1934. Mata came to live with us, and we began to ask her which road she was in the middle of. She saw the point, and eventually came to see things our way. She was in constant correspondence with her sister Alice, whose husband Arthur Hosking was a conservative. Aunt Alice was essentially non-political, but she carried on a running argument with Mata until they died. They never broke off personal relations, and Nanie continued to see their children (her cousins) though only at long intervals.

Nanie's brother David was sympathetic to the Left, and continued to put us up on our auto trips from Kansas City to Sandwich, only specifying that if we were being pursued by the police we should not stop with them. But brother Ralph was a conservative and bitterly resented Nanie's politics, which he thought might jeopardize his career as an engineer (guilt by association was not rare in the Nixon period). So, after a period when we had visits from Kay and the children at Sandwich, relations were broken off completely.

My brother Hal had been a liberal in college, opposing the First World War actively before the U.S. got in; then dropped politics for many years. He lived in St. Louis, and became increasingly embarrassed when we stopped with him on our way east. Finally he wrote a letter saying that the visits were at an end. He wanted to do a piece of research on problems of hearing in the armed forces, and thought he had to get security clearance. As it turned out, he did not need that, but he did the research and then did not resume relations with us.

His position at the Central Institute for the Deaf and Washington University were not endangered, but he was after bigger game: he hoped to get a Nobel prize some day. Actually he never did, but he was recognized as a top scientist and would have been if he had continued to see us. He never apologized and seemed to think that we would forget how he had acted. We didn't. But much later, at the urging of sister Sal, I did attend his 90th birthday celebration.

My mother's brothers and sisters and their respective spouses ran the gamut from conservative Republican to liberal Republican(?!), with a good admixture of non-politicals like Aunt Sue. Uncle Pen was far right, as noted. But his two oldest children, Mary (Crocker) and Hannah (Bigelow) both contributed to the MDSF, Mary on a regular basis. Uncle Jack was a Hoover Republican.

Aunt Rebecca was strongly anti-Communist, but her husband, my Uncle Bob, was broad-minded, and they put us up two nights a week when we were living in Bradford and teaching at Simmons, in 1936-37. Uncle Arthur Morse was very conservative, but his wife, Aunt Esther, was both smart and sophisticated. I gave her Albert Kahn's "The Great Conspiracy Against Russia", and she read it and said she agreed with every word! Uncle Arthur's brother Tom Morse, a private school principal, had married a girl who was one of my social set when I was growing up. She turned out to be a poetess and quite a radical. Uncle Lawrence Brooks was a liberal Republican, or so he said, and we had to take his word that there was such a species. So, we had no solid phalanx of opposition in the family, and maintained good relations with the Hallowells all the way through, avoiding confrontations.

But the relations with my father's sisters could not be kept up, as noted earlier.

XXIII

Bradford Junior College, 1934-36
(Look for Trouble, Find It)

Talking over the telephone is not generally considered the best way to get a job. Yet the fact is that I got two jobs on the basis of telephone conversations (and other things of course), and the first was a conversation not with me but with my father. I was in Brazil at the time but my record was on file with a teachers' employment agency and the principal of Bradford Junior College had seen it and was duly impressed. But since she was an aristocrat catering to the daughters of aristocrats, she wanted to know whether I was a gentleman. She was put in touch with my father by telephone, and since he was so obviously a gentleman I got the job--a three-year contract.

Bradford is part of Haverhill, an old shoe town which formerly had a powerful union and a class-conscious working class--at least enough to have elected a Socialist mayor around 1900. But like the other shoe towns Lynn and Brockton, Haverhill had been ruined by the migration of the industry caused by the higher union wage, or rather by the inability of the union to penetrate the small towns. Shoe manufacturers work largely with machines rented from the United Shoe Machinery Corporation, and it does not take much capital to start a factory, especially in the women's branch of the industry where fashions are always changing and mass production is hard to develop. So it was common for a manufacturer to move into some nonunion town, often quite nearby, and cut his costs that way.

There were still factories in Haverhill when we got there in 1934, but although the workers had a union they were demoralized. At a time when there was a real swing to the left in the working class (and in the country as a whole) the Party member who undertook to sell the *Daily Worker* at the plant gates met with a rather poor reception. The district organizer said this was the only city on his beat to make such a report.

Bradford Junior College called itself a pioneer in the higher education of women. In the days before women went to college, it had trained up the daughters of the aristocracy from all over the country. Along with Abbott Academy in Andover, it had high standards, which however were not altogether maintained when it

177

became a junior college. William Allen Neilson, the president of Smith, wondered why they had to change a first-rate academy into a second-rate junior college. The president of Bradford thought that was a great joke.

Pitar had died when we were in Brazil; Mata came to live with us, arriving at the beginning of our stay in Bradford. She fitted in well with the family--no mother-in-law traditional role.

Chan and Barbara went off to school and immediately Chan was in deep trouble. He was put in a class that corresponded to his age and he found it uninteresting. He began acting up, as he had done to some extent in his schools in Brazil. The principal lectured him, saying the same thing three times, and at the third time Chan hit him. As Nanie put it, Chan discovered, by trying it, that you can't sock the principal with impunity. He was sent home, and lectured also by his father. He was moved up a class, found the work more interesting, and settled down. Barbara put on glasses at this time. She had not been in school before and we hadn't realized how nearsighted she was. Mina was four years old but was able to have an argument about religion with her neighbor and best friend, who was a loyal Catholic and went home crying.

My book *Labor and Steel* had come out while we were in Brazil. I was summoned to Washington, by my friends, to go on the radio as an expert on the industry (this was before the days of TV). The principal had no objections. I doubt if she tuned in. The family of course did, and Mina was mystified. She recognized the voice but said. "I can't see his face." I said that the U.S. Steel Corporation would "break a lance" before it would see its plants organized by the unions. I had no idea at all that U.S. Steel would sign without a strike, after the unions penetrated the auto and rubber industries.

We got to know a pair of Party members in Amesbury, the next town to Haverhill. They had been spotted as radicals, and were socially ostracized. Haverhill had its Communists too, and they operated more or less openly as such. The Party leader was Joe Figuereido, of Portuguese extraction; while we were there he went for training in the S.U. He told the shoe workers like Alfred Porro and Marino Brandolini what to do, and since they trusted his leadership they did their best to carry out his suggestions. We struck up a friendship with him and his wife Eula, and with Marino, who had a boy Chan's age, and Porro, and comrades Rose and Sam Cristofaro.

There were also Fascist sympathizers in town, and it might have been thought that the (proto-)Fascists and the Communists would be at each others' throats. But Porro, soliciting funds for the *Daily Worker*, was able to hit up the Right-wing leader for a quarter. He himself also contributed a quarter to the organization of the rightists!

A problem that deviled the Communist movement all through the 1930's (and before and after) was whether to come out openly with the whole Marxist paraphernalia--which of course would have to include opposition to the (capitalist) government--or to lay low, deny Party membership, and try to participate in organizations whose aims the Communists shared, even though they did not involve full acceptance of the Communist philosophy.

Enemies of the Party sought to get at it by laws requiring teachers to take a pledge of allegiance to the U.S. Government and Massachusetts actually adopted such a law in the early 1930's. The result was not what was intended. Communists took the oath. But some religious sects, and certain non-religious bodies like the ACLU were opposed to such pledges on the ground that they interfered with freedom of conscience and with the whole idea of freedom of speech. For what good is the "right" to express oneself on a political issue if the immediate result is that he is fired from his job?

A group on the faculty at Harvard Divinity School objected on religious grounds to taking the oath. Among them was Henry Cadbury, who had been fired from the faculty of Haverford College for opposing the First World War.

Henry Cadbury and his group went to the State House and explained that they wished the government of the United States well but had moral scruples against oaths like this one, and surprisingly they were excused, although this was a deep secret. But a Quaker by the name of E.M. Winslow, teaching in an up-state Massachusetts college, refused absolutely to take the oath and was fired from his job.

There was some stir about the Winslow case and he found people rallying to his support--enough so that he later ran for Congress (unsuccessfully of course). He was invited to come to Haverhill and debate a State Senator by the name of McCarthy (no relation to Joe). The debate was duly held, and attracted quite a crowd. In the question period a blow-hard minister named Bozarth tried to put Winslow on the spot (as if he had not already been pilloried enough) and called on him to take the oath of allegiance to the flag. Winslow politely refused.

McCarthy might have frothed at the mouth, but he wasn't playing it that way. There was no question where he stood on the issue between Fascism and Communism; he was for Fascism (he was announced a little later as giving a course of lectures on German and Italian nationalism). But he didn't rant at Winslow; he just said, "Well, the professor doesn't choose to salute the flag. For me, when I see the flag, my hand just naturally goes up." He was so mild that you couldn't be mad at him.

I took the oath, partly because that was the Party line and partly because it was a rather innocuous oath anyway. Later the attempt to pry into peoples' politics became intolerable, and both Chan and I lost our respective jobs on that issue, but that's another story.

The Party line changed actually while we were in Haverhill. Eula was active in her union and had some following when she refused to salute the flag soon after we got there, in 1934. But a little later when a delegation organized by the Party went to City Hall to protest some restrictive measure, the proceedings were interrupted when someone asked that they take the oath of allegiance to the flag. They took it in chorus. The oath ends "-- with liberty and justice for all", and the group repeated the words "FOR ALL." The heresy-hunters were discomfited.

There was one occasion when the liberals and radicals had clubbed together to present a petition against some local repression. We took the petition around to various ministers and professionals, and a good many of them signed, but not the local leader of the ACLU. This did not surprise me after our Memphis experience with the ACLU, but it shocked some of the local liberals.

The local paper, the *Haverhill Gazette*, was not any more progressive than it had to be, but it did run an open correspondence column, and a certain amount of political education took place thru this medium. One of our friends, a young radical who had been studying Marx, used to write in his ideas, and they were published, with sarcastic headlines supplied by the paper: "How Simple Things Are to Youth", etc. The lad, Clint, could not get a job in Haverhill and had to leave town. Marino was also unemployed, and Porro, who had been business agent of his local, had to do carpentering for a living. The Party group had little activity. There were about a dozen of them. The Jimmy Higginses sold the *Daily Worker* on the street corner and that was about it (Jimmie Higgins was a character in one of Upton Sinclair's novels--a left-winger who did the routine Party work loyally and without complaining).

Nanie was a natural born politician, with an eye for what was possible. She joined the P.T.A. in Bradford, and when the time came for the annual school appropriation she got the P.T.A. to pass a resolution specifying that the school budget should not be cut. This was the only expression of opinion that the politicians had to go by, and the appropriation was maintained.

I did not sell the *Daily Worker* on the street corner, but a group of us did go to Amesbury, selling pamphlets attacking the Fascist-minded priest Father Coughlin. And there I made a big mistake. I asked a man if he would buy a pamphlet on Father Coughlin, and he did. It turned out that he was a Coughlin sympathizer, and he reported us to the police, who picked us up. My companion at the time had the wit to give an assumed name, but I thought they might look at my auto license and chose to give my own name, which got in the papers and caused a major scandal. I was investigated by a member of the board of Bradford Junior College.

I rode that one out. But a little later the Party decided to throw a birthday party for Mother Bloor in the municipal auditorium, which had been used by the Republicans and Democrats, so why not by the C.P.? The Mayor and Council refused, but they did hold a hearing on the subject. Dale Mitchell of the college faculty went down with me. The American Legion was not active politically, but the Veterans of Foreign Wars were there with little American flags. The case for refusing the hall to the C.P. was so weak that first Dale and then I told the Council off. Dale was given a 3-hour lecture by the head of the college, and I was fired although my contract had another year to run. Eventually they did pay me half a year's salary. I might have been able to get a whole year's pay if I had pushed for it, but by that time Simmons College had offered jobs to both Nanie and me, and we did not fully understand our rights.

The municipal auditorium was not made available to the C.P. But the incident had evidently shaken the Council, which decided to break up the hall into offices.

I had barely started looking for another job when an offer came from Simmons College. The head of the economics department, Sara Stites, was a liberal who had heard of my activities in the Harvard Student Liberal Club, and approved of them. Needless to say I was amazed.

Bancroft Beatley, the President of Simmons, had pretensions as a liberal, and he came all the way to Haverhill to close the deal. A little later that spring Simmons needed a teacher of statistics, and I suggested Nanie for the (part time) job, which she got. It was arranged that we would continue living in Bradford and we would commute, Nanie being away from home three days and HBD five. We got Uncle Bob and Aunt Rebecca to put us up, which was quite a thing for them to do as Aunt Rebecca was just as bitter against Communism as anybody.

My shift from Bradford to Simmons was not especially announced, but the Boston Post heard of it and ran a story with the headline, "Attacked as Red, Quits College."

XXIV

The Sacco and Vanzetti Case

The anarchists Nicola Sacco and Bartolomeo Vanzetti had been convicted in 1921 of a payroll murder in South Braintree and were in prison while attempts were made to appeal the case. Actually the appeals were made, but all that the higher courts did was to pass on the question whether legal forms were observed, and apparently they had been. No court other than the original one, presided over by Judge Thayer, ever passed on the merits of the case. So, various new angles could not be brought up for judicial review. There was, for instance, the matter of the testimony of the ballistic experts, who were called in to pass on the question whether the murder bullet was fired, or could have been fired, from Sacco's gun.

I had a personal feeling about this one, because the half day of the trial that I attended, in Dedham in 1921, had been devoted to this question. It will be recalled that the state and the defense each presented two witnesses, who split as expected; the state witnesses van Ambergh and Proctor testifying positively and the defense witnesses negatively, or so it was made to appear. Later, after the convictions, Proctor said privately that he had not seen anything to make him think that the bullet had come from Sacco's gun, as van Ambergh, a man whose testimony was apparently for sale to the highest bidder, had tried to convince him. Proctor did not want to be in the position of letting down his employers (the State), so an answer was cooked up which seemed to endorse van Ambergh's position but without actually saying so.

It must be admitted that the defense did not press him to clarify his rather ambiguous answer. If they had succeeded in eliciting his real opinion, that would have made three experts to one against the state's position, and the prosecution would have had to abandon that line of argument.

In the period after Sacco and Vanzetti had been found guilty of the payroll murders and sentenced to die in the electric chair, the defense team had not been idle. They had not only given to the public the true story of the views of the ballistic expert Proctor, they had got two of the witnesses for the prosecution to repudiate their testimony implicating Sacco and Vanzetti in the crime (they later repudiated the repudiations). So, as the date for the execution approached, pressure had built up for executive clemency to the point where Governor Alvan T. Fuller felt the need of some additional backing for allowing the execution to take place. He appointed a committee of three--ex-Judge Grant and the presidents of Harvard and MIT--to evaluate the evidence, including that which had surfaced since the trial, and make a recommendation to him. It was thought that Judge Grant would take the lead in this committee, but President Lowell of Harvard quickly assumed the leadership, and the report of the committee became known as the Lowell Report.

President Lowell confided to Achim Friedrich, a special friend of his, his motives for taking his appointment seriously. We had known Achim Friedrich from way back, and he told my mother what Lowell had said to him. He said that he would try to bring in a report that would give the people of Massachusetts confidence in their courts of law. In other words, he was not exactly impartial, and this of course was shown by his conduct at the hearings. The net result of his thoroughly dishonest position was not that the people of Massachusetts came to have more confidence in the courts but that they came to have less confidence in him. In any case, the Lowell Report in effect summed up the case for the prosecution.

Felix Frankfurter, while he was still a Professor at the Harvard Law School, had written at Mrs. Evan's instance a little book on the case. He had concluded that the men were innocent. In my Labor class at Simmons, I later had the girls read the Lowell Report and Frankfurter's little book and make up their own minds about the guilt or innocence of the accused. Almost all of them sided with Frankfurter.

Certain liberals helped the defense in various ways. The defense was always headed by the anarchists, the group to which Sacco and Vanzetti belonged. They imported lawyer Fred Moore from Los Angeles, but this was not a happy selection. Not only did he antagonize Judge Thayer, but Sacco disagreed strongly with his idea of the way to conduct the defense. Moore left the defense team in 1924, and later certain liberal lawyers volunteered their services. Sacco at a certain point became paranoic; he thought that poison gases were being wafted into his cell, and the food was suspect. The anarchists would not help him; they said he was the responsibility of the government which had locked him up. It was the liberal committee which got a judge to intervene and have Sacco transferred to a hospital, where he recovered. Some of the liberal women gave English lessons to the men and struck up a warm friendship with them. Mrs. Evans befriended Mrs. Sacco. My mother was treasurer of a committee which raised money for the defense.

Sacco and Vanzetti would probably not have been executed in a country like France with its militant labor movement. In 1927 Nanie and I were in Paris, and on the Sunday before the execution, we saw 150,000 demonstrators in the Bois de Vincennes marching arm in arm and chanting "Vive Sacco--Vanzetti." They were not voters in the U.S. When the execution actually took place, the *Humanité* gave the whole front page to it.

Pressure of another kind, from the right, was exerted on a fair-minded lawyer, one Thompson, who had come forward to aid the defense in its legal moves in the period from 1921 to 1927. The pressure finally became so strong that Thompson was unable to take it any longer, and asked my uncle Lawrence Brooks to take over. Uncle Lawrence had not followed the case as my parents had done. He believed that the men were innocent, but at the time was fighting a battle with arthritis (a battle which fortunately he won) and begged off for reasons of health. As it happened, the governor, who could have pardoned the men or commuted their sentences, was a member of the same political grouping as Uncle Lawrence and might have paid more attention to the arguments of the defense if they had come from a sympathetic source. As it was, the position he took was not exactly sympathetic--quite the reverse. He told the defense they had to present something in writing to back up their contentions.

Vanzetti had been convicted of an attempted holdup that had taken place in Bridgewater on Dec. 21, the year before the South Braintree murders. He said that he had been on his usual route selling fish on the South Shore. He remembered the day because his Italian customers had been buying eels; it was customary for them to eat eels on Christmas. The Bridgewater holdup was not directly related to the payroll murders, but the credibility of Vanzetti and his alibi witnesses was involved. Art Shields was part of a group who set out to prove that the eel story was not just imagination. He tells the tale in the second volume of his autobiography, which appeared in 1984. The group examined the stubs of bills of sale of fish dealers in Boston and sure enough, there it was: a barrel of eels had been shipped to "B. Vanzetti" just before Dec. 24 of the year in question. The governor still would not pardon the men or even commute their sentences.

Later, quite early in the administration of President Franklin D. Roosevelt, the Writers Project of the Works Progress

Administration was producing a series of tourist guides, one for each state, and the editors of the Massachusetts guide, which was in preparation when we were at Bradford, turned out to be good leftists: Joseph Gaer and Merle Colby. (Nanie, working in her quiet way, had had Merle Colby in to Bradford as a speaker for the P.T.A.) These editors were stumped over how best to handle the Sacco-Vanzetti case, which they had decided to feature in one of the introductory paragraphs. They appealed to me and I produced the crucial wording, which ran like this: "It was believed by many that although legal forms were observed, the key to the case lay in the political views of the defendants."

This was the wording adopted, and the *Guide* was duly published. The general editor of the *Guide* series came up from Washington and presented a copy of the *Guide* to Governor Hurley in a ceremony to which the press was invited. But when people began to dip into the *Guide*, the sentence about Sacco and Vanzetti met their collective eye. The American Legion complained to the Governor, and by evening he had disowned the *Guide*! The furor attracted national attention. The *New Republic* reprinted the offending sentence, inquiring "What's wrong with that?" It was just not possible to excise the sentence, so they had to let it ride.

Later fictional treatments of the case, especially *Winterset*, play and movie, by Maxwell Anderson, gave a lot of people the impression that the judge had qualms of conscience after the event. Actually Judge Thayer was rather proud of what he had done, as indicated by his remark to a Dartmouth professor, "Did you see what I did to those anarchist bastards?"

1936 was the year of Harvard's tercentenary (1636-1936) and the University took the occasion to stage a celebration, with visitors invited from abroad. Martha Gruening got the idea that this would be a good time to revive the memory of Sacco and Vanzetti, pointing out the role that had been played by Harvard's president A. Lawrence Lowell in doing them to death. So a brochure was written and printed and circulated at the tercentary celebrations, under the title *"Walled in This Tomb."* It was signed by a number of liberal (and radical) Harvard graduates, including Roger Baldwin, Ernest Gruening, Horace A. Davis, Horace B. Davis, and Granville Hicks. Granville Hicks and I entered a kind of minority report on the actions of the Lowell Committee, which had reviewed the evidence and concluded that the men were guilty. We said that the actions of Lowell & Co. were not to be considered personal aberrations of those men, but were the natural,

186

if gruesome, reactions of members of their social class and standing.

As we have seen, the case was internationally known, and in the course of time a movie about the case was produced in Italy and shown in the United States. I went, with my daughter Quentin and her then husband John Bassett. I explained the case to them, and a young man sitting behind us took careful note of my remarks. As we came out of the theater he introduced himself--Sacco's grandson. After the executions, Rose Sacco, Sacco's widow, had remarried and moved to Portland, Oregon. The anarchist tradition in the family had died out. The lad we met was studying religious music: "My grandfather would not have liked that." But just at this time the Massachusetts General Court adopted a resolution to the effect that at the time of the Sacco-Vanzetti case public opinion in the State was so inflamed as to make a fair trial all but impossible. Sacco's grandson was on hand to receive a copy of the resolution.

The case refuses to die. I fully expect to live to see a tablet in the two men's memory erected on Boston Common!

As I write this, a book has just been published on the relations between Brandeis as a Supreme Court Justice and Frankfurter as a professor at Harvard Law School. Frankfurter went to bat for Brandeis's ideas. One of the reasons given for disqualifying Abe Fortas from continuing membership on the Supreme Court was that he had advised the President on current political matters while he was on the Court. I never thought that that was fair; Supreme Court Justices should take an active interest in current political affairs, and should disqualify themselves from ruling on a case only when they have been actually connected with that particular case. Brandeis's last minute refusal to halt the execution of Sacco and Vanzetti was due to his over-strict interpretation of that canon. His family had befriended Mrs. Sacco and the Justice himself certainly had an opinion on the case. With the conservatives against them anyway and the liberals on the court refusing to intervene, Sacco and Vanzetti were doomed (just why the liberal Justice Douglas voted against review of the case I don't pretend to know).

XXV

The Communist Party in the 1930's: Boston

Nanie and I had no idea at all of helping in the formation of Party policy, which as already noted was imported from Moscow anyway. Nanie was like Grace Hutchins, defending Party policy even when she didn't necessarily agree with it.

I wrote a few articles for the Party press, under assumed names. One arose out of *Labor and Steel,* and was published in *The Communist,* and was entitled *"Political Connections of the International Armament Firms."* by Jan Reling. Around 1937 I did a piece on the depression and its causes, which appeared in *The New Masses* with Lowell E. Willis as the author. I also wrote a few pages in criticism of the slogan "the sit-down strike of capital", the slogan used by the Party to explain the recession-within-the-depression in 1937. I said that that implied that the capitalists could have kept recovery going if they had so opted. I thought they were compelled by the (il)logic of the system itself to do what they did. This contribution to the convention discussion was turned over to the district leader (Phil Frankfeld) for submission to the national office, but no notice was taken of it.

The fact was that all through the 'twenties and early 'thirties I had been getting my theories corrected by people who were better informed on Marxist theory than I was, so that when I adopted Marxism I was still trailing along some semi-discarded liberal ideas. But I did fail completely to go along with certain Party policies, such as self-determination for the Black Belt.

The theoretical articles in the Party's organs consisted largely of attacks on "bourgeois" economists, bolstered with quotations from Lenin and Marx. I could not do this kind of thing. At the same time we were content to follow the SU's political line, even when that involved the slaughter of so many Soviet functionaries--with their apparent consent! Our friend Ben Alper read the proceedings of the trial of Bukharin, Radek and co. in 1937 and found it convincing; the case against the three had been "proved". Also, they had confessed.

During this period some were following the lead of Trotsky; A.J. Muste became a Trotskyite. I could never become enthusiastic about Trotsky's theoretical work. Several liberals whose judgment I respected visited the SU and came back with glowing reports of

188

economic progress while not caring to inquire into the reasons for all the shootings. We did not have any idea of the extent of the shootings. Harry Ward, Colston Warne, and the *New York Times* Moscow correspondent Walter Duranty misled a lot of people about what was going on. We did not think that Stalin was above criticism, but his critics were mostly against the revolution anyway, and we did not feel called on to add to the reactionary chorus. Also, the Party leadership (Browder, Foster *et al.*, who must have known what was happening) had no doubts and failed to keep the membership abreast of events. I later got very bitter about their silence. And I regretted that we did not insist on a more open discussion of the purges. Others who took the criticisms seriously reacted by dropping out of the Party. The turnover was very high all through the 'thirties, for this and other reasons.

The Party participated actively in the great unionization drive of the 1930's, and had the leadership of several important unions. The members often thought of the Communists as union leaders without even realizing that they had a political program; the Party did not especially push the candidacy of its nominees but advised the unionists and the public which of the old-party candidates to vote for. The story was told of a member of the New York Transit Workers union who was all for the Communists--in the union. But he came to work wearing a Lemke button (in 1936, when the Party was advising that Roosevelt be reelected "at all costs"). When the Party people remonstrated with him, he said, "In the union, yes, I'm a Communist, but me politics is me own affair."

In Boston a grafter by the name of Curley had been elected mayor of Boston, then reelected, and had served a term in Congress. At one time he had played up to the Fascists. So, we were not a little shocked when Otis Hood, speaking for the Communists at Simmons on a panel with three other speakers from different parties, made a case for voting for Curley for governor. I did not go to all-city Party meetings very often, but I did show up at the next one to protest about supporting Curley. Phil Frankfeld the District Organizer defended Otis Hood's speech, which he had not heard. Curley was a Democrat and was thought to be a little more progressive than the Republican candidate.

Somehow word of this exchange got back to New York, and a representative of the national office came to town and gave Frankfeld a dressing down. Frankfeld apologized to me and said that if he and the top officers were arrested, which they always considered as a possibility, I was to take over the leadership of the district! Of course, it didn't come to that.

At this time (the mid-'thirties) the Party was a factor politically. Otis Hood ran for the Boston School Committee on the Communist ticket and made a good showing. In New York Communists Ben Davis and Pete Cacchione were elected to the City Council. There were no Communists in Congress but the Party's program was presented by Vito Marcantonio of the American Labor Party.

It is hard today (1990) to picture how completely the institutions of liberal democracy had been discredited by the middle 'thirties. The liberal economists had failed absolutely to predict the depression (called the "crisis" by Marxists), and the whole system of democracy was tottering; it had not been able to survive the Fascist onslaught in Italy or Germany. The need for a change was so evident that in Germany people could say, "If I wasn't a Nazi I would be a Communist," and vice versa.

Marx was finally recognized in the U.S. as a great thinker; it was almost respectable to be a Marxist. But here a difficulty arose. To be a Marxist meant to be a revolutionary. Lenin, whose writings were taken as gospel, was a revolutionary with all that that implied. To be sure, the situation with which Lenin had had to contend was a very different one; he had no choice but to work underground, because the authorities were after him; he even had to live abroad. He could not work within the system but was committed to overthrowing it. The image of the Party, which the old-line parties sedulously cultivated, was thus that of a conspiratorial organization which did not recognize the ordinary canons of morality. It was fashionable in the Party to scoff at bourgeois morality. Lying was a policy of the Party, when it came to questions like affirming or denying Party membership. So, people had some basis for saying that Communists could not be trusted. They of course overlooked the fundamental dishonesty in the system itself, and the way in which the 'acquisitive interest' treated the Communists.

The Party in the '20s and early 'thirties had cultivated its revolutionary image. Before being taken into the Party a candidate had to undergo a searching examination to make sure that he was not a liberal. I myself was refused admission at the time of my first application, even though Nanie was already in the Party.

But by 1935 the Party, which had earlier rebuffed all attempts to come to an understanding with the Social Democrats (in the U.S., the Socialist Party), was seeking to make a "united front" with practically everybody to stave off the Fascists. The bars were let down. By the end of the 1930's, the Party was soliciting memberships on a door-to-door basis.

Not that that made it safe to be a Party member. On the contrary. The FBI under J. Edgar Hoover made a policy of going to the employer of a suspected Communist and trying to get him fired. The Committee on UnAmerican Activities of the U.S. House of Representatives was set up in 1938 under the chairmanship of Martin Dies of Texas, and used to conduct hearings with the object of fingering known or suspected radicals and causing them to lose their jobs. (There had been earlier committees like the Dies Committee: the Lusk Committee in New York just after the First World War, for instance, and a House Committee around 1930 chaired by Rep. Hamilton Fish; the Fish Committee got hold of a letter from Nanie and published it, so that she was spotted very early) It was the Committee on UnAmerican Activities that got Chan's job, and a sister committee of the U.S. Senate, chaired by Senator Jenner of Indiana, did a similar job on me.

The atmosphere of terror which was created by the activities of the FBI (and later the Dies Committee and the Jenner Committee) can be imagined. The FBI would come around and engage known radicals (and liberals) in conversation, and try to get them to name their associates in radical (and liberal) causes who could then also be persecuted. I used to tell the people I knew that they didn't have to talk to the F.B.I., but many did anyway. One time I was visiting New York and stopped in on my friend Lillian Arnold, who was in the theater world as job-getter for actors (and actresses). She was friendly with a journalist in the rear apartment by the name of Tabitha Petran, who used to write for the *National Guardian*, as it was then called. Lillian had made a date to take me to the theater (she had more complimentary tickets than she could use). One evening there was a knock on her door; it was the F.B.I. They wanted to talk to Lil about Tabitha Petran. Lil heeded my advice and said rather confusedly, "I wouldn't talk to you guys-- not even if it was my own mother--" They had no choice but to leave. Lil was upset for three days. The theater party was forgotten.

Those who did talk to the heresy-hunters used to say that they thought they could outsmart them. In the case of an experienced left-wing politician like Scott Nearing, that might make some sense, but I always thought the people who did talk overestimated themselves (or underestimated the FBI).

The program of FDR's liberal New Deal did not include any proposal to clip the wings of the FBI, nor can I remember that the ACLU waged any campaign against the blatant, illegal persecution of radicals that went on in the 1930's under government auspices. Indeed it was during the administration of FDR that the infamous Attorney General's list of "subversive" organizations was promulgated and circulated without the authority of either Congress or the courts.

XXVI

Communists In Boston Continued:
Simmons Gives Me the Gate

Simmons was of course a college, not a university, and the instructors were not under pressure to produce learned studies as the staff of a university is. Nevertheless the college did provide some funds to be paid to students working their way who would do collection of material for professors engaged in writing articles. I wrote several articles with student assistance. One examined the occupations of Massachusetts legislators over the years, showing how craftsmen and merchants and farmers in the early years had given way to lawyers in the modern period; I suspected and said that they were largely corporation lawyers doing the bidding of their sponsors in the legislature as they had done for pay before. Another study had to do with the mortality of firms in the shoe industry, a highly competitive one. This proved to be a trick subject because so many firms had moved from union to nonunion centers to get lower wage rates; nothing changed about the firm except the name. The most ambitious study was "The Theory of Union Growth," which appeared in the *Quarterly Journal of Economics* and was completely disregarded by all students of the subject. Even after I had proved that it is not whether business is good or bad that determines whether unions grow or not, but the direction of movement of business, writers continued to be perplexed by the fact that unions had failed to grow in the 1920's but had sprung up in the 1930's.

I was quite prepared to do something of book length, and for a while considered doing a text in economics especially for women students, with emphasis on consumer problems. This might have been expected to meet a warm reception among Simmons students, some of whom were actually majoring in (home) economics. Most of the Simmons girls, although career-minded, expected to get married and manage a household in the course of time. But I presently found out that the conception of economics that they had was of something that they could talk to their boyfriends about; they wanted to use the same texts that the men were using. So I dropped the idea of an economics text, but could still have written a labor text, and might well have done so if the war had not intervened. As it was, I managed to complete the book on *Shoes:*

The Workers and the Industry for the Labor Research Association, just as the war in Europe was getting under way.

Simmons was frankly a vocational college. The courses in economics and sociology were patronized for various reasons, but the core of the classes was the group that planned to go into social work. In fact originally that had been the only training that they would get toward social work; but by the time we got there, a separate School of Social Work had been set up, and even the graduates of Simmons were expected to take a year there before they could get recommended for a job in the field. For the students from other institutions, which meant most of the enrollment at that school, a course in Economics was required for those who had not had the subject as undergraduates. The emphasis was on labor problems. When I was assigned to teach the course, I expected to have problems, because it was a required course and everybody tried to get out of it if they could. So it was a pleasant surprise when a student informed me during the first semester that I was one of the more popular instructors.

At Simmons College proper also, the teaching went well enough, both in economics and in sociology, into which I had been initiated at Bradford and in which I found myself quite at home. I did not waste the students' time with long personal disquisitions as some other instructors did. But Nanie was miles ahead of me in popularity. Partly this was because her grades were a cut above mine for the same quality and quantity of work, and partly because she succeeded in getting across to the students some of the enthusiasm she felt for her subject, statistics. She had always contended that women's inferiority complex where math was concerned had no basis whatever in natural aptitude. For herself, she objected strenuously when she was told that she had a "masculine mind." She could handle the math and she persuaded the girls that they could too. When she had finished one semester of statistics with them, they insisted that she give a second semester, for which they enrolled joyfully. Incidentally this experience was to be repeated much later, at the Abraham Lincoln School in Chicago, where the subject was not statistics but classical economic theory! Nanie was a good teacher, not an excellent one, and was recognized as such.

The economics department as a whole had a special standing with the students, not only because of Dr. & Mrs. Davis. Miss Stites had been in the habit of meeting once or twice a year with elected representatives of the several classes to talk over teaching methods and subject matter and make suggestions for

194

improvements. In most other departments there was no such contact, and in some, the student discontent reached the boiling point. A self-appointed committee undertook to post on the bulletin board a list of courses rated from good to "stinker". The administration succeeded in heading off this initiative, but it did become aware that attention needed to be given to student opinion, and a careful evaluation of all the courses, or rather of all the teachers, was made.

The results were not announced publicly, but interested instructors could find out where they stood with the students. When I inquired, the president said he was satisfied with my performance--"more than". But later, when he had made up his mind to fire me, he would not put this estimate in writing. And as far as promotion was concerned, although I had been a full professor at Southwestern, I was still only an Asst. Prof. at Simmons after five years, with a very modest salary . The President justified the low salary on the ground that Nanie had a job too, so that the family income was adequate! He overlooked the fact that 2/3 of Nanie's $1500 a year went for a living-in maid, while we paid income tax on the whole amount!

The influence of the CP, of Marxism, and of the Soviet Union increased dramatically from 1933 to 1936. The depression, called in Party literature the crisis of capitalism, had demonstrated the complete futility of the supposedly self-regulating mechanism of capitalist society. A mass movement, led in large part by the CP, had resulted in the unionization of basic industries. Capitalism was on the defensive. It was good politics to be liberal and almost respectable to be radical.

Nanie and I were available to reinterpret the world scene in terms that made sense. Nanie gave a number of talks to women's groups and community organizations, while I was circulated to many Jewish groups, some Unitarians, and even a specially organized group of liberal businessmen. I worked with Otis Hood and others in arousing union groups to the need for unemployment insurance, which was then a relatively new idea. At the end I was even called on to participate in a symposium on the air. Nanie continued her speaking after she became pregnant, and lost a baby after a long bumpy drive to Lynn.

I used to make up little stories to illustrate the futility of the liberal approach. One college acquaintance recalled one of these stories many years afterward, indicating that it had helped him to get things straightened out. It ran like this:

A man was rowing against the current in a narrow canyon. When he gave his full attention to the job he was able to make headway. But every so often he would stop rowing and shout, and his voice echoed back and forth from the walls. His friends on the bank urged him to stick to his rowing,' but as he was carried down into the white water he shouted back, 'You see. I'm a liberal, and I want to hear both sides!"

I remember the actor Will Geer doing a recitation in Symphony Hall: "One step forward and two steps back--That is the method of the liberal attack."

So, our views were nearly fashionable for a time. The C.P. was losing the persistent advocacy of revolution that had characterized it in the 1920's and becoming in effect an adjunct of the Democratic Party; Browder called for the reelection of Roosevelt in 1936 "at all costs". Some of us asked, "Does he mean, at the cost of giving up the C.P. organization?" Some years later, it actually did come to that. But in the period in question, the mid-thirties, the Party exercised a remarkable amount of leadership. Causes that had been lost began to be won; initiatives that had seemed completely unattainable only a few years before proved successful.

In those days, when some non-Party person came up with what looked like a good idea, I would point to it as an illustration of the point that others beside Party people could have good ideas. The Party people would smile knowingly and wink at each other, and it would turn out that the move in question had been suggested by the Party. The Party had enough of a following, and enough devoted comrades to organize many more, so that Congressmen of dubious liberal backgrounds could be pressured into taking a good stand.

There was a small and struggling local of the American Federation of Teachers to which Nanie and I belonged, and it elected me to represent the local in the Boston Central Labor Union. I used to bring in resolutions endorsing proposed New Deal legislation, and these usually passed.

After 1937 the temper of the times changed, for a number of reasons (we do not overlook the fact that the Wages and Hours Act was not passed until 1938). The CP was criticized at the time, and has been castigated many times since, for certain policies which were probably wrong, or at the least wrongly applied. But it would be a complete distortion of history to make out that the decline of radical sentiment after 1937 was the fault of the Party, or that it could have been somehow avoided if the Party had acted differently. The European Parties also declined, even to the point of ceasing to be mass parties as they had been in the 1930's or before. The CPUSA had special problems and met them as best it could, not always in the best way. But we must get down to cases.

One field in which the Party had a real base which later evaporated was in the unions, especially those in the CIO but including also some AFL unions. The American Federation of Teachers has been mentioned. The tragic debacle of its progressive wing was probably not necessary: it was brought on because the CPUSA attempted to apply in the AFT a policy that was suggested ("dictated") by Moscow and which had no real relevance to the American scene.

The policy in question was the so-called United Front. After the middle of the 1930's the Party policy was to make a united front with practically everybody except the out-and-out Fascists. This was in order to stave off the menace of Fascism. Thus the Communists, who had rejected the United Front when it might have paid real dividends (in Germany in the pre-Hitler period), actually forgot who their real friends were in a futile effort to play up to the reactionaries. The result in the AFT was, as we have seen, that the progressive coalition that had elected Jerome Davis President was disrupted and the pseudo-liberal Counts was elected in his place.

I never thought that the Party understood the nature of the problem in the unions. In order to organize a union it is necessary to appeal to liberals, radicals, and relatively conservative wage workers (and there are many of these latter) on the basis of their common interests as workers. Sometimes, as in the fur industry of New York City, the membership is predisposed to Marxism and the Communists have led a spectacular campaign to drive out the gangsters, as Ben Gold did. Then the membership will gladly contribute money and effort to left-wing causes, and adopt resolutions in favor of freeing the Scottsboro boys and endorsing the foreign policies of the Soviet Union.

More usually, the membership includes many who have been conditioned against radical causes, perhaps in their respective churches, and the effort to educate them in class consciousness can even be counterproductive.

Since red-baiting had split so many unions, Communists in the unions used to pretend not to be Communists. One Party member was attacked as such in a union meeting. He denied the charge heatedly, and even demanded an apology! The Party objected to this, and called it "hiding the face of the Party." Nevertheless it was the policy of the Party not to have Party members flaunt their membership.

One Party member, Jesse Prosten, in the Packinghouse Workers, never denied that he was a member so far as I know. And got away with it. He was a very valuable trade union worker. In his union he rose to the very top. He had excellent judgment.

But too many Party members took Lenin's view on the unions literally and attempted to apply in the U.S. in the 1930's policies which were intended to apply to Czarist Russia. The Party was everything: the union should be an adjunct of the Party, and a training ground for Party activity. Such a misapplication of Leninist theory could result in isolating the Party members and exposing them to victimization.

Somewhat tardily and unwillingly, the Party policy of denying membership when confronted was changed to a refusal to answer. This solution had the advantage that it was a position that could be adopted by non-party sympathizers and "fellow travelers". Charles Hendley, the Secretary of the New York Teachers Union, when asked if he was a Communist, used to say, quite correctly, "I consider that question to be inconsistent with the principle of the secret ballot," which put the onus squarely on the questioner where it belonged.

Bancroft Beatley, who was president of Simmons during the years that we were there, had pretensions to being a liberal. He used to make impassioned speeches on academic freedom at Commencement. But when the test came, he folded the same as the rest of the college presidents before the pressure of conservative opinion.

In June 1941, after Commencement, when the students had scattered, Beatley called me into his office and informed me that he was not renewing my contract, and furthermore that he would not recommend me for a teaching position in any other institution of higher learning. He said that his feeling toward me was personally friendly (not a statement one would expect when he had just announced his intention to drive me out of the academic profession) but--. He explained how he had gone around campus trying to find some pretext for the dismissal, and had hit on the idea that I was not considered suitable for committee work. I tried to point out that he had not put me on any committees, that the only committee I had served on had been as a substitute for Marian. I was ready to discuss my record on that committee, but he was not interested in the merits of the case. He had made up his mind. He mentioned some bits of malicious gossip which also I was not permitted to discuss. He said he did not like the way I walked down the hall!

I did not say at the time whether I was prepared to make a fight. I could have stayed another year and carried on a campaign. I have no special reason to think that the Trustees would have overruled the president, but his reputation as a liberal, and that of Miss Stites, who supported the dismissal, would have been seriously compromised. With regard to the student body, the situation was more favorable than it had been at any previous time. There was an active political club with leftist orientation which would certainly have stood up for us. I was not on tenure, so that the AAUP would probably not have come into the case. Marian was involved too. She was charged with having said that the Dean was anti-Semitic. In the new dormitory, Jewish girls had applied in a group for one section and the Dean had said that it would be a mistake to have that section, and the dormitory, to be known as Jewish.

Nanie and I wanted to do what would most benefit the movement. But here a complication arose. We were told that if we won the fight we would be expected to stay for "a good long time." And Nanie had decided that she did not want to work under Bancroft Beatley.

We had thought that the faculty might have supported us, but it turned out that even the Teachers Union local would not. After the vote, which was taken in our absence, Lawrence Wylie, who afterwards became a Harvard professor of Romance Languages, tried to tell us that we could not expect any better treatment from the faculty as a whole. He had the chutzpah to tell us, "We are your friends." I was tempted to say, "With friends like that, we don't need enemies."

The lone dissenter in that meeting I have always thought was Harrison Harley, who was a psychologist but still Miss Stites's superior in the hierarchy; he was chairman of the division, while she was chairman of the department. (It was a question whether he and Miss Stites were eligible for membership in the union, since they had some authority in hiring and firing, but the local was small and struggling and they were sympathetic, so they had been allowed to belong) Harley made it clear that he thought we got a raw deal.

In the end I accepted two years' dismissal pay and Nanie got one year's pay. Beatley wrote a glowing letter of recommendation for Nanie but was not willing to state that I had been a satisfactory teacher; he referred the question to Prof. Harley.

199

A public battle even if we had won it would have seriously affected my (our) chances of getting another college job, as I did some years later. Also, while I hated to leave teaching, I was quite prepared at the time to go into the labor movement, as in fact I did. I got what comfort I could from the remark of a lady friend who said, "There's no trick about having a job, and getting promoted, but how does that help the radical movement?"

It was hard to figure out the mental processes of the head of the department, Sarah Stites. She had been at Simmons for many years and under her leadership the Economics Department had acquired a reputation in the community for treating current issues from a liberal point of view. Nanie and I of course did nothing to dispel that tradition. We had disagreed with her on the choice of a text for the elementary economics course but our personal relations had remained friendly so there was no question of a personal grudge. Yet she laid her reputation as a liberal on the line when requested to do so by the President. It is perhaps mean to suggest that she was jealous, but the fact is that Nanie and I were apparently rated as high as or higher than she was as teachers.

Pres. Beatley had showed his hand earlier, in a speech he made to the faculty. He said in carefully guarded language that he hoped we would not do or say anything that would discourage potential donors from making bequests to Simmons College. I did not challenge him at the time but I had felt sure that he was aiming at me.

XXVII

In the Labor Movement:
1. United Shoe Workers, Cumberland

My interest in the shoe industry dated all the way back to 1921: the first job I had after graduating from college was in a wage arbitration case in Rochester, New York, for the shoe workers union there; the brief was prepared by Harry Chase with my aid, for the Labor Bureau. Thereafter I collected some material on the shoe unions and at one time even applied for a job as a shoe worker; having had no experience I was not taken on. When we settled (1934) in a shoe town, Haverhill (Bradford was a part of Haverhill), I set to work collecting data for the LRA Labor and Industry series, on the shoe industry. The book was published in 1941 as *Shoes: The Workers and the Industry*, and wound up the series. Bancroft Beatley read it and remarked that some people were not going to like it, which was true enough. Actually it may have been one reason why he decided shortly thereafter to dispense with my services on the faculty at Simmons.

In the course of collecting material for the book, I had established contact with the United Shoe Workers (CIO), and had got to know the officers. The President Frank McGrath, used to stop by my house when he came to the Boston area. The union had a research director and editor named Leo Goodman, but he was on his way out. So, when I lost my job at Simmons, the USW was glad enough to offer me the job that Leo Goodman had had.

The place the family moved to was Silver Spring, Maryland, just north of the District of Columbia. The Party immediately tried to get Nanie to take on the job of getting Browder out of jail, but she was exhausted by the move, and by Russian War Relief before that, and could not handle it. Later she did take on the job of organizing domestic workers in the area.

I had already done a couple of jobs for the union. One was on a wage arbitration case in Boston, which we lost. The other was in connection with a national minimum wage for the shoe industry, and involved appearing at a hearing in Washington.

The Wages and Hours Act, passed in 1938, established a basic minimum wage for both men and women of 35 cents an hour, but this could be raised to 40 cents after hearings in which the decision was made by nine people, three each from labor, employers and the public. The unions--United Shoe Workers, Boot and Shoe Workers (AFL), and the Brockton Brotherhood of Shoe and Allied Craftsmen--petitioned for a minimum of 37 1/2 cents an hour, and set out to get a unanimous decision from the board.

The outcome was probably predetermined, since the International Shoe Corp., the biggest manufacturer, which had a representative on the Board, had apparently decided not to make a fight; their man sat silent through the proceedings. The other employers did put up an opposition, and had a specialist there who argued against the raise. My job was to show that the industry was being demoralized by migrations from organized to unorganized centers, to get a lower wage rate. I was loaded with material, which was shortly to appear in my book. Data on the migrations had been collected by the Lynn Chamber of Commerce: and indeed it was an old story in the industry; Lynn and Brockton along with Haverhill had seen the jobs move away for many years. When the industry was riddled with unemployment in Haverhill, we happened to drive by Somersworth, New Hampshire, just a few miles north of Haverhill, and found a nonunion plant working two shifts, full of orders.

I had supposed that I would be subjected to cross-examination by the employers' man; so, when I had finished my presentation, and questions were called for. I was amazed to hear him say, "No questions!" The board did vote unanimously for the raise to 37 1/2 cents an hour. A man with wide experience in hearings in Washington, one Oppenheim, was quoted as saying that mine was the best presentation before a public body that he had ever heard. The unions were so pleased that they clubbed together and gave me a gold watch. (I already had one!) So, I started on my job as Technical Director of the United Shoe Workers with a considerable reputation.

My job included doing research, preparing briefs for collective bargaining negotiations, editing the Shoe Workers' edition of the *CIO News*, and presumably lobbying if there had been any legislation pending that was of special interest to shoe workers.

In New England, Powers Hapgood was put in charge of organizing shoes: he was followed later by Michael Widman, who was also a coal miner. When the organizing drive hit Auburn-Lewiston, Maine, the employers fought back and Powers and his whole organizing committee were thrown into jail on trumped-up charges. The strike was lost. In spite of the best efforts of the CIO, the shoe industry remained only partly organized, though there was now a nucleus of dues-paying members to furnish a treasury for later drives.

Also, the migrations had slowed way down. The minimum wage was raised to 40 cents an hour in 1942 with little opposition from the employers.

The research directors of the various unions got to know each other. My special friends were Lyle Cooper of the Packinghouse Workers and Lincoln Fairley of the West Coast Longshoremen (Harry Bridges' union). The most capable was probably Jim Wishart of the United Auto Workers: but he was purged in the witch-hunt against the lefts when the CIO joined the AFL, or before. Ben Riskin, who I think was with the Mine, Mill & Smelter Workers, caused a furor when he suggested that all employees, not only miners be paid on a "collar to collar" basis, pay to start at the time they entered the plant.

Part of the creed of the Left movement was that leaders are suspect, the people to trust are the rank and file. The I.W.W. were the ones who spelled this out in so many words, but the idea was quite widespread in other branches of the movement. The United Shoe Workers were under left leadership and I had a chance to estimate the validity of this contention. In the national convention, in spite of efforts to keep down the number of paid officials among the delegates, it turned out that the majority of them, or nearly, were on the payroll. But the leaders were the ones most interested, the best informed, and on the whole the most progressive. Of course this does not say that officials cannot become "pie cards" who sit on their behinds and do nothing. But there is no magic in being a member of the rank and file. Except, perhaps, in times of great agitation and excitement when change is in the air and things have moved faster than the officials realize. Then a rank-and-file movement may be the only way to get important things done. Like starting a revolution, for instance. Rosa Luxemburg thought that a revolutionary general strike, which she favored, would be started, not by the union officials nor even by the organized workers but precisely by the unorganized, the rank and file.

The family pulled up stakes in Newton, even though this meant that Chan had to finish the year at high school while living with our next-door neighbors the Haugheys, and came to live in Silver Spring, Maryland, a suburb of Washington.

I had expected that the job with the shoe union would last for some time, but actually it lasted only a little over a year. The President of the union, Frank McGrath, was out of the office most of the time, traveling around the country. The Secretary, Scotty Mitchell, was in the office but was not given the authority to make decisions: he did not belong to the left faction which was in control of the union. though he got along with all factions. McGrath wanted to delegate authority to me, but I did not feel that I could run the union.

The question may be asked, why did I not stay on with the United Shoe Workers? I surely could have done so, and would have lasted longer than McGrath, who was no great shakes. I might have spent the rest of my life as a union official.

For one thing, I was not too sure of my ability to solve the union's problems. Actually nobody else did either; a generation later, the industry was still only partly unionized, wages were low, and the rival Boot and Shoe Workers Union persisted even after the AFL and the CIO came together. For another thing, I had no taste for the kind of politics that one has to play in a union (or any other organization). It was some satisfaction to have made my way so near the top in a union, albeit a struggling one, but I still thought of myself as an intellectual in the labor movement and tried for some time afterward to catch hold in a bigger, more stable union, in a position where my technical training would be of some use.

I quit the job with the United Shoe Workers at the beginning of 1943. For two weeks I worked in the Office of Strategic Services, under a good guy named Maurice Halperin. The personnel department, which had been checking up, got my record from Brazil and the job with the O.S.S. was at an end. I sounded out a few more government jobs, but presently discovered that a little red flag had been placed opposite my name in the Civil Service file, and this meant no government job for me. So, when Mel Fiske came to me with the suggestion that I take a job as editor of the Western Maryland edition of the *CIO News*, in Cumberland, Md., I was in a mood to accept.

We moved to Cumberland from Silver Spring, Maryland, in the beginning of 1943. A greater contrast could hardly be imagined. Silver Spring was a residential middle-class suburb of Washington, while Cumberland was a small industrial city which served also as commercial center for a number of coal mines to the South (in West Virginia) and West. From our house on the side of a hill we looked out over the rail yards below. The war was on and everybody was busy; the skilled mechanics worked overtime regularly and sometimes did a double shift when one was out sick.

Nanie was busy keeping the house going and caring for little Terry, who had been born in 1940.

Chan had already started college; he took a semester out and worked in the big textile plant, the Celanese. Barbara was in her sophomore year at high school. She played the flute in the school band, and worked on the school paper. In her senior year she would have been news editor; in fact if she had been a little more aggressive, they would have made her editor-in-chief. But we did not stay. Mata was with us full time now, not interrupted by frequent visits back to Minneapolis as had been the case when she first came to us, in Bradford. Mina rounded out the household: and in 1943 Cynthia Quentin was born. That was her name on the birth certificate. Her mother erased the Quentin, but she later restored it.

My job was to edit the Western Maryland edition of the *CIO News*, whose Washington editor was Len de Caux. I had known Len from my days with the Federated Press, and we always got along well. The paper was printed in Washington. We had the outside sheets, the same as with the Shoe Workers edition which I had edited: the middle of the paper was the same for all the sub-editions and was the work of the Washington office. I would write the copy for our part early in the week, then stay up all Thursday night "putting the paper to bed," and put the product on the train for Washington early Friday morning. In addition to my duties as editor I was the representative in Cumberland of the CIO, and was supposed to do some organizing on the side.

The pay was not very high, and the income of the paper was cut way down when I feuded with the leadership of the Celanese local, our biggest chunk of subscribers, and it withdrew support. However I was able to get the paper on a sounder financial basis and even add to my own income by being more aggressive in soliciting ads than my predecessor had been.

Mel Fiske, whose job I took over, had expressed the opinion that the advertising had reached its peak; there were not any more ads to be got. I decided that that might be the case; but I was not going to take his word for it. So one day I went to a furniture store that had never advertised in the *CIO News*, and to my great surprise they took a contract for a whole year. Thereafter a number of other businesses also came in, and the finances of the paper took a bound forward. The board that supervised the paper was impressed, and voted to allow me a commission on the extra advertising that I was bringing in.

We had a sports editor who knew something about the early history of Babe Ruth, a Maryland product; he ran a whole series of articles on the Babe, including his astonishment when he learned that someone was willing to pay him money to play ball.

The outside organizing was concentrated as it turned out in three plants: in each of them the workers themselves came to us and we did what we could to get them organized and functioning as a union. Two campaigns ended in failure for the union, but very different was the story in Moorefield, West Virginia, where the workers at a sawmill had decided almost unanimously that they wanted a union, and wrote us a letter to that effect. We got up a delegation consisting of Boyd Payton of the Textile Union, John Sharp of the Rubber Workers, and myself, and went down to Moorefield. The crowd signed up as members of the United Furniture Workers, and before long there was a signed agreement.

The dispute that had prompted the unionization move was over the firing of a man who had objected to carrying out certain orders of one of the straw bosses. The man in question, Bill Smith, had lost several weeks of work, and when the union forced his return, he actually got back pay for the time he had missed. This was arranged through the NLRB. Bill Smith himself was in some respects an unsavory character, with racist proclivities. A few of the others were both racist and anti-female. We had to argue with them pretty strongly to save the anti-discrimination clause that was standard in United Furniture Workers agreements (West Virginia people, it seems, still think of themselves as part of the South). But "Bunk" Smith, Bill Smith's brother, was a solid union man and favored solidarity of black and white, and the same was true of Ray Saunders, the head of the union, an older man who had never learned to read and write but could remember conversations in a remarkable way.

The Furniture Workers had no representative in Cumberland, so I was assigned to work with the Moorefield local as from the International. I used to go down to their meetings every other week, and presented their grievances to the management. When there was a particularly knotty problem to be straightened out we called in a government mediator. With government help, the union won all its grievances and seemed to be firmly established. But at the renewal of the contract there was no question of a wage increase; the company wouldn't consider it, and as we were working under a no-strike agreement, there was nothing we could do.

The international union, the United Furniture Workers, was well pleased with the way things had gone, and at a certain point they asked me to come to New York and offered me the job of business agent in Baltimore, servicing the surrounding district, which included Cumberland and Moorefield. Here was another chance to make unionism a way of life, but I turned it down. Ironically the United Furniture Workers had been one of the unions that I had approached when I was fired from Simmons about giving me a job as organizer!

In the 1980 census Cumberland was listed as having a population over 100,000, but this referred to the urban aggregation: at the time of World War II it was barely 20,000 for the city proper. It was a labor town, sociologically speaking, but was not run by labor. The politicians trod carefully where labor matters were concerned, trying not to antagonize labor openly while they fulfilled their commitments to their sponsors the special interests. Delegations from the Western Maryland CIO Council called on U.S. Senator Glenn Beall from time to time to get his position on pending legislation of interest to labor. He would usually not commit himself, saying only that he would listen to the debate and vote according to his conscience. But he took the Council seriously and even came to one of its meetings (he was himself from Cumberland).

Labor would have been in a stronger position if its ranks had not been so divided. The split between the AFL and the CIO had not been healed, and the important group of railroad men was not in either one. The Mine Workers had of course been charter members of the CIO, but at this time were playing an independent game as usual and were violating the no-strike pledge which had been given by the rest of the labor movement for the duration of the war. The miners had their District 65, which was raiding both AFL and CIO unions and signing up anybody they could; they had a group of railroad workers in Cumberland. The mayor of Cumberland was not as careful as he should have been not to antagonize labor, and just at the end of our stay in the city, when he ran for reelection against a frankly pro-labor man, Tom Post, he had lost enough support so that Post was elected.

In Cumberland, the position of women in the family was something that we found very hard to get used to.

When I went to see Albert Kline the first time, his wife was there, and Nanie was with me; she struck up an acquaintance with Mrs. Kline, a rather subdued type, and before we left Nanie had arranged for us to take Mrs. Kline to the movies. When we went around on the appointed day, Mrs. Kline was dressed to go, and obviously wanted to go, but she could not; her husband wouldn't let her. This was in the family of a good union man and solid citizen.

There was even some feeling among the mill workers that women ought not to participate in the affairs of the union, but that was in the process of being broken down. The women, such as Eva Chaney, a friend of ours and a comrade, did participate and even played a leading part.

George Meyers, a "good guy", had been a leader in the big Celanese local of the Textile Workers. In fact he had been president of the state CIO Council. Unfortunately he was drafted and left Cumberland soon after we arrived there. He was stationed at Fort Devens, not far from Boston: and when his stay there became prolonged, we put him in touch with our friend Lillian Arnold, who worked in the Boston Public Library. She introduced him to her friend Allie, and George, who was single, hit it off with Allie. They were married a little later.

George was a Communist, and was known as such. When he finished his period in the service he became national labor director of the Party, a position he held for many years. As a member of the top brass, he became a target of the persecutions after the Second World War, and served a sentence in prison for trying to overthrow the government.

He and Allie had two children, a boy and a girl. They all used to visit us as Sandwich. During one of his visits, he was under surveillance, though not under arrest, and the dicks came and parked near us keeping an eye on him. When he drove to New York at the end of his visit, I drove down with him, and we had a government escort the whole way.

Being in the top brass of the Party had its perquisites too. He got to visit the Soviet Union as guest of the government, and later went to the Mongolian Peoples Republic with all expenses paid. Like the other top brass, he retained his faith in the Soviet Union untarnished until the end. His children grew up and found places in the U.S. educational system.

Another Celanese worker who was in the party and active in the union was Boyd Coleman. He and his wife visited us at Sandwich.

Boyd Payton had been president of the Celanese local of the Textile Workers and went from that job to one as organizer for the union's national office. I was interested to find that the Textile Workers, who were under Social Democratic leadership, kept watch over what their organizers read, at least to the extent of supplying books for them to read.

208

"Pop" McCulley, another party person, was quite a character. He was married, and his wife was one of a pair of identical twins. The twin sister's husband died and she came to live with Pop's family. The twins were known as "Pop's wives." They were characters in their own right. One time Pop had been in trouble with the law for bootlegging, and his "wives" had developed a healthy dislike of the sheriff. That official had an accident to his car and came to Pop's house requesting to use the telephone. Mrs. McCulley was there with her sister. She permitted him to use the phone, but held a gun on him while he did, with the admonition, "If you make a false move I'll let you have it." The sheriff used to shake his head when he talked about "those McCulley women."

The McCulleys had as one of their little circle of friends one Andy Moreland, who was a social outcast because of the fact that he had befriended the hunger marchers of the 1930's when they came through Cumberland on their way to Washington. Andy had been out of a job thereafter and had finally managed to catch hold as a janitor, but the "respectable" element in the town would have nothing to do with him.

Pop on the other hand was able through sheer strength of character to survive an amount of obloquy that would have sunk a weaker man. He became shop chairman of the cellulose acetate department. I well remember our parting from him. He broke down and cried. So few workers had heeded his advice politically. "I tried to tell them, " he lamented.

Al Lannon, a former marine worker, was Party organizer for the Maryland area. At one time he sent an earnest but inexperienced Party member to work in the Cumberland area. A reporter for the Cumberland newspaper discovered that he was there and interviewed him for the paper. The guileless lad said he was hoping to advise the unions about their policies. He had to leave Cumberland with nothing accomplished except to make things difficult for the Party people who were there.

The period in Cumberland was one of the few times when we functioned actively in the Party, for what that was worth. I was a delegate to the state convention in 1944. Browder had come up with the extraordinary policy of abolishing the Party and withdrawing from the international scene, as set forth in his book *Teheran*, which became available just at the time of the convention. The policy included abandoning work in the South, although this was not announced to the membership. I got a copy of *Teheran* and read it between sessions of the convention. It seemed very off color to me, and the idea of abandoning the Party also. I said as much on the floor of the convention. It developed that in the largest local unit of the area, in Baltimore, about a third of the membership had opposed the new policy. But they made no fight in the convention, and in the end the only delegate who supported my position was Pop McCulley.

Browder's policies were later attacked as non-Marxist in the famous Duclos letter, and Browder was expelled from the Party. I never understood how the other leaders could have fallen so completely under his spell. Even Foster, who was to take over as leader, was obliged to speak privately when he disagreed with Browder. Anne Timpson, who was on the National Committee, furnished the reason. If Foster had challenged Browder openly, "We would have expelled him!"

When we had been in Cumberland a while, my mother died and left me $25,000. To my amazement and dismay, the news of this legacy was published in the Cumberland newspaper. Harry Porch, a railroad union leader whom I knew, told me that I wasn't "one of the boys."

What would have happened if we had stayed on in Cumberland? After a couple of years during which the big Celanese local was run by an appointee of the national office (Dundon), the left wing took heart and elected Roy Craze, a "fellow traveler" though not a Party member, as President. The support of the local for the paper might have been resumed and life would have been easier.

But Cumberland's future as a labor town was already jeopardized, although people did not realize it at the time. The big Celanese plant closed down for good. It left behind a large number of workers whose lungs were impaired. George Meyers, who got out in time, said years later that all his friends from Celanese days were dead. "Brown lung" had taken its toll.--As for the sawmill at Moorefield, the workers there lost their union--why I never knew. Probably they got fighting among themselves.

The CIO meanwhile had been moving to the right. Len DeCaux lost his job as editor of the national *CIO News*, which was presently discontinued when the AFL and CIO were merged in 1954. Len was completely out of a job and had to learn a manual trade--typesetting--in order to earn a living.

XXVIII

In the Labor Movement Continued:
2. Chicago.

The left-wing Farm Equipment Workers Union had heard of me while I was still in Cumberland and had invited me to come and give an educational talk at a 3-day seminar they were holding for the membership. I came and gave a sympathetic talk about the Soviet Union, and they were delighted. They offered me a job. I was to take charge of the Peoria local, where the main plant of the Caterpillar Tractor Co. was located. This was quite as big a job as the one the Furniture Workers had offered me and even more challenging. The only thing was, I did not have the background for this kind of job and did not know how to go at it. I declined, but they still wanted me on the staff and offered to put me in the publicity department under a young chap named Ed Schoenfeld. This job I accepted, although the duties were undefined and the salary rather low. We spent $1000 moving the family to Chicago, and bought a house in Winnetka with Munga's legacy. Nine months later, I was fired.

The leftist Farm Equipment Workers were due to be absorbed by the United Auto Workers, but that was not evident at the time I went to work for them.

I had hoped to be able to work out a niche for myself in the national office, but this was not to be. Publicity remained in the hands of Ed Schoenfeld; bargaining was turned over to a young man newly imported for the purpose; and research, which I had thought might be my field, was not set up as a separate department or function. Later, after I had been eased out (by Jerry Field), I was called back to do research in connection with a strike in which the union was engaged; but when I found that it was not intended to be a permanent position, I declined.

Meanwhile I had been offered the job of research director in the Mine, Mill a Smelter Workers Union, a highly suitable arrangement. I held the job just three days. The salary of the Research Director was being paid by the CIO, and when the national office of the CIO (Haywood) heard about my appointment, they refused to pay my salary. Mine-Mill could have shifted titles around and kept me but they did not choose to do so and I was out, again.

The job with Mine-Mill was one that could have lasted a long time, maybe until the end of the chapter. It was only a short time thereafter that Mine-Mill was eased out of the CIO for being too leftist (it was the successor to the famous Western Federation of Miners, and the metal miners of the west had a long tradition of radicalism). The man who took over as research director made good, and even got some power in his own right; he was elected president of one of the divisions of the union. The union sponsored a fine movie, *Salt of the Earth.*

But the time came when the union was absorbed by the United Steel Workers; and even before that merger, Clinton Jencks, the man who had played the union organizer in the movie, a real leftist, was given his walking papers as being too radical for Mine-Mill. (He ended up as a college teacher of economics!).

The war was over, Hitler and Mussolini were dead and Fascism in their respective countries was gone too, but Franco was still in power in Spain. The veterans of the Abraham Lincoln Brigade thought that a suitable amount of pressure from the Allied Powers might topple him, and they set about to lobby the United Nations and the individual governments to that effect. They set up a Chicago Committee for Spanish Freedom, and it was run for a time by a comrade who did a creditable job. When she had to retire for personal reasons, I took over.

There were three main things that I accomplished in the six months I was there. First, a delegation to the United Nations in New York. This was a followup on a similar delegation some months earlier, but it was by no means without importance. We had set as our objective to contact Helen Gahagan Douglas, who was one of the U.S. delegates to the U.N., but we could not get through to her. We were intercepted and talked to by an underling from the State Department. We spoke our piece, which was duly noted, and asked him what the State Department purposed to do about it. He said it would act in the light of circumstances. We said we were speaking for a considerable section of public opinion. He said foreign policy was not made by public opinion, it was made by the State Department, and that was all we could get out of him. For our delegation it was something of an education. Milt Wolff the national head of the Lincoln Brigade veterans was pleased with our efforts, such as they were.

I also got out a newsletter to the mailing list that I had inherited. One of the Veterans of the Brigade came and helped on a volunteer basis. His name was Mel Allen, and he had been wounded in one arm, but he could still fold and stuff.

There were a number of other Brigade veterans in the Chicago area, and I visited them to get support for the Committee. Their fortunes were completely varied. One had made good financially and dropped out of the movement; he gave us some "conscience money." One had been running a little photographic business, but it was not making money and he was about to move to the Pacific Coast. The others were strung out along the scale from affluent to indigent.

The third activity in which I engaged was to organize a meeting in support of the Committee's efforts. We had as speakers Abel Plehn, who had just written a book about Spain and the Popular Front; and Russ Nixon, who was then doing political work for the CIO. These were not as big names as we might have secured, but experience had showed that in Chicago the big names are very unreliable. In New York they are usually on the spot and if they go out of town they can come back. In Chicago they either don't come, or when they do, they have other engagements, or they just can't be reached, or they change their time of coming (the commonnest experience). Our two speakers were not great orators, but we knew they would come, and they did.

We also picketed the Spanish consulate. For this occasion, and for speaking to neighborhood groups, we enlisted the support of John T. Bernard, a former Congressman from the Iron Range in Minnesota, a Corsican who had cast the sole vote in the House against the boycott of the Spanish Loyalists. He had been defeated for reelection and was acting as a kind of political trouble-shooter for the UE in Chicago. I well remembered how he had come to Boston during the Spanish Civil War and what a hit he made with his stories of the political activity of Italians in heading off the attempts of the Fascists to penetrate the Italian community in Duluth.

Soon after the picket march got under way, a detachment of mounted police clattered up, and I thought we were all going to be arrested, but we were not. The newspapers paid us no heed.

The leftist euphoria just after the war had been shattered when the U.S. refused to move against another presumed Fascist dictator, in Argentina. Since this was a violation of pledges, it came as a real shock. The solidarity of the anti-Fascist front had been broken. It became evident that nothing could be hoped for from the new Secretary of State, Stettinius, whom I thought of as "little Eddie" from the days when I had known him as a little boy in Dongan Hills.

It was at this time that Browder's misleadership of the C.P. came to an end. It took a push from outside the country to do it. The Duclos letter, finding that the Party's policies were not Marxist, was at once accepted as gospel and Browder was out. He had changed his line while in prison. Apparently he had come to see the State Department's point of view, originally on China. To his credit be it said, he did not thereafter attack the Party. He made a living by retailing literature from the S.U., to which he remained ever loyal. Eugene Dennis, who was not nearly so closely identified with the S.U. as some others in spite of having worked for the C.I., was General Secretary. Foster was the actual leader and thereafter all movements to replace him or to change the Party's policies met with frustration. The C.P.U.S.A. was the most loyal follower that the C.P.S.U. had. Even the occupation of Czechoslovakia, even the invasion of Afghanistan, did not shake the loyalty of the hard-line C.P. stalwarts, among whom incidentally were several whom I still (1983) consider good friends, even relatives.

The Party had long since ceased to be a revolutionary organization, but the leaders were sent to prison anyway, thus completing the rout of the Party organization. Interestingly, young idealists have continued to join the Party, although when they find out what is (not) there, they generally drop out; the turnover is high, as it always was, including in the 1930's. In 1946, when we were in Chicago, there was still organization and activity, and a number of good people were still in the Party. One such was William L. Patterson, an old friend from the days of the ILD. He was the director of the Abraham Lincoln School, which was conducting evening classes in the Loop attracting a fair number of students. Nanie and I were both impressed into service and gave courses there in economics.

The sponsors of the School, the ones who got it going, were not Communists but they thought the community ought to know more of Marx's teachings. They secured as chief of the faculty Alvin Winspear, who had been fired from the University of Wisconsin in the red hunt. His field was ancient Greek philosophy and Literature, and he was a good teacher; his classes were well attended. Also connected with the school were Henry Noyes, a former professor of English from the University of Missouri, who had not been fired but had quit his job to go full time into the movement, beginning at the bottom with a manual job; and Herman Schendel from Milwaukee, whom I had known as Harold

Christofel's secretary when I went up to give a talk to the Allis-Chalmers local of the UAW (or was it UE?).

Nanie was assigned to economic theory, in which her grounding was excellent; she had taken some graduate work in that field with Prof. Garver at U. Minn. and learned how to fling the logical arguments--Ricardian style. She gave them a go at the labor theory of value, and they liked it so much that they insisted she come back the next term and continued along the same lines, just as the statistics class had done at Simmons. My classes went well, and whetted my inclination to get back into academic work, though still not to the point of my seeking actively for a teaching job.

Bill Patterson was a fine man and an eloquent speaker, and no doubt did a good job with his course(s), but as director he was misplaced. He had scheduled a course at the Lincoln School for the coming term, and had scheduled the same course at the same hour on the same days at a Party school in the South End! Henry Noyes and Herman Schendel approached me about taking over the administration of the school. I ducked because at that time I had a job, and I had doubts as to how long the school would survive-- doubts which wore realized all too soon. Also the approach was not authorized.

We had bought a house in Winnetka, as noted. The selection was made rather hastily, and largely because Sal and Cliff were already there. It turned out that there was a good crowd of lefties there, and we kept up with some of the friends we made there-- retired now, of course.

Winnetka did not disappoint us in the matter of schools. The kindergarten that Terry went to was very progressive, with a rabbit hopping around; the kids loved it. Mina (and Barbara for a year) went to New Trier High School, which served several North Shore communities. The Latin teacher there translated a number of popular songs into Latin, to the great delight of his students. Mina (known there as Wilhelmina) had a circle of friends, and several of them came to Sandwich in the summer--two summers, in fact. The standards of the school were high, the incidental expenses also. In giving a going-away present to a teacher who was leaving, the students taxed themselves $3 a head, equivalent to something on the order of $15 in 1983.

The Winnetka schools with their progressive ideas had been so well advertised that people had the impression of Winnetka as a progressive center, but it turned out to be lily white. Indeed the only North Shore town with any considerable black population was

Glencoe, next to Winnetka. So strong was the anti-black feeling in Winnetka that a little dry cleaning business run by a black who did not even live in Winnetka was forced to close; the landlord, under pressure from the racists, would not renew his lease. We argued and pleaded with him, but to no avail.

We tried to get the liberals together for this and general purposes, and got strong support from Atlantis Marshall, a long-time progressive, and a number of others. We organized a North Shore Civil Liberties Committee, held meetings and invited in speakers. We had no national affiliation, specifically not with the ACLU. Archibald MacLeish came from that area, and his mother was still there; she sided with the ACLU, but we got support from the family of Harold Ickes (Roosevelt's Secretary of the Interior and a well- known liberal) and other big names, and quite a few smaller ones.

When it became evident that the efforts of the Chicago Committee for Spanish Freedom were not going to unseat Dictator Franco, the Committee was wound up. About that time I received an offer from Murray Latimer, head of the Chicago Civil Liberties Committee. Graten Little, a black from Evanston, and I were to join with him in expanding the work of the Committee, at the same time raising our own salaries. I had little choice but to accept. Latimer was known as a good progressive; he was even a Party member, although I was not supposed to know that.

He was the son of a former Socialist mayor of Minneapolis, and had been running the Chicago Committee for some years. In spite of his having a rather abrasive personality, he had managed to hold onto the support of the Chicago liberals, especially the Jewish community, and had won some victories.

The Chicago Committee had a rather different conception of free speech from the ACLU. Whereas the latter defended the right of the racists and other fascists to meet and march, the Chicago Committee contended that a meeting to stir up race hatred was against public policy--that it was illegal. This question was debated in the courts when the question of breaking up such a meeting arose, and a court in Chicago did actually decide that the meeting in question-one called by the followers of Gerald L.K. Smith--was illegal.

Since we were campaigning against the native fascists, we had to know what they were doing, and at one time I found myself in a meeting addressed by Gerald L.K. Smith himself. He was a former Methodist minister and had an ingratiating manner, but showed also that he could talk tough. One of his followers, who was

216

apparently working full time for him, had got to know us as we had him. He came up behind me and warned me that if we tried to start anything we would get crowned. We didn't, and we weren't.

We did, however uphold the rights of those who undertook to discuss sex in public places, and found ourselves defending a company that had tried to put on a movie in Wilmette, on the North Shore, with accompanying remarks to which some of the audience objected. The remarks may indeed have appealed to the prurient interest, but the Wilmette "solid citizens" went too far and attempted to put a ban on the books that had been used and recommended. So, we were in the picture and held them up to scorn for putting books on trial. The company concerned was naturally grateful and contributed to the Committee. They even offered to take me into the business, I suppose as a public relations man. I ducked.

The LaSalle Hotel was refusing the use of its ballroom to organizations of blacks, and we sent a delegation to protest the decision. The management defended itself on the ground that having blacks passing through the lobby would offend their white customers. Not only did we make no progress with the LaSalle Hotel, but the hotels in the Loop all got together just at this time and decided not to serve black customers or service black organizations. There was nothing we could do about it at that time. Of course such an agreement would be illegal today (1983), but it took many years of agitation on a national scale to swing public opinion to our side.

One of the issues of that day was released time for religious instruction. The public schools were not allowed to have ministers come into the classroom, but the schools were often willing to cooperate with the churches so that the children received religious instruction anyway, in released time.

The Chicago Committee helped with the campaign against released time, but the Jewish liberals had their own organization that was working on that specific subject, and they carried the ball. An active leader was Boris Steinberg. He was so active in this and other ways that he did not take proper care of his eyes, even when blindness threatened. So, he went blind at an early age. He refused to collapse, and became the first blind golf player!

Vashti McCollum won a suit against released time, but the custom lingered on for many years in spite of being in flagrant violation of the principle of separation of church and state. When Cynthia Quentin was going to school in Kansas City, her school would suspend classes at a specified hour and the pupils would troop to a nearby church or synagogue of their choice for religious instruction. Cynthia Quentin and a German boy were the only two who did not go. What German she knows was learned in that released-time hour.

Paul Robeson was in and out of Chicago, which was his headquarters while he was playing Othello there. I got to know him a little, but especially his wife Eslanda, who was an interesting person in her own right; her hobby was African folk culture. It was only later that I heard she was the one largely responsible for his leaving the practice of law and taking up singing and acting, at which he of course made an international reputation. I always thought he would have made a real contribution in the field of law if he had stayed in it. He had everything: all-American tackle at Rutgers, phi beta kappa, and an outgoing personality.

I can't fault him for opting for the wider audience which his life in the arts gave him. I saw him starring in "Emperor Jones" already in 1924. Also, he was one of a very few who ever played the part of Othello to take the leading role, which in the script belongs to Lago (that at least is my idea; others dispute it). Paul went into a decline in his later years, and some tried then to pretend that he had gone back on his leftist ideas, but I never saw any proof of that, and in fact it was denied.

Graten Little and I were discharged from the staff of the Chicago Civil Liberties Committee, and the Committee itself folded soon after. I heard later that Murray Latimer had become Public Relations man for a trade association. The Lincoln School also folded, in spite of having a man sent on especially from New York to try to keep it going. It was evident that making a living in the left-wing organizations was a vanishing proposition.

On the other hand higher education was booming, with GI's leaving the service and taking advantage of the government-sponsored scholarships to get some college training. I made the round of Chicago educational institutions and thought for a time that I might pick up something. Nanie then suggested that I follow up on an offer I had had while still in Cumberland, to come to the University of Kansas City. I contacted President Decker, who had got my name from Harvard on a trip to the east. I visited Kansas City, and actually began work there in the middle of the academic year, living in one of the dormitories. The family moved down during the summer. We sold the house in Winnetka at an advantageous price, bought a new one a mile or so from the campus, and set aside the legacy from my mother to finance the higher education of the remaining four children, or rather for all five, since Chan was going for his Ph.D.

My idea of being an intellectual in the Labor movement was not a bad one, actually; there were quite a number in the end-- Cooper in the Packinghouse Workers, Lincoln Fairley with the West Coast Longshoremen, Ben Riskin with Mine-Mill, succeeded by (me and then) another man whom I never met; Jim Wishart in the Auto Workers whom I did know, Solon de Leon in the National Maritime Union. In the Packinghouse Workers, the political factions were evenly balanced, so the lawyer took over and ran the union. I might have done the same in the United Shoe Workers, but did not have the yen for it. The examples of Powers Hapgood in the United Mine Workers and the CIO and Don Henderson in the Agricultural Workers show that college men can make good organizers. I could have had jobs with the Furniture Workers and also with the Farm Equipment Workers, running a section of the union, but I passed up both chances and went back to teaching. The Chicago Committee for Spanish Freedom and the Chicago Civil Liberties Committee were stop-gap jobs. The editorship of the *Western Maryland CIO News* could not have lasted more than a few years, if only because the national *CIO News* did not last very long.

Being a professional Communist was never a job that appealed to me. At first, I was not equipped, through not knowing Marxism well enough; I made one mistake after another, and had to be corrected. These were not mistakes in theoretical reasoning so much as in knowledge of the movement. Luckily I was not churning out articles for the press like (for example) Maxime Rodinson in France, and so did not have the embarrassment of changing my line when the Party did, as was his experience. He survived because in France Marxism is a respected discipline, as it is not in the U.S. (too bad for the U.S.!). Maxime Rodinson, a Party intellectual, wrote the article on Marxism in the Encyclopaedia!

XXIX

Kansas City - The University, In and Out

We lived in Kansas City seven years, from 1947 to 1954. The house that we bought was in a neighborhood populated by wage-earners and small businessmen mostly. The faculty usually settled closer to the University, in areas where the income level was higher. We did not do much entertaining. Nanie did not especially enjoy cooking and had no feeling for the social whirl. We did get to know my colleagues, through University functions, and it was really amusing when I knew the men and Nanie the wives, how each had got the kind of mate that he or she deserved.

The colleague that I saw the most of during the 1/2-year that I was baching it before the family came, was Eugen Altschul, also in economics. In Germany in the pre-Hitler period, he had had an important role in the intellectual life of that period. As Professor at Freiburg, he had been editor of an internationally circulated economic periodical. Being Jewish, he had to leave when Hitler came in, and came presently to the U.S., with his wife and a son and daughter. He himself was able to find work in Washington, then came to K.C.U., arriving shortly before I did. Although he was not politically in my camp he considered Marxism a respectable discipline. His wife had died and the family was broken up, so he also was baching, and we frequently ate together, along with a math prof named Biser who was going through the last stages of divorcing a wife in the east.

Altschul's son had been a lawyer in Germany, so in the U.S. he decided to go into academic life and studied for a Ph.D. in political science. He failed his exam for the Ph.D. and his father gave him a dressing down. He was found dead soon after in the garage, overcome by carbon monoxide fumes. His daughter, who had become a social worker, blamed the father for her brother's death.

She came to visit Altschul in K.C. and the four of us went for a walk in the park. The daughter laid hold of Biser and they came back from the walk arm in arm. They were married soon after and produced a family. Altschul used to visit them but he could not stand the racket in their house and spent most of his time in a hotel near by.

The University paid little attention to learned articles, and there seemed to be no faculty members working on a book. I produced a manuscript on imperialism, but could not find any publisher in the U.S. that would even read it. Finally Blackwell's, in England, condescended to do so, and found that the book did not hang together as such; they suggested breaking it up into several articles, and I did. The articles were published by *Science and Society*: one on "Hobson and Human Welfare", one on "Conservative Writers on Imperialism," and a third, which attracted the most favorable attention, on "Schumpeter as Sociologist," including a slashing critique of Schumpeter's theory of imperialism. I also produced an article on "The End of the Holmes Tradition," which came out in the *Kansas City Law School Review*, in which I took to pieces Holmes's attempt to define the limits of free speech (the "clear and present danger" doctrine). I concluded that Holmes (who so nearly became my great-uncle) was not a liberal but an honest conservative, if that is not a contradiction in terms.

Professor Hodges was not any older than I was, but he had come to the University before I had, and was promoted to a full professorship ahead of me. The first year after my opening semester was 1948, a presidential election year, and there was an independent political movement of liberal tinge; Hodges let on to be a liberal, and the new movement coincided with his ideas, so it was arranged that he would attend their regional convention and present our ideas, which he did. A little later, President Decker hailed me on campus and brought up the subject. The question was whether Hodges' ideas were liable to get the University into trouble. I should no doubt have told him then that Hodges had gone at my suggestion and I was just as "radical" as he was. In the end Decker found out that I was much more so. But on the occasion in question, he said it was his idea to do nothing about Hodges, and nothing was done.

Decker was still in office when a three-year contract was offered to Ralph Spitzer in the Physics Department. Ralph had been active in the 1948 political movement when he was at Oregon State, and had lost his job as a result. He had asked Linus Pauling to write him a recommendation for the job at U.K.C. Pauling had done so (in glowing terms), but his letter arrived after the decision to hire Ralph had been made. Pauling included a final paragraph saying not to attach any importance to the Oregon State affair, that Ralph was not at fault. This was the first the administration had known about an Oregon State affair. They were of course much exercised but after investigation decided not to reopen the matter of the Spitzer contract. I mention this because it showed that U.K.C. under Decker was making no special attempt to check up on the political activities of the men it contemplated hiring. This of course was to Decker's credit.

The Educational Director of one of the unions in St. Louis approached K.C.U. with a proposal to have the University act as host in a one-day program to give unionists in Kansas City a glimpse of what higher education had to offer. I was assigned to prepare such a program, and at the appointed day 20 or 30 union members from a number of different unions showed up and were exposed to the program. A sample of what we gave them was a talk, with slides, by Klaus Berger on the social content of art. The undertaking was adjudged a success and was repeated each year for the next four. The organizer of the program in St. Louis showed up at the fifth annual session, and heard me make a mild anti-imperialist talk at the dinner. We had her to tea after the sessions. She turned out to be a Socialist and was married to Maurice Taylor from Boston. We had worked with Maurice in the Teachers Union, although the difference in our political orientation sometimes made that difficult. In fact after some quite uncalled-for red-baiting by Maurice (with me as the target), the local had voted to censure Maurice. Nanie was prepared to forget all that and sent her regards to Maurice. But the five-year program came to an end.

Our best friend on the faculty, Klaus Berger, who unfortunately left shortly to take an important job at the University of Kansas, was a refugee from Germany. He was a left-wing Social Democrat, and in later years we had to admit that his estimate of the Soviet Union had been more nearly correct than ours. He was an art historian, and in the years just before the Nazi takeover he used to lecture to packed houses in Berlin about the social content of painting (Kathe Kollwitz et al). It was his proudest boast that he had been #32 on Hitler's list of public enemies. When the Nazis took power he left Germany (just in time) and for the years until World War II busied himself in Paris with looking after other refugees; then fled again just before the Nazi invasion and spent a year in England before coming to the U.S. He married Margaret Anderson, whom we had known when she came to meetings of the State Council of Teachers Unions in Massachusetts.

The faculty at K.C.U. was not especially broad-minded, nor dedicated to scholarship as one might expect to find at a university. Even the best of them were prejudiced against foreigners or Catholics or both. Not many of them did any writing for publication: I was exceptional in this regard. So, there were not many discussion groups, although an attempt was made to set one up and it met in a neighborhood drug store at uncertain intervals.

The students were neither very bright nor very well-to-do. The youths who fell in either category usually found their way to the higher-level schools in the east. On graduation from K.C.U., our students gravitated to various kinds of small businesses, or it might be to a professional school. The trials of the small business man in this age were more than some of them could take. One student who had taken a couple of courses with me graduated and set up a small laundry business. He had borrowed some money from his Spanish instructor. But the business did not pay, and he was unable to discharge his debts. At a certain point he decided that everybody was against him, took a gun, and set out to pay them back. He went first to the house of a girl he knew, marched up the steps, and rang the doorbell. The girl and her mother were both inside and the girl started to answer the bell, but her mother restrained her. There was something she didn't like about the man's approach. She saved both their lives. The man waited a while, then left and went up to the University, where he shot and killed the Spanish instructor. He had a list of several others whom he had planned to treat the same way.

It might have been thought that some at least of the students would go into the employ of some one of the big corporations which had offices in Kansas City, and some did indeed do so. The University made an attempt to play up to their needs, and arranged a two day seminar on what it meant to work for a corporation. Speakers were invited in from other institutions. The advice the students got was sometimes rather contradictory. At one session which I attended, a visiting speaker seemed to be telling them just the opposite of what a K.C.U. prof had just said. I took the floor and explained to the students that in order to get promoted in a corporation the important thing was not to have any enemies, since any one of them could veto an advance. The old American virtues of initiative and innovation were dangerous, I told them, since they might well involve treading on someone's toes. The students loved it, and gave me a big hand.

At another time, students took an aptitude test to give them a steer on what kind of work to go into. One of them came in and remarked that he had tested well for real-estate salesman and corporation president, and he was trying to decide which to shoot for!

A man in his 'thirties showed up in one of my classes and said he had given up a reasonably well-paying job to go back to school. I used to use him as an example of opportunity cost--the income for one being counted as a cost in some calculations. What I didn't know was that he had not given up his job at all; he was on assignment from the F.B.I. to listen for subversive remarks and report them back. This he confided to a student who was a friend of mine and the student reported it to me. Our visitor was worried because he hadn't had anything to report. He did undertake at one point to write a paper involving an interpretation of history, and I gave him a pamphlet by Plekhanov on "The Role of the Individual in History." He returned it after a bit, then came and borrowed it again; he said he wanted to show it to his father. I had no idea of who his "father" was. Plekhanov of course had written a book that is still considered one of the classics of Marxism, but the pamphlet was not doctrinaire though it presented the materialist conception of history. Our visitor's contribution to the class discussion was strictly negative. He would talk at considerable length without touching on the subject supposedly being discussed.

I never knew whether the F.B.I. had contacted Pres. Decker and tried to get me fired. I do know that it was while Decker was president that I was put on tenure, which is supposed to be a protection against arbitrary firing. Decker cast the deciding vote.

My comparatively good standing with the student body may have had something to do with it. I played on the faculty basketball team and the soft-ball team and once finished No.3 in the tennis tournament; Ernest Manheim and I reached the semi-finals of the doubles. The students appreciated my athletic ability, such as it was; some of them even said I was a "good fellow." As for classes, some of the students noticed, when their attention was aroused, that I always saw to it that the progressive point of view was fairly presented. But there was no general revulsion against my teaching--certainly no boycott.

The subject of academic freedom was not much discussed in faculty circles, but one case in a neighboring institution showed that a second look is sometimes required before one makes up one's mind. A small denominational college--Presbyterian I believe--fired a member of the faculty for attending a Unitarian Church. This looked like a clear cut case. The facts were not in dispute. But someone of the faculty told a friend at K.C.U. that the man in question was superannuated, his teaching was no longer

224

satisfactory, and the administration had taken this method of getting rid of him with the idea that it would do him less harm in his search for another job than if he were fired for incompetence, the real reason. The fact that a college could make such a decision shows how little the colleges regard their reputation for liberalism and broad-mindedness. We were shortly to have another illustration of that point much nearer home.

President Decker was a connoisseur of both art and music and was recognized as such in the community. But the University had failed to grow as anticipated and was facing financial difficulties as a result. A group in the faculty perceived the situation as a menacing one and launched a campaign to get rid of Pres. Decker, and the campaign was successful. Decker was replaced. It should be noted incidentally that superannuation was definitely not one of the charges: Decker was one of the youngest college presidents in the country.

As a footnote we may remark that the University's financial problems were not resolved by Decker's replacement, and after an interval it began receiving money from the state; it was a branch of the University of Missouri.

I realized that with Decker gone my position would be jeopardized even though I was on tenure, but I did not participate in the campaign for his ouster either for or against. I figured that my support would not help him appreciably; it might even be the kiss of death. The cold war and the red-baiting of Nixon and McCarthy were reflected in an increasingly chilly attitude toward me which extended to social relations: we were not invited out socially.

I was increasingly worried about manifestations of anti-Semitism in the Soviet Union, and even tried to look up the subject. The leading anti-Sovieteer in the faculty was a former Menshevik named Soloveichik, and he lent me a book on Soviet anti-Semitism; we also had several discussions on the matter. The evidence on the convict labor camps could not be laughed off, although I had the feeling that the data were being inflated. So, my attitude toward the S.U. had cooled, to put it mildly. However, I was still not ready to attack the S.U. I had been put on tenure without making any disclaimer of C.P. membership, and indeed I never did make any such disclaimer, on principle rather than out of love for the S.U.

The University of Kansas City acted as host to a week-long training session for people expecting to lead groups reading Great Books. On the list of Great Books was the *Communist*

Manifesto. The Dean of a little college across the river from KCU bridled at the name, and Dean Royal of KCU said he had a semantic block, and the left it at that. At a banquet concluding the week, the participants were asked how they had liked it. One man said it was all fine, except when Dean Royall had called the other Dean a Semitic blockhead.

Soloveichik was considered the expert on the socialist countries and U.S. relations with them. At a meeting of faculty people to discuss foreign affairs he took occasion to remark that Mao Tse-Tung was a stooge for the Soviet Union (This was in 1950). He even got K.C.U. to extend an invitation to Kerensky, the former premier of Russia who was overthrown by the Bolsheviks, and Kerensky, who had been living in retirement in New York, came to Kansas City for a semester and presented his version of the events of 1918 to anyone who could be induced to listen. A student also turned up at K.C.U. who had been in a Soviet military prison for a short time after World War II. This made him an expert on Soviet prison camps in general, and the University used to meet the community's demands for information or this vital topic by sending out this student, who presented the misinformation then current with the aura of authenticity.

In the tide of intolerance which swept the country in the early 'fifties, and which was to sweep Richard Nixon into the White House, many government agencies took part. The F.B.I., as already noted, had for many years made it its business to keep track of radicals and report to their employers or prospective employers about an individual's political activities so as to prevent, or terminate, his employment. The UnAmerican Activities Committee of the U.S. House of Representatives was set up with the avowed purpose of driving radicals out of employment. Senator Joseph McCarthy gained a great deal of personal notoriety when he used his Government Operations Subcommittee for the same purpose. Senator Jenner got into the act with an investigation of radicals in higher education, conducted by his subcommittee of the Judiciary Committee of the U.S. Senate. Later, it was an assistant district Attorney of Middlesex County (Mass.) who questioned our friend Dirk Struik about his politics and put an end to Dirk's teaching activities at M.I.T. The number of two-bit politicians who sought to make a career out of red-baiting, on the Nixon model, proliferated greatly during this period. Several states had witch-hunting committees of one or the other house of the legislature.

It was never clear just why Senator Jenner carried out his attack on free expression of opinion in the universities. He announced during the course of his investigations that he was retiring from politics, and he did at the end of his term. Also he was badly advised in selecting the University of Chicago for investigation. The young president of the University, Robert Hutchins, a flaming liberal, had conceded the main point to the investigators when he had stated earlier that there were no Communists on the faculty. Actually the University had been investigated twice within a few years, once by a committee of the Illinois legislature and once at the insistence of Mr. A.B. See, an elevator manufacturer, whose daughter had told him that subversive doctrines were being peddled on campus. The press was getting bored with the subject, even the *Chicago Tribune.*

When the Committee came to Chicago, I had expected that the next stop would be Kansas City, and I was making preparations to disappear for a couple of weeks. I had not expected to be summoned to Chicago but I was, along with Ralph Spitzer, and we both went. Before leaving the City, I notified the chairman of the department, the vice president, and the Chairman of the Board of Trustees, of what was pending. None of these seemed especially impressed.

In Chicago, the hearings opened badly for the Committee. The list of those who were summoned to appear included no radicals, only liberals; some were not afraid of being pilloried. One law school professor, Malcolm Sharp, sent word that he was terribly sorry, but he could not attend the hearings as he had important business in New York (he was there trying to do something for the Rosenbergs). He got away with it. The Committee devoted a day to holding hearings in secret--why I don't know. Two of the liberal profs declined to go into secret session. They were not even called before the Committee! The press was finding the going rather slow.

This does not mean that the Committee was scorned by the intended victims. Some of them were scared to death. One that I remember, a minor character of liberal leanings, was actually trembling when I saw him in the pre-hearing room. But in the end the Committee came up empty as far as the University of Chicago was concerned.

The contingent from Kansas City was rather different. The questioning was done not by Senator Jenner but by a lawyer from New York. I asked right away what the Committee was investigating, and he said, "Soviet espionage."

At this point I could have said, "I don't know anything about it. You have come to the wrong address," and any further questions could have had the same answer: "What has that to do with Soviet espionage?" This was in effect the way Lee Lorch had avoided testifying in Dayton, Ohio; when he asked what the investigating was about, the counsel said they were investigating Communist activities in Dayton. Lee proved that he had never been in Dayton, and the investigation stalled (Lee of course lost his job anyway, but for quite different reasons).

Instead, I refused to answer on the grounds set forth in the first and fifth amendments to the Constitution. This defense was not sufficient to prevent the Committee from spreading my radical past on the record, and this they proceeded to do. When I mentioned that I had been in Brazil--a point that the Committee's research assistant, a former business manager of the *Daily Worker*, had missed although it was no secret--the inquisitor asked if I had been engaged in actions against the interests of the U.S. I might have stopped him there and demanded an apology, but I did not think of it in time.

When the witch hunt first began, the Hollywood ten had taken the First Amendment, to no avail. Later victims took the Fifth, and did not go to prison but usually lost their jobs. The following year, after I was called, a group including Chan went back to the First and got prison sentences of six months to a year (Chan actually served 5 months).

Communists were treated harshly. Although they disavowed revolutionary aims-- a point that was missed in the publicity--the top leaders of the Party were given five years, and served them.

During my stay at Kansas City I had attended a meeting of the Midwest Economic Association, a regional grouping of members of the American Economic Association. I had presented a resolution condemning the witch hunt as an invasion of academic freedom. It had got six votes. The opposition, led by Dale Yoder of the University of Minnesota School of Business, impeccably dressed even to his spats, was riding high. I realized that the annual meeting of the whole American Economic Association would be no different politically.

Ralph Spitzer, as noted, had been called to Chicago along with me, and his record also was spread on the books. He had just finished a 3-year contract of employment at K.C.U. and realizing that he would not be reemployed, he sold his house and went back to school, in Canada. He already had a Ph.D., and he now studied for an M.D. and eventually got it. He remained on in Canada, doing research for the University in Vancouver.

Back in Kansas City, the atmosphere had changed. The Chairman of the Board of Trustees, who had been unimpressed when told that I was being called by the Jenner Committee, now emerged as an implacable red-baiter. I was asked to appear before a committee of the Trustees. Actually they got all the Trustees they could reach. I got Leonard Boudin to come on from New York to sit in on the meeting.

I pointed out to the Trustees that I had half a year coming to me on sabbatical, which I purposed to take. I also lectured them for half an hour on the nature of free speech, and they took it. Fligg, the lawyer for the University, said afterwards that he thought I was swell; he would like to take a course with me. This did not prevent him from doing a job on me later.

I was permitted to take my sabbatical leave, and went off to Mexico with Nanie and Cindy Boo (Quentin).

The body which made the decision to fire me was made up of three groups, equal in number: the faculty (chosen by the faculty council), the administration, and the Trustees. I was not being tried by a jury of my peers, but by a body composed of elements presumably conservative or hostile, and it so developed. Even the faculty representatives were conservatives, as it turned out, and this although the whole faculty council had voted shortly before to put me on tenure. The University was challenged on the fairness of the setup, and changed it after my hearing, thus admitting implicitly that it had been unfair.

The charge against me was that I had refused to answer the Trustees' questions about my political orientation. There was no dispute about this: I had so refused. What the Trustees' lawyer, Fligg, set out to prove was that I was a radical. On this point also there was no dispute. I had never denied that I was a radical, although when Fligg looked for radical activities in Kansas City he found precious little: I had not been active in those years. It was considered a great triumph when he showed that I had been in touch with a radical organization of intellectuals.

On my early radicalism the Jenner Committee had filled a comprehensive book, and the *Kansas City Star* had made its contribution by publishing the full details of the Jenner Committee hearing, not at the time of the hearing itself (in June) but later, in the fall, when it could hardly be considered news.

The hearings covered a wide range. Fligg had discovered that one of the founders of the C.P.U.S.A., a certain Boudin, had the same name as the man who had acted as my counsel in the meeting of the Trustees in June. The connection between the two had been supplied by me: I had told Fligg that it was that of uncle and nephew. Anti-Semitism in the Soviet Union was a trump card: Fligg read into the record, not once but twice a long letter from Soloveichik attacking anti-Semitism in the Soviet Union. But I was not personally accused of anti-Semitism, nor of supporting anti-Semitism in the S.U. Innuendo, guilt by association, any stick was good enough to beat a dog.

Soloveichik was called as a witness, but when he was asked whether he thought I should be fired, he said, No, he was against Communism (meaning me) but he was even more against Committees (meaning the Jenner Committee and its ilk), and so was on my side(!). The other faculty member who was called (presumably at his request) was Prof. Misbach, from the psychology department, who had been president of the chapter of the AAUP at the time it had invited "Scoop" Phillips, expelled prof from the Univ. of Washington and an admitted Communist, to come and address the chapter. Misbach was anxious to avoid responsibility for the invitation.

For my part, I sought to show that my teaching had not been slanted and that if I was a radical I was still intellectually honest. Prof. Altschul took care of this latter assignment. He dissociated himself completely from my politics but insisted strongly on my intellectual honesty and, by implication, my right to my opinions. I called as witness, one Evans, a student who had taken most of my courses because he liked them, although he was not, and was not charged with being, a radical. At no time was my competence as a teacher called in question.

I could have called the hearing body back into another session and pointed out to them the lack in the hearing of the ordinary safeguards afforded to people charged with a crime. In a sense there had been double jeopardy, in that the conservatives on the faculty council who were on the hearing board had voted against putting me on tenure and then voted again against keeping me on the faculty. The great mass of material not strictly related to my case would have been excluded in a court of law. But the charge itself was illegal and unconstitutional, however much it might have been considered sanctified by its having been used by a committee of the U.S. Congress. The decision to fire me was unanimous. When I asked that the decision be withheld until after the Christmas vacation, so that I might have a chance to get myself another job at the meetings of the American Economic

Association, the chairman with a smirk on his face denied the request. It was a great joke to him but a serious matter for me.

A professor from the University of Missouri had come to the hearings to act as observer for the American Association of University Professors (AAUP). He submitted a report, and the AAUP later sent a committee to investigate the case. Their method of procedure interested me no end. They went to the campus without contacting me and asked questions designed to show that I had been a difficult man to work with. They did not call on me (although I was the complainant) until I called them up and asked them to see me. They were planning to include in their report that I had objected to teaching a certain course (on the business cycle) but I was able to show that I had taught the course, twice: so, they left that out. I was getting ready for them to report that I had been discharged for cause, but that they did not do. They said that the University should have made an estimation of the case including my value to the University, and this it had not done. They recommended that the University be censured, and it was censured at the next annual meeting of the AAUP.

The *Kansas City Star* put my dismissal on the front page, and rather surprisingly printed in full a statement that I gave them. I said that the charge against me was heresy, and continued: "They sneered at my efforts on behalf of suffering humanity. I say, Shame on those who sneer at the people." This was not strictly a case of logic but conveyed the idea. Thereafter the columns of the paper remained closed to me.

The legality of discharging, for political reasons, a faculty member who was on tenure was open to question, and I proposed to question it. A lawyer from Nashville who had been in the public eye as a defender of the peoples' rights came to mind and I asked him to prepare such a case. His name was Fyke Farmer. At first he ignored my communications, but when I sent him a check to pay his fare he decided that I was serious and did come to Kansas City.

Fyke was an old-style liberal in the Clarence Darrow tradition--not as tall as Darrow and not sloppy in his dress, but still a fighter. He had the idea of making my case a major landmark in the history of academic freedom, and prepared a brief. He went through the necessary steps to challenge the decision of the Trustees in firing me, and requested an oral hearing. The request was refused by Judge Whittaker in a brief decision which was noteworthy for its disregard of both the facts of the case and the nature of the judicial process. He said that my conduct in a public institution was such that the people would not stand for it.

K.C.U. was a private institution and what the people will or will not stand for is not supposed to be something that judges take into account. Fyke decided that we were not getting to first base and we dropped the matter.

Judge Whittaker was a corporation lawyer from St. Louis. He had been put on the federal bench presumably at the instance of Arthur Eisenhower, brother of the president, who was a force in St. Louis financial circles. Whittaker was quickly elevated to the Circuit Court of Appeals and then to the U.S. Supreme Court, after he had passed on my case. How so undistinguished a man could ascend so high is explained partly by the custom of observing a certain geographical distribution in the personnel of the top court. Whittaker's predecessor on the court, Justice Reed, from Kansas, had been as undistinguished as it is possible to get; he was never in the minority. When he retired, it seems they had to have somebody from the plains states, and Whittaker was named.

I always thought that I would not have been fired if Decker had remained as President of the University. But he was gone, and his place had been taken by a former U.S. Commissioner of Education named McGrath. He had done a study in the early 1930's on the composition of the ruling bodies of universities in the U.S., and I thought this might show liberal tendencies on his part. So when I was brought up on charges I telegraphed him--he had not yet come to K.C.--but got no response. When he did arrive it soon became clear that he would not intervene on my behalf.

I sometimes used to wonder why I had not taken the opportunity to go to Berkeley and become a professor at U. Cal., as I could have done. I did not realize at the time what a privileged position such professors enjoy. But Nanie never regretted our choice. She said, "It would have come out the same way." We of course both missed the mental stimulation that would have come with academic high-level association. But Nanie was naturally a happy person, and her family and other work occupied her time.

She found that teaching opportunities in K.C. were limited. So not being able to find college teaching, she set out to teach high school. Her years of successful college teaching were not considered sufficient background. She had to take courses, some by correspondence, on the administration of the high school, the history of education in the U.S., and other vital topics. One of her teachers was a man named Speer, at K.C.U. School of Education. He scamped the job, missed a lot of classes and came to others unprepared. It was Speer who brought the charges against me that resulted in my dismissal.

232

But eventually the preliminaries were satisfied and Nanie got a job teaching high school in the southern part of the city. One of her classes was composed largely of students who had not finished the high-school course and were forced to continue on although they were past normal high-school age. They had no idea except to disrupt the class, and Nanie was completely unable to handle them. She spent the rest of the year working in the school library.

At the time I was being fired she had got herself another job, in a private secondary school for girls, which incidentally did not have the gruesome prerequisites for teaching required by the high school. After her contract was signed, one of the trustees undertook to red-bait her and she lost the job, although they did pay her a year's salary.

After I was fired, I was subjected to a boycott in the community which really surprised me. I thought of driving a milk-wagon like one of our neighbors, and there was a position open; but it was in the aristocratic Southwest area and I was told that the people there would not stand for me delivering their milk! More appropriate would have been a job in the big reference library which was right next to K.C.U. but under entirely separate management. One of my colleagues at K.C.U. had developed cancer of the larynx which made it impossible for him to continue as a teacher, although the progress of the disease was checked by an operation. He took a course in library science and got a job in this library. I thought I might do the same thing. But the director of the library, although personally friendly, said that it would be quite impossible; there was too much interlock in the boards of the two institutions. When I was preparing a statement of my case to be mimeographed and circulated, it was even difficult to find a reduplicating firm that would do work for me!

The sentiment in the city about my case was very difficult to judge because so few people came forward on either side. One man who did write in to the *Kansas City Star* in my support, an insurance worker whom I did not know at all, came at my request before the investigators for the A.A.U.P. and said that he was endangering his position by doing so. Leonard Walker, a research worker whom I had not known previously, thought that a community movement in my support could be organized and even set out to do it; he was supported by Dr. Hilliard Cohen, but no real movement developed. We continued to have friendly relations with some members of the faculty, such as Prof. Buschman in philosophy, Prof. Scott in the Art Department and Prof. Newman in drama, but they never had any idea of organizing support for us. The local branch of the A.A.U.P., which I had spent considerable effort building up, did object to my being fired, but let the matter rest there. The Secretary, as already noted, was strongly against me and resigned his position.

It was not only the temper of the times that accounted for the reluctance to take a stand. Nor was it any special conservatism of Kansas City as a city. Just, peoples' attitude on such things is overwhelmingly, "You can't fight City Hall," and they don't. Leonard Walker was himself in trouble a little later on his own account because he did fight "City Hall" on a different issue. Marty Leavitt, a colleague of mine, a liberal who was active on relatively safe issues, appeared at the annual meeting of the A.A.U.P. a year later in company with Prof. Misbach, trying to get K.C.U. taken off the censured list!

The American Economic Association at its annual meeting took no notice of my case, although a number of so-called liberals were aware of it and could have raised the issue. I was small potatoes. The Association did protest about this time against Paul Sweezy, a former Harvard instructor and editor of *Monthly Review*, being forbidden to speak at the University of New Hampshire. The tenure issue in my case did not interest the A.E.A. at all.

I contacted a few liberal profs in the East (H.H. Wilson at Princeton and Robert Lynd at Columbia) and found them mainly worried about how soon the red-hunters would be getting after themselves. The National Emergency Civil Liberties Committee arranged meetings for me in New York and Boston, with Harvey O'Connor as an additional speaker to attract an audience. My friends in the movement dutifully showed up in both places and expressed sympathy.

I also made a quick trip by bus to the Pacific Coast, thinking that I might catch hold in a Quaker college. I went to Whittier, Richard Nixon's alma mater. It was arranging a special day in honor of its most distinguished graduate, Richard Nixon. I told the president that I did not think I would be happy there. He was not about to offer me a job, but he nevertheless spent three quarters of an hour, telling me how liberal the faculty was. There is a certain feeling in academia and elsewhere that one must appear liberal and open-minded even when one is not prepared to do anything about it.

I had thought naively that a contact in Hollywood who was (presumably) making plenty of money might help to finance my legal case, but this was not to be. In the places I visited on the coast, and in Denver, where I stopped off briefly on the way back, in fact all over the country, people had their own local cases to fight and were not taking on any responsibilities from other parts of the country. The witch-hunt was nationwide.

Since it was evident that I would not be able to get a high-level job anywhere in the U.S., I wrote to Canada and to Maurice Dobb in England. The Canadians replied that it was impossible for them to offer me a job at a sufficiently high level (Chan a little later did get a job in Canada; he was at an employable age, while I was in my 'fifties). The Labor Research Association knew about my situation and set about to use their contacts in the academic field. Maurice Dobb actually did get me a minor research job, in England, but I did not follow up on it.

I thought of going into library work and wrote to a friend from Mission days, Bill Webb, and he wrote a fine letter but not very encouraging. Actually so much close eye work would probably have been beyond me. New Hampshire was engaging on an interesting project of reforestation, and I sounded out some other friends about possibly getting some sort of supervisory work there, but it was too long a shot.

Eventually, after not too long a wait, I was hired by a free-lance photographer named Christie to do journalistic work for him. He specialized on taking pictures of earth-moving machines, which pictures the companies could then use in their advertising. In addition to the pictures, the ads had to show something on the machines' performance, and this data it was my job to assemble.

I went with Christie from one job to another, getting the necessary material and writing it up. He usually had a pretty good idea of where to go, but when driving along the street he might see a construction job in the next block and go over and photograph it. He did a lot of work for the Caterpillar Tractor Company, and they would have given him a steady job on salary, but he preferred to remain independent. Somebody--we never knew who--informed the Caterpillar people that Christie had a subversive assistant, and the company raised objections. They said they wanted to be able to get pictures on defense jobs among others, and the government might not go for having a potential spy at the site of a forthcoming airfield. So, I was fired.

I got my next job because the wife of the man doing the hiring thought I had a nice voice over the telephone. The job was delivering, and selling, household articles from door to door, for the Great American Tea Co. This company was actually the parent of the great Atlantic & Pacific Tea Co., with its chain of stores, which presently far outdistanced its parent and continued as a separate company. I had a delivery truck which I drove on a regular round, serving old customers and getting new ones. I never looked on this as a continuing job, but it served to bring in some money to supplement my dismissal pay from K.C.U.

The F.B.I. did not try to follow me on my daily routes, but one time I found myself near Cliff Hill's office and stopped in to see him. The F.B.I. knew about that. This perplexed me as I could not see why they would have been keeping watch on Cliff Hill, who was not active in the movement. Perhaps it was his connection with me. I could understand why Cliff's wife and mother of his three children was leery of his association with me. But he remained loyal and even, at the time he was riding high, offered me a job! I declined gratefully.

A distressing occurrence at this time emphasized how much the witch-hunt had come to affect peoples' private lives. I had been jilted a couple of times by people I had considered friends turning against me. There was Prof. Joseph Davis, who had known me as a student at Harvard (in Statistics and Accounting) and had corresponded warmly afterwards. And much tougher, Carroll Binder, who had married Dorothy Walton and succeeded as a journalist, become chief of the editorial page on the *Minneapolis Tribune*. He reacted coldly when I asked him to write an editorial about academic freedom, and our friendship came to an end.

Just to wind up on my appearance before the Jenner sub-committee: I had the curiosity to look up Senator Jenner's report on his sub-committee's activities investigating the academic establishment. The only positive achievement he had to report was getting me discharged. He retired at the end of his term as he had promised.

XXX

Black Colleges in the South: South Carolina, North Carolina

Nanie had been having pains in her breast but had said nothing about it because she thought I had enough trouble as it was. But eventually she went for a physical examination and got the shocking news that she had cancer. I blamed myself because at the time Cynthia Quentin was born the doctor had pointed to a certain hardness in one breast that might portend cancer. Nanie brushed it off and forgot about it. I did not forget but failed to have her go for periodic examinations as I should have done. By the time the pains began, things had gone too far to be headed off. She had the operation but the doctor was pessimistic about her eventual recovery. A Dr. Lowell, a friend of Mina's, came to Sandwich with his family and camped out in our back yard. He said to Nanie, "I suppose you realize you've only got six more years to live." Actually it was only five.

She recovered after the operation sufficiently to be able to go about her business. She was still determined to show she could teach high school, in spite of her sad experience at the first attempt, and she inquired around, not only in the city but in communities at a little distance from town. At one small town she was turned down when it was discovered that she was not a churchgoer. But she eventually landed a job in the northwest corner of Missouri, too far away to commute except weekends. And then, just as the academic year was starting, I got an offer of a job teaching college in South Carolina. I was to be head of the Department of Humanities (!) in Benedict College, Columbia, a small college then attended exclusively by Blacks.

I was surprised to hear from Benedict, because this was one of a number of black colleges that I had written to offering my services, and Benedict had not even answered my letter. What had happened was this:

Grace Hutchins, having been apprised of my situation, took it seriously and kept on the lookout for a college teaching job for me. She was in touch with a man named Spencer Kennard, who was politically O.K. and had been a missionary in China, like Grace's parents. Spencer had spent many years in the Orient, first in Japan and then in China, and in his sabbatical years had pursued higher

237

degrees; he actually had three Ph.D.'s, from Yale, the Sorbonne, and a German university (Heidelberg!). So when he found himself unable to continue in China or Japan, he came back to the U.S. and accepted a job at Benedict. He was head of the Social Science Department. When the college year was about to start, in 1953, the man who had been slated to come as head of the Humanities Department got other plans; he stood Benedict up. Spencer told Grace about this and she said he must get the job for me. Spencer persuaded the President, one Bacoats, that while my field was social science I was certainly trained in English and had a Ph.D., which is considered very important; so Bacoats offered me the job. Neither he nor Spencer nor Grace knew that I had started to major in English at Harvard and had taken several courses in the field; I had a minor in English. So there was no question that I could do the job, and I departed for Columbia (S.C.) almost immediately. This meant that the household in Kansas City was left with Mata in charge, and she was beginning to show signs of age; but she managed somehow, with Nanie coming in on weekends. Nanie's teaching at her high school went satisfactorily. I came back to K.C. for visits at infrequent intervals.

Education for blacks in the South had been through several phases. Immediately after the Civil War, a number of schools for blacks had been set up by whites from the North who were concerned about the future of the freedmen. Calhoun School where Cousin Milly taught and which I had visited during my schoolboy days, was such a school. The faculty at such schools was mostly white and the schools, though intended primarily as trade schools-- like Tuskegee, which could not have been run without Northern money, and like Calhoun--had standards; their graduates were literate. Dean Payne of Benedict College was an alumnus of Calhoun School; he had known Cousin Milly.

Later the South adopted the philosophy of free public education for everyone, and public schools, on a strictly segregated basis, were set up in all the states. To train up black teachers for the black schools, colleges for blacks were set up, usually under the auspices of one or the other of the black churches. Benedict was a Baptist college; Allen University, across the street in Columbia, was under the Methodist church. The black churches were independent of the white churches, so the colleges also were not directly controlled by whites.

I had been prepared for the idea that students entering Benedict would have had few educational advantages. But I had still thought that they would have some intellectual ambition. Since the

238

church was such an important part of their social life, I had thought that they would have some acquaintance at least with the Bible. This was not the case.

Actually the ignorance began at the top. The President, Bacoats, had been chosen for his ability to balance the books; he did not know the difference between a monograph and a monogram.

There were a few black colleges which had standards equal to those of the white colleges. Howard University in Washington, D.C., financed by the federal government, was one such school; Tuskegee and Hampton also qualified, and Fisk, in Nashville, and Atlanta University, where W.E.B. Dubois taught, were on a high level. But for the most part, standards in both the black schools and the Black colleges in the South were lamentably low. Students coming to the black colleges from the black schools--most of which of course were rural--were often functionally illiterate, and classes in remedial English were an urgent necessity.

The situation was bad enough in South Carolina, but it was much worse in Mississippi. We had a couple of students from Mississippi; they could read after a fashion but were quite unable to answer an essay question on the examination; they passed courses on the strength of so-called objective (true-false) tests. I taught remedial English among other subjects, and learned that practically none of the students could punctuate properly; they never used an exclamation point, very rarely quotation marks or question marks; they did not know what colons and semi-colons and dashes were for.

The faculties of the black colleges were a mixed group. A few of them were there with a missionary spirit similar to that which had attracted the faculties of the early black colleges. My sister Sal, after she finished Radcliffe, went to Hampton and taught there for two years. I had come measurably close to doing the same kind of thing. So, teaching blacks in the South was quite in the family tradition. There was a sprinkling of other Ph.D.'s and others who were there for political reasons. Forrest Wiggins, teaching at Allen, had been on the faculty of the University of Minnesota for five years, but when it came time for him to be put on the regular faculty, he was bounced out, for no other reason than that he had been vice-chairman of the state Farmer-Labor Party in the campaign of 1948, and had worked for Wallace's election.

There were a few other white Ph.D.'s, some politically minded and some not. The bulk of the faculty were blacks, but practically none of them were Ph.D.'s. They had not even all of them been to college, although most had. Some were there for religious reasons, training up future missionaries. They put up with the sloppy work of the students and even encouraged it by some sloppy work of their own. So, Benedict and Allen were sending out graduates to teach in the black schools and raise up another generation of badly prepared black students.

Black nationalism had made no entry into the black educational system in the South. The black students and faculties with few exceptions accepted perforce the system of white supremacy. They had little self-respect. The text-books in the schools were chosen by whites in control of the system, and the graduates of the black schools had been taught to regard General Lee as something of a hero.

I make an exception in the case of the better students, and there were some. The really top-grade students either did not come to Allen and Benedict, or if they did, did not stay long; they gravitated to northern schools. A good student is a good student wherever found, and even with their poor preparation they gave the instructor somebody he could talk to. They led the other students by their good example. But the great bulk of the students were not doing work of college level.

Confronted with this situation, the teachers were somewhat baffled. Forrest Wiggins, who taught Spanish, used to say that it was a real challenge to him to write a test that at least some of the students could pass. Spencer Kennard had one class in which he failed all but one student (12 out of 13). But that was obviously no solution, although it gave him the feeling that he was maintaining standards. I was up against the same problem in my course in English literature, a large class. In the first of three trimesters, I failed the bottom third of the class. In the next trimester, another third of the original class went out. By the third trimester, some new students had come in, but there were still some very weak students who had survived the first two cuts but were still not doing college-level work. They were knocked out in the third round. So, nobody who was really of failing quality had passed the whole course, and to that degree standards had been maintained.

It should not be imagined that the low standards at Benedict and Allen passed without protest in the black community. There was one black writer who cited numerous instances of such disregard of standards and labeled them a betrayal of the interests of the black community, in a book which had a certain circulation. He was not exactly hailed as a hero; in fact his later career was filled with difficulties.

The handful of black leaders in Columbia who had national status, such as Septima Clark, paid curiously little attention to the local colleges. Septima Clark did not even know about the dismissal of the radical professors when it took place.

Things were changing during the time that I was in the South. The teachers in the black public schools had been paid far less than the teachers in the white schools. State legislation was passed establishing the same salary schedules in both white and black schools. So, white teachers who could not get a job in the white schools began competing for the jobs in the black schools; and being better prepared they usually got them. This development of course improved academic standards in the black schools but did nothing to overcome the feeling of race inferiority which is so deeply ingrained in blacks, especially of course in the South. Also the graduates of the black colleges found that they did not have a place to go to get a job.

The religious control of the colleges was felt in various ways. One way was the so-called religious emphasis week which disrupted the normal course of events in the second trimester. Speakers from outside were brought in to lecture, and even came into the classrooms to harangue the students. Compulsory chapel at the beginning of the school days was a regular feature all through the school year.

The city of Columbia was partly segregated, partly not. In the downtown area, where the aristocracy had lived, it was customary in the early days for the rich white people to have their houses on the main streets and their slaves, on the side streets. This pattern continued after slavery. For the rest of the city, neighborhoods were quite completely segregated. When the rest of of family moved to Columbia at the end of the school year, and we were confronted with the problem of where to live, we did not settle in the black neighborhood.

The system of segregation as practiced in South Carolina at that time required not only that no blacks attend a white institution but that no whites attend black institutions like Benedict and Allen. During my first year at Benedict the State Department circulated thru the country certain "freedom fighters" from Hungary, who had left (or been expelled) for their opposition to the Communist regime. The students at Allen and Benedict were not sympathetic with them--not that they held any brief for the government of Hungary, but they resented keenly the way the exiles were being given so many favors when they were getting none at all.

One of the Hungarians found himself quite at home at Allen, and decided to stay and enroll as a student, which he did, and stayed a year. He got along well with the students and was prepared to stay longer, but the governor heard about his presence and forced him to leave. Ed and John had not found him objectionable; actually he was interested mainly in the arts and did not campaign against Communism as "freedom fighters" are supposed to do.

The students at Benedict and Allen were conventionally patriotic and supported any war fought by the U.S. as a matter of course. They were also conventionally in favor of the economic system as they found it; they saw no connection between the exploitative economic system and the exploitation to which they were subject as blacks. That is, until Dr. DuBois came to town, as he did. The very first thing he said was that he missed any mention of socialism on the part of the other speakers at the banquet where he spoke. The students sat up and blinked; afterward for a time they were inquiring at the Library for books on socialism. I admit I was appalled when somebody asked Dr. DuBois in the question period who he considered a leading socialist and he answered without hesitation, "Nehru!" At that time DuBois was not a member of the Communist Party, although he did join before he died--and after the Party had abandoned its totally wrongheaded insistence on "self-determination for the black belt."

Senator Eastland of Mississippi came to town during that year and gave a speech to an all white audience. The people at Benedict wanted to know what he would say, and delegated me to go and listen in, which I did. The Confederate flag was on display and Eastland, who was rather the business-man type than the rabble-rouser, gave a conventional white-supremacist speech, proving to his own satisfaction that the blacks were no good; the white supporters of integration in Washington, D.C., he said, did not send their children to the public schools where they would have mixed with blacks but patronized all-white private schools, and this I suppose was true of a number. But I got the impression that the crowd did not feel the note of victory in their fight. They felt that the ground was slipping from under them. Incidentally there was one black spectator who could see without being seen; he had worked as a stage hand and kept out of sight behind the scenes. He spotted me and wondered what I was doing there. My presence was explained to his satisfaction.

During my first year at Benedict, there was a disturbance one evening at a tavern not far from the campus. The police came and shot one of the Benedict students, who as it happened was one of

242

the stars of the basketball team. Miraculously, he was not seriously hurt and was presently back playing basketball, though without the same zip that he had formerly had. Needless to say, the cop was not disciplined in any way.

Less than a month after I had gone to Benedict, I was approached on campus by a man who said he was from the F.B.I. He wanted to get my recommendation for a student from K.C.U. who had given me as a reference. The name was slightly garbled and I did not recognize it at first; I said I did not know him. Later when I thought it over I realized who the student was, but I did not try to follow up and give him my endorsement. I thought it might be the kiss of death. Actually while I was still in Kansas City a former student who had been drafted and gone into officers' training was dropped from the program after the military learned that he had been a student of mine. It was never proved that this was more than a coincidence, but it certainly was that. I thought at the time I was approached in Columbia that the F.B.I. wanted me to know that they knew where I was.

In my classes I did not teach American history, but I did take occasion to let the students know where Lincoln stood on segregation. I had a copy, which I had from my grandfather, of the only "book" that Lincoln ever wrote. It was a reprint of the speeches that Lincoln made in the U.S. Senatorial campaign of 1858, when he was defeated by Stephen A. Douglas. The issue in that campaign was whether Lincoln was in favor of integration. Lincoln denied vehemently in a whole series of speeches that he had made any such proposal. He said if the Lord had intended blacks and whites to mix socially he would have made their skins the same color. Incidentally I was rather shocked when I found that even the Abolitionists had a very low opinion of slaves. James Russell Lowell's poem "The Present Crisis" started from the assumption that a slave is less than a man (or woman), though he did give him credit for having a soul. The students at Benedict apparently knew about "The Present Crisis" and would have none of it.

When the fight against bus segregation began in Birmingham, Ala., the students at Allen immediately organized under the leadership of Ed and John and took to riding the buses in Columbia, sitting up front. Ed and John collected bus fare from everybody on the campus, including all the faculty right up to the President.

The family's move to Columbia was accomplished with so little difficulty that we realized it would have been possible to make it at the beginning of the school year, or at the middle. Nanie's services were utilized by Benedict, in the English Department, and could have been a year earlier; Benedict was really short of well-prepared teachers.

The Communist Party had been reduced to a shadow of its former self, but I had been glad enough to be connected with that shadow when it came to job-hunting time. When the confirmation of Judge Whittaker was before the Senate Committee on the Judiciary, Fyke Farmer appeared at my instance before the Committee to oppose confirmation. At the same time I tried to contact some Senator who might be supposed to respond to evidence of the Judge's position on academic freedom. The choice fell on Senator Hennings of Missouri. I wrote to him requesting that he oppose Whittaker's confirmation. Hennings passed my letter on to the Judiciary Committee, on which sat, as it happened, a Senator from South Carolina. So, it was out in the open that I was teaching at Benedict. The South Carolinian said he would see about getting the tax exemption of Benedict withdrawn.

The pressure on Benedict became so strong that I went to President Bacoats and offered to resign, an offer that was immediately accepted. The resignation was not exactly voluntary; I had been forced out. There was weeping and lamentation on the part of women faculty members at Benedict, but the resignation stuck. The President held no hard feelings toward me; in fact, he wrote letters of recommendation for me to other black colleges, and one of them, with standards actually superior to Benedict's, presently offered me a job which I took. This was how I came to teach at Shaw Univ. in Raleigh, N.C.

While we were still in Columbia, the bus-riding campaign brought unlooked for results. Black students riding in the front of the bus had of course been a defiance of the unwritten segregationism of the South, and even of the law as it then was. So, a test case was taken in which the local NAACP challenged the constitutionality of the segregation ordinance. Judge Timmerman, the father of the Governor, upheld the ordinance and fined the students. But on the appeal, which went all the way to the U.S. Supreme Court, the segregation ordinance was struck down as unconstitutional and the case remanded to the District Court for Proceedings consistent with this opinion. When it came before Judge Timmerman again, he again found the students guilty on the ground that that was the law when the act complained of had taken place! Of course, he was overruled. But his son, who was governor at the time, placed an agent of the State Bureau of Investigation

(SBI) on the Allen campus, where he presently discovered who the leaders and instigators of the movement were. He also dug into the past of some of the faculty, and found out about Forrest Wiggins having been fired by the University of Minnesota, and why. So, at the governor's insistence, Ed and John and Forrest Wiggins, were all fired. At the same time Spencer Kennard and Nanie and an English prof who had become politically sympathetic to Ed and John were also fired from Benedict, also at the governor's insistence. This was after I had gone to Shaw. Nanie's firing was particularly vindictive because she had already resigned with the perspective of joining me in Raleigh.

Allen and Benedict were presently placed on the censured list of the AAUP, where they remained for many years. At last the president of Benedict, Bacoats' successor, found that this censured status was impeding his recruiting of faculty, and took steps to correct the situation. The AAUP referred him to us, the injured parties, and eventually Spencer received the equivalent of a year's pay, and I settled for 1/2-year's pay; both of us turned the money in to the MDSF (Nanie had died meanwhile).

It was a welcome innovation when the AAUP adopted the policy of getting financial compensation for the victims of political firings. Of course the ruining of one's academic career which some victims of the witch-hunt experienced could not be remunerated in any such simple way. Most such victims, including the avowed Party members at the University of Washington, did not even have the satisfaction of seeing their respective institutions put on the censured list.

Ed and John and Forrest Wiggins all found jobs elsewhere. Ed went to West Virginia; Forrest to Georgia and then Florida; and John to Thunder Bay, Ontario, where he taught for many years. He remained a strong supporter of the Soviet Union, which he visited at one point.

My shift from Benedict to Shaw was arranged rather hastily, at the end of the academic year, and Nanie continued to teach at Benedict. We knew by this time that she had a terminal case of cancer. One of her colleagues paid her high tribute afterwards; he said she never complained about her illness--one would not have known there was anything wrong with her. We were going to Sandwich each summer, and our hope was that medical advances would make it possible to halt and even reverse the deterioration that had set in. We knew a doctor on Cape Cod, and each summer we would make the pilgrimage to his place to see if there had been the beginnings at least of a break-through. There never was.

Raleigh was an afternoon's bus ride from Columbia, so we were able to spend the weekends together--a big improvement over the first year at Benedict. Terry was off at Smith and Cindy (as she still was then) continued in school at Columbia. The household was rounded out by Mata and by Timmy Bulge, the blue dachshund with the big appetite. After a year of this split-household arrangement the main part of the family moved to Raleigh and we took a house on the north side of the city, at a little distance from Shaw.

We were used to the idea that the acuteness of tension in the relations between black and white in the South was in proportion to the black-white ratio in the population. Thus, it was at its maximum in the bottom lands of the Mississippi, the Delta country, where the ratio could reach 3 or 4 to 1, but much less in areas where whites predominated. It was not accident that it was to require a national movement to break down the systematic terrorization and disfranchisement of the blacks in Mississippi, where the black-white ratio was higher than in any other state. In the Deep South, race relations were tougher than in the not-so-deep South. North Carolina was more relaxed on the subject than South Carolina.

The contrast, it is true, was deceptively great just at the time we made our move. Gov. Timmerman in South Carolina was a typically bigoted old-school conservative, while North Carolina was just coming off a term under the liberal governor Terry Sandford. It was not then apparent that the racists were by no means ready to retire from the battle in North Carolina, which thereafter sent the notorious Jesse Helms to the U.S. Senate for three straight terms (the last in 1984). North Carolina was also the site of the Klan murders of the Communists (at Greensboro in 1971); of the near-civil-war in Monroe in 1966; and of the persecution of a pre-teen black boy in a notorious frameup, also during the time that we lived in N.C. The state as a whole was industrialized, with furniture and textiles the leading products. But much of the agricultural area was still in cotton, and in little pockets throughout the state there were communities where the black tenants could not send their children to school in the winter because they were unable to buy them proper clothes. I could have worked up quite a scrapbook of case histories along such lines from the stories that my students told of what they had observed.

Shaw was one of the chain of colleges (and schools, like Calhoun) that were set up by whites from the North for freedmen in the South after the Civil War. The founder, Elijah Shaw, came from Wales, Mass. Shaw University had been through the same developments as Benedict, but on a higher level; it had some pretense to academic standing. It was ironic that I should have moved from a lower-level to a higher-level institution (for once) but such was the case.

Even then, the standards were pretty low. Shaw was called a University but did not really have any graduate schools. The best student I had during my time there, Glenford Mitchell, came after graduating from Shaw and attempted to enroll at the Columbia School of Journalism. They gave him tests and told him he would have to take a whole year of undergraduate work at Columbia--in American history and politics--before he would be ready for the School of Journalism. He did that.

The reasons for the low standards were basically no different from those at Benedict. These were the poor preparation of the bulk of the students (although N.C. schools were plainly better than S.C. schools), and the influence of the church with its emphasis on missionary work, its compulsory chapel and its religious emphasis week (the Baptist Church had taken over the responsibility for the college at an early date).

As Glenford Mitchell had discovered, many of the courses offered at Shaw were not of college level. This was of course especially true of those in the field of religion, as noted; but a major offender also was the field of business. The business school, so called, came eventually under my jurisdiction as head of social science, and I found myself in the position of approving, and offering, courses in stenography and typewriting which had no academic content at all and were valuable only as imparting certain manual skills. I realized that the system was too deeply ingrained to be pushed over by my expression of disapproval. If things had broken differently and I had stayed at Shaw, I might have tackled the job of relegating these courses to a secretarial school outside the college.

The Shaw faculty was mixed, with several black teachers who were going for the Ph.D.; three of them got the doctor's degree while I was there. It was common for them to move on then to a better institution. The market for black Ph.D.'s was not overcrowded and many of the big Northern institutions, with an eye perhaps to affirmative action trends, were hiring them as opportunity offered.

While I was at Shaw, the wife of Communist intellectual V.J. Jerome, who had been teaching at Kittrell, was fired for what seemed like obviously political reasons. I had not known she was there, and she found out about my being at Shaw quite by chance. She was not planning to do anything about her discharge. This seemed to me like a mistake and I advised her to at least raise an outcry, which she did, but without avail.

The Korean War was over before we reached Raleigh, but the Vietnam War was going on and one of the black draftees was seen and recognized in a newsreel. His family was alerted and applied to the movie theater for permission to see the film. They were not admitted, even in the balcony. The theater had formerly admitted blacks in the balcony but that privilege had been withdrawn sometime before.

George Stokes was a student of mine, perhaps the best fan that I had at Shaw. He took all my courses and I knew him quite well. He and Glenford Mitchell cooked up a scheme to begin the desegregation of the movie houses. George was rather light-skinned, whereas Glen was quite dark; he was a Jamaican, and a natural leader in the desegregation fight because he had never acquired the habit of subservience that is forced onto blacks in the South. The teacher of accounting was a Nigerian, solid black. They persuaded him to go to the movie house and ask for three tickets, which he did. The ticket seller said, "We don't serve colored."

"Colored!" said my colleague, "I'm not colored. I'm a Nigerian." He was using "colored" in the South African rather than the North American sense.

The ticket seller must have thought he had diplomatic status. She sold him the tickets and he and the two boys started to enter the theater. They were stopped by the usher who went through the same routine but ended up by admitting all three.

This bit was repeated later, at which point our Nigerian friend decided he had had enough. But the sit-ins had begun (1960) in Greensboro, and they presently spread to Raleigh. We did not know it at the time, but students from black colleges in several cities had got together before the school year began and planned the whole campaign.

In Raleigh, the students marched through the streets. The police did not interfere. The cops only saw to it that young racist whites on the other side of the street did not attack the marchers. I was marching and did not notice any undue tension. One of the students thanked me for marching with them. I said, "Oh, it's my fight too," and was tempted to add "--as a Communist."

The students formed a picket line at one of the movie theaters. They sang freedom songs, led by the white music instructor Clyde Appleton. This time the cops did interfere; they arrested 30 or 40 students and including Clyde, and these were kept in jail overnight. When the students came out in the morning, the Acting President of the University was there and shook each one by the hand. There was no question where Shaw stood.

It was actually at Shaw that the Student Non-Violent Coordinating Committee (SNCC) was formed, later that academic year. Glenford Mitchell, Albert Hockaday, and other students of mine took a leading part. The story of that movement was written up by Glen Mitchell, who brought out two books actually--very bitter against whites. Glen Mitchell was the first grantee of the Marian Davis Scholarship Fund. He later became international secretary of the Bahaists, with headquarters at Wilmette, Il.

Desegregation then proceeded apace, in Raleigh, not only at lunch counters and movie houses but eventually also at the more exclusive hotels & bars.

Clyde Appleton was a veteran of another battle over civil rights, in Arizona. He and other teachers in the school system had objected to signing a loyalty oath. Clyde had left and come to Shaw.

The family that we knew best in Raleigh was that of Anne Tyler who was about to embark on a successful career as a novelist. Her parents were contemporaries of mine and I used to see them frequently during my first year in Raleigh. Her brother had adopted the name of Israel, apparently as a gesture of solidarity with a persecuted minority; he was known as Ty. He visited us in Sandwich.

However the Tylers were not a sufficient social group and after some hesitation I elected to mix with the Unitarians who had a liberal young minister and a number of congenial families. When the family moved to Raleigh, Cynthia Quentin and I used to go to church sometimes and when the minister was in a political mood it was a rewarding experience. We also drew some blanks, when he could think of nothing better to talk about than theology. There was no Quaker meeting in town.

The Shaw faculty was very sympathetic when Nanie died. All except one of them wrote or phoned, and many came to the house. They also came to a memorial meeting at the University, where people told of their contacts with her; she had helped several with personal problems. It was an eye-opener to many that such a meeting could be held without any religious overtones.

Nanie's body was never buried; it was donated to science. Instead of a monument, we established the Marian Davis Scholarship Fund in the following year as a memorial to her. Her body was cremated and the ashes scattered in a field in back of the hospital, which was in Durham.

Many years later Nanie's grand-daughters Sarah and Leah, who had been born after her death, visited the hospital and were shown where the ashes had been scattered. They picked up a pine cone and brought it to Sandwich. They did not know that "Pine-cone, Pine-cone" was the beginning of a nonsense rhyme that Nanie had made up to amuse their respective mothers!

It was in Raleigh that Cindy became Quentin. She had discovered, as bright students do, that she could handle the English language, so she decided that she would be a writer. Cynthia Davis was not a distinctive enough name for a writer; so she first revived the middle name Quentin that I had given her (but which Nanie had erased on the birth certificate) and then asked to be known as Quentin.

I could not maintain that Cynthia Davis was a distinctive name; after all, there was a girl with that name then attending Shaw. I might have argued that Cynthia Q. Davis was distinctive, like the name of the liberal student leader Thomas Q. Harrison. But in any case she became known as Quentin. Her school work was excellent. She won a National Merit scholarship and chose to attend Radcliffe. After she had gone, I moved to a house that was practically on campus and took in students as lodgers.

The members of the Unitarian church also rallied around, and I was glad enough to have their sympathy too. It was then that I discovered that there are some people who intervene in other people's affairs with constructive effect.

I had always enjoyed games, and when I had no family around, I read up on bridge and chess and took to playing regularly. I enjoyed both games, but in the end, especially after I "took to the road," it was bridge that occupied more of my time. It was quite a resource to go to a strange city and be able to look up the local ACBL affiliate. This was important for me because my eye cramp prevented me from reading more than a limited number of hours in a day. I never developed into a champion, but still played well enough to make it fun.

Chan meanwhile had been fighting it out with the UnAmericans. A member of the (House) UnAmerican Activities Committee came from Michigan and thought he could make some political capital out of red-baiting the faculty of the University, where Chan was then teaching. The Congressman had the names of three faculty members, including Chan, and called them to the stand. One, in effect, turned state's evidence and got off; the second, in pharmacy, left for a satisfactory job in Canada; and Chan was the third. He took the first amendment, the same as the Hollywood Ten had done at the beginning of the witch hunt, and was duly cited for contempt of Congress, the same as Corliss Lamont, Harvey O'Connor, Paul Rosenkrantz, Barenblatt and others.

Corliss and Harvey got off on technicalities, and Chan, who was defended by a lawyer from the NECLC, could perhaps have done the same. The lawyer, one Wittenberg, had an imposing mop of white hair, he couldn't understand anybody's wanting to go to prison. Chan insisted on posing the constitutional issue. His differences with Wittenberg got so heated that I though they might part company. I arranged for Royal France, former U.S. Senator from Maryland and a civil libertarian, to take the case. But the defense was handled by Wittenberg in Chan's way and Chan got six months for contempt of Congress. Barenblatt and Paul Rosenkranz also served terms in prison.

Chan was living in Providence at the time, working for Mathematical Reviews. He was assigned to Danbury, Connecticut and Natalie used to drive the kids over from Providence to see him. He spent his time (5 months) learning Russian among other things, and presently got so he could read Russian fiction for pleasure.

The *Providence Journal* was not famous for its liberalism, but it came to Chan's defense, and kept the case alive, running a cartoon during the time he was in prison. An English instructor at Brown arranged a welcoming delegation when he got out, and the pictures of his arrival were on the front page of the *Journal* (The English instructor was not reappointed). So, McCarthyism (as it was called) was on the wane. But Chan was blacklisted in the U.S. and still was twenty years later. He landed a good job at Toronto.

Another law-enforcement officer who sought advancement through red-baiting was the district attorney of Middlesex County in Mass. He drew up an indictment against our friend Dirk Struik, who had been at M.I.T. for many years, accusing him of seeking the overthrow of the gov't. of Mass. He denied membership in the C.P., with the full approval of the Party. I told him that was not the thing to do. He thought it over and changed his testimony--said maybe he had been a Party member after all. M.I.T. suspended him with full pay. He kept his office at M.I.T. but was not allowed to meet with students. The case against him was not pressed; it was still pending when he reached retirement age.

During our time in the Carolinas, we were going back & forth to Sandwich every summer as usual, and our friends were visiting us. This resulted in our having other visitors. George Meyers came with his family. The FBI kept watch on him, parking at times in the neighbor's driveway. They also followed our movements, but Nanie outsmarted them. Our friend Eula, who had been married to Joe Figueiredo, was due to be deported. She had proved that to be deported to her country of origin, Portugal, would be a sentence of imprisonment and maybe death, as Portugal was a Fascist dictatorship under Salazar. So, she had secured permission to go to Poland. But some financial obstacles had to be overcome--bail or fees. The Party could not find the money. So Nanie went downtown in Sandwich ostensibly to shop, then kept going all the way to Little Compton, R.I., and got Jessie (Lloyd O'Connor) to put up the money ($5,000). (The F.B.I. of course knew about Harvey & Jessie. When I was trying to get a government job in 1945, one of the questions I was asked was whether I know the O'Connors, who were supposed to be part of the Communist conspiracy. But it would still have been embarrassing to Jessie to have the F.B.I. trailing us to her house).

We also had visits from Anne Timpson, who thought she was "wanted" and went "underground" for several years. It will be recalled that her daughter Kathy stayed with us in Kansas City for part of that time.

But even before we hosted George and Anne, Shawm Hill had become known as "Commie Hill" because of the Reeds.

Ferdinanda Reed was one of three women who became technical owners of the *Daily Worker* when it was decided that the Party should separate itself from the daily. She was also a great booster for the S.U., which she visited every few years; her elder daughter Mary spent most of her life there after the revolution, doing translation for the C.I. (Mary was in Leningrad during the siege in World War II, and her son lost his life at that time).

But the major event that gave the Hill its name was Nancy's attempt to help the lefties in the National Maritime Union. Various documents showing Party activity in the union were concealed under the floor of Mary's little house. Unfortunately her pals in the union such as Blackie & Hedley Stone, left the Party and Joe Curran, who had been picked by the lefties to head the union, became a violent red-baiter. The documents were exhumed under government supervision. Nancy told all the details of what was happening to her friend Bub Powers, thus insuring that the whole town would know about it.

252

Our relations with the Powerses, our nextdoor neighbors, had been very good for nine years, after we moved in, and we were also friendly with Nancy's Uncle Robert Wesselhoeft. A feature article in a local paper gave a full account of the contributions to the arts & letters of the country by Ernest Hutchinson (piano) and other residents on the Hill, showing that Communist activities were only a small part of the story.

But when the witch-hunt began in earnest, the Powerses broke off their friendship, and Uncle Robert waged a vendetta against us and also against his niece Nancy. He owned the land bordering the lake, and tried to keep us from crossing his land and using his dock. He put up a sign on the pump-house, "Communists Keep Out." He tried to get Frank Lovell to stop supplying us with milk, and accosted me belligerently in the post office. He called on the police twice to arrest us for trespassing on his land, but they wouldn't do it.

Frank Lovell continued to supply us with milk. When the police came around, we showed them the letter Uncle Robert had written inviting us to buy the property. Nancy laughed the whole thing off, and the police decided not to intervene. We and Nancy had an easement; uncle Robert's property rights were not as absolute as he thought. His wife Lucille had no stomach for the vendetta. But it was only after many years of strain that she pointed the way to a solution. Uncle Robert liked to swim at 11 A.M., and we learned at long last to keep away from the dock at that time.

XXXI

Storming the Pentagon: 1967

It was in October 1967, that public indignation at the country's foreign policy reached a new high and it was decided to stage a demonstration against the Pentagon. John Bassett and Quentin and I went down to Washington together with Sarah (8 months old!).

At the march, a crowd collected at a little distance from the Pentagon, separated by a grassy lawn. John and I went out and sat on the grass, as did a number of others. The police came and asked us to move. I indicated unwillingness, and was picked up and carried to the paddy wagon. John had not expected to be arrested, but when he looked around, the others who had been sitting just behind him had discreetly moved away. He was marched off to the wagon too.

The cops did not beat us up, but some youths in another area did not get off so easy. Several were put in the van with us who had displeased the cops, and they were really bloodied. The total number arrested was around 250. This was apparently too many for the District jail. Some 20 miles away, in Virginia, was a center that had been used at one time for rehabilitating alcoholics. The policy had changed and the authorities were no longer engaging in rehabilitation, so the facility was standing idle. It was pressed into service for this occasion.

In jail I got into conversation with Norman Mailer, who had not been content to sit on the grass but had run at another part of the Pentagon until he was intercepted. I thought of the "Writers' Committee" that had gone to Pittsburgh in 1931 and investigated the coal miners' strike. That committee had consisted of Theodore Dreiser and me, as noted. I tried to interest Mailer in forming a writers' committee, but he walked away.

At the same time an argument had been going on in another part of the jail, where a small group of dissidents was planning to put out a statement attacking the leadership of the demonstration. After an hour when I arrived the talk was still going on. I remarked that if such a statement was issued it would get front-page space in every commercial newspaper in the country. The conversation ended. The statement was not issued.

Mailer later wrote up the whole episode in *The Armies of the Night*. He did not claim to have acted creditably: in fact he

254

admitted he had acted like a cad. But he did try to take part of the credit for heading off the statement in question, although he had arrived after the idea had been in effect dropped.

We spent the night in jail and were all released next day, except for a few who refused to pay a fine that had been imposed. The offense of everybody had been the same, but the sentences were quite varied. Some paid $25, some $50, some nothing at all.

XXXII

The Marian Davis Scholarship Fund

In 1961, the year after Nanie's death, we organized in Sandwich the Marian Davis Scholarship Fund, to grant scholarships for higher education to veterans of the fight for equality and social justice who might not have been able to get enough scholarship help from other sources. The Trustees included not only me and my children but a number of like-minded friends.

One of these was Sarah Gordon, who for many years had attended meetings in the Boston area which were raising money for worthy causes and responded immediately and enthusiastically to the moneyraising appeal. The sight of Sarah waving a $20 bill at such times was a familiar one.

At first, of course, the Fund was not known (its existence still remained unknown to most people many years later). However as the decade wore on, the Student Nonviolent Coordinating Committee (SNCC) changed its character and was dissolved, and the young people who had been carrying on its work found themselves in need of further education and applied to us. We also sometimes applied to them. But these were only a fraction of the students who were helped.

The work of the Fund was unpaid, and was carried on by members of the family--HBD, who was always the Treasurer and often Secretary as well; Chan; and Terry. The Trustees who were most active in raising money included Steve Fritchman, a Unitarian minister who had been active in the Boston area and then moved to Los Angeles. Among those whom he interested in the Fund was the Secretary of the American Humanist Association, who steered a bequest of $25,000 our way, from a moribund Humanist who did not know what to do with his money. Steve also interested a former Canadian farmer named A.C. Severson, who had a good-sized income from an invention that his brother had made and who gave the Fund $500 a month for many years.

At first the income of the Fund greatly exceeded the grants, but we resisted the temptation to keep our capital intact and make grants only out of income, and after some years the receipts from our donors stabilized at around $30,000 a year, and grants at the same level. Thus we could grant $1500 to each of 20 students, with some getting more and some less.

For many years, foreign students studying in the U.S. were included among the grantees. But after some unfortunate experiences, we had to conclude that we did not have the facilities to check up on the credentials of foreign applicants, and these grants had to be discontinued.

The raising of new funds depended at first on personal solicitation, like Fritchman's. But before long we began circulating an annual appeal, which was prepared by Anne Braden, of Louisville, Ky., a professional journalist who with her husband Carl, since deceased, was giving her full time to worthy causes. Her main interest was in the Southern Conference Educational Fund, and it was from the list of contributors to that fund, obtained of course by Anne, that the Davis Fund got many of its early contributors. Anne was also invaluable to the Fund in other ways. In her travels through the South she contacted many potential grantees who then applied and were given financial assistance. In this and other ways the Fund was prevented from becoming a strictly regional organization--even though the bulk of the grants are still (1985) made to candidates who are studying in the Northeast. A majority of the grantees over the years have been from minority groups, including especially Blacks.

XXXIII

Conclusion

Liberals do a great deal of good. They carry out reforms, keep things that are bad from getting worse, make changes for the better when these are not too sweeping. After all, I was a liberal for many years.

Why then did I become a radical?

Because of the Depression, in the first place. It became apparent then that the liberals were not getting to the roots of things, and were not going to. Of course, the fact of the Russian Revolution, and the fact that we had been to Europe and had seen flourishing Communist movements in France and Germany had prepared the way. In fact, it was lingering pacifist scruples that held me up for a long time when I was otherwise ready to abandon liberalism.

The behavior of liberals in time of crisis also soured me on liberalism. In the 1930's, I well remember Will Geer's performance in Symphony Hall, Boston, acting out the rhyme, " One step forward and two steps back--That is the method of the liberal attack." (In the original, the liberals said, "We read the *Nation* and the *New Republic* too"; the management had him delete the names, and he just said, "We read the *Ta-da* and the *Ta-da-da-da* too";--the *N.R.* was then of course a little to the left of center). Lucien Price had looked up the history of the Salem witch trials and had found out what the liberals then did, getting into action too late to save the lives of the victims, overwhelmed by the witch scare (His article "Witchcraft Then and Now" was published in the *Nation* in 1922, after the Palmer raids).

The failure of the American Civil Liberties Union local branches also became apparent to us. I make honorable exception of the Boston and Los Angeles chapters, and of course of the Western Penna. Committee with which I worked. But when the national ACLU turned to red-baiting, it was no great surprise to me. Naturally I regretted (the loss of) Roger Baldwin as a friend to whom I had looked up.

Lawrence Brooks was another who folded under pressure. He resigned from the Joint Anti-Fascist Refugee Committee and the American-Soviet Friendship Society in order to get appointed judge of the Malden District Court. So in the Nixon-McCarthy

258

period when Chan and I lost our academic jobs, we had another chance to see liberals in action. I interviewed a number of nationally known liberals and their reaction was, "I wonder when this is going to get to me!" The idea of organizing an opposition was just foreign to their way of thinking.

When Corliss Lamont made public the debate in the ACLU about removing Elizabeth Gurley Flynn from the Board, and it became perfectly clear that the ACLU had gone over to red-baiting, Corliss as noted set up his own organization, the Emergency Civil Liberties Committee (later the National ECLC), and people wondered if this would be a radical civil liberties organization. However it became more a personal vehicle for the lawyer who handled its major cases, *viz.* Leonard Boudin. Boudin won several major cases which the ACLU would not, or at any rate did not touch. He was a major force. But he absorbed all of the ECLC's budget with his $25,000 retainer fee. At one time the ECLC brought in a pair of young lawyers who got into many smaller cases; they had 10 or 20 of them on the griddle at once. But Boudin killed all that. Dorothy Douglas was on the Board of ECLC and formed part of a group which objected to Boudin's domination of the Board. But she died and Edith Tiger the Director who had worked cheerfully with the younger element, withdrew into a rather inactive role. She was in effect an observer. Boudin found himself often preoccupied with the defense of his headstrong daughter, who was involved in a group that undertook to manufacture bombs and got blown up themselves. She participated in a bank robbery to get money for her group, the Weather Underground; but the group failed, Miss Boudin was caught, and sentenced in spite of her father's efforts, and neither she nor Leonard furnished leadership to the radicals of their day.

The liberals didn't want to change the system, and I did. For many years I thought the system could purge and correct itself, but it was not until I read Marx that I saw how different the radical philosophy was and how superior. The discovery came easy to the textile workers of North Carolina. They said, "We were dialectical materialists all the time and never knew it." (That was Elbert Totherow who said that).

Liberals, and liberalism, do a lot of good, as noted. They are a necessary--inevitable--part of the picture, if only because there has to be some middle ground even between the right and the far right. What is not generally realized is that the liberals are actually part of the Establishment, which they have no intention of challenging or upsetting. The cozy relationship between the ACLU and the FBI

259

has not been due to errors in judgment on the part of Roger Baldwin and Morris Ernst, although Roger plainly misapprehended J. Edgar Hoover's role. The relationship was in the nature of the case. William Keller, writing on *The Liberals and J.Edgar Hoover*, in my opinion gives a false impression when he speaks of a break between the liberals and the FBI in 1965--1970. Actually most liberals are still red-baiters and work closely with the FBI.

All through the 1920's, I stuck to my liberal philosophy, although some of my best friends, like Bob Dunn, were radical and getting more so. It was only in Germany, in 1928, that I finally attempted to set down what goals I had in mind for the liberal state to achieve. I found to my dismay that there was almost nothing there. I was becoming aware that the German Social-Democrats had achieved their goals. They killed the leaders of the left wing, Rosa Luxemburg and Karl Liebknecht, and put down the Communist upsurge in 1924. They did this in the name of democracy.

We used to ask Fred Lohn at Braddock just what the German "revolution" of 1918 had accomplished for the working man, and aside from the abdication of the Kaiser, all he could point to was the eight-hour day, which was being established at the same time in the United States (with the steel industry falling in line somewhat tardily). The Social Democrats were prepared to fight for the retention of capitalism. I had to ask myself whether that was my philosophy too.

In France and Germany, we saw flourishing Communist Parties and realized that in those countries we would have been in that camp. In England, the lines were not so sharply drawn; the Labour Research Department, where I had worked, continued to serve the Labour Party even when Page Arnot and Palme Dutt came out as Communists. The Communist Party even applied for affiliation to the Labour Party.

Marian and I were in fundamental disagreement with the basic tenets of capitalism, with the principle of unearned income. The Marxist class analysis enabled us to see that the capitalists would not give up without a struggle; that there were limits to what could be obtained by the process of gradual reform. So we gravitated to the Communist Party. She gave up her pacifism quite readily, as Grace Hutchins and Anna Rochester had done. I was quite shocked at this, since pacifism was much more a part of my individual ethos. But eventually I came to agree.

The Great Depression (called the Crisis by the Communists) was man-made; it was not an Act of God. Since the institutions of liberal democracy did not furnish any automatic cure, as Hoover and the Republicans thought it should, people began to line up with the parties that stood for a firm central control to obviate such crises. In Germany, and to some extent in the U.S., people were saying, "If I wasn't a Fascist I would be a Communist," and vice versa, a point of view that I could never understand.

The Second World War had its conscientious objectors, just like the First. Some of the same people were involved, like my friend Leslie Heath. I am still not sure that they were wrong. It seemed important at the time to check the spread of Fascism, but it might have been predicted that the Allies would continue fighting to extend the sway of imperialism, as they have done. The devastation of Southeastern Asia and Korea was as bad as anything the Nazis could have brought.

A radical today (1990) has to be against atomic war. He also has to be against unearned income, and the inheritance of the same (I still believe that my favorite reform of the 1920's was a correct line). So, it is not correct to say today that "communism has failed," much less that capitalism has succeeded.

Marxism was correct in stressing the importance of classes and of class exploitation. But it is possible to be doctrinaire and fail to recognize other forms of exploitation, such as sex (gender) and national exploitation. Race exploitation is recognized as such and is being fought as it deserves. I believe that Marx and Engels were against all forms of exploitation and fought them each in its turn.

It is still an open question whether men can ever learn to live at peace with their neighbors. Intertribal wars were the rule in the years before the rise of nations.

The power struggle is perennial and shows no signs of abating. It is possible to argue, as our friend Smitty the astronomer does in all seriousness, that man is bent on self-destruction and will achieve it. A radical is at least an optimist on this point. But not without reservations.

What has the 20th century taught us? We should have learned that democracy as such achieves little toward solving the great pressing problems of the power struggle and the struggle against inequality. But with regard to the latter, we have even some reason to be optimistic. The French Revolution was committed to "liberty, *equality*, and fraternity," the Russian Revolution and the Chinese Revolution no less. Egalitarianism has an honorable pedigree. The fight against exploitation is also perennial and cannot be looked on as lost.